WINGS OF THE RISING SUN

OSPREY
PUBLISHING

If you know the enemy and know yourself, you need not fear the result of a hundred battles. If you know yourself but not the enemy, for every victory gained you will also suffer a defeat. If you know neither the enemy nor yourself, you will succumb in every battle.

Sun Tzu, *The Art of War*

WINGS OF THE RISING SUN

UNCOVERING THE SECRETS OF JAPANESE FIGHTERS AND
BOMBERS OF WORLD WAR II

MARK CHAMBERS

OSPREY PUBLISHING
Bloomsbury Publishing Plc
PO Box 883, Oxford, OX1 9PL, UK
1385 Broadway, 5th Floor, New York, NY 10018, USA
Email: info@ospreypublishing.com
www.ospreypublishing.com

OSPREY is a trademark of Osprey Publishing, a division of Bloomsbury Publishing Plc

First published in Great Britain in 2018

A catalog record for this book is available from the British Library.

ISBN: HB 978 1 4728 2373 1; eBook 978 1 4728 2372 4; ePDF 978 1 4728 2371 7; XML 978 1 4728 2370 0

20 21 22 23 24   10 9 8 7 6 5 4 3 2

Edit and photo captions by Tony Holmes
Index by Zoe Ross
Originated by PDQ Digital Media Solutions, Bungay, UK
Printed and bound in India by Replika Press Private Ltd.

Front cover: PO1c Tadayoshi Koga's Zero-sen arrives at Dutch Harbor from Akutan Island, where it had been spotted by a US Navy PBY-5A Catalina flying boat on July 10, 1942. (*NARA*)

Back cover: (left) Koga's Zero-sen in flight, October 15, 1942. (NARA); (right) An E16A1 from the 634th Kokutai. (US Navy); (bottom) J1N1-Ss, G4M3s, D4Y2/3s and J5N1s at Yokosuka Naval Air Base in September 1945. (US Navy, Naval History and Heritage Command)

Spine: (top) EB-2 in flight above Wright Field, October 1, 1943. (NARA); (middle) A damaged J1N1-Sa "Irving" of the 302nd Kokutai. (NARA); (bottom) An MXY7 Ohka flying bomb. (NARA)

Flaps: (front) A B6N2, photographed on March 3, 1945. (NARA); (back) P 5016 was delivered to Wright Field in July 1943. (NARA)

Cockpit artworks on pages 67, 75, 81, 87 and 97 by Jim Laurier, © Osprey Publishing, originally published in the following titles: (p. 67) DUE 16: *Seafire vs A6M Zero*; (p. 75) DUE 8: *P-40 Warhawk vs Ki-43 Oscar*; (p. 81) DUE 26: *P-38 Lightning vs Ki-61 Tony*; (p. 87) DUE 82: *B-29 Superfortress vs Ki-44 "Tojo"*; (p. 97) DUE 73: *F4U Corsair vs Ki-84 "Frank"*.

Osprey Publishing supports the Woodland Trust, the UK's leading woodland conservation charity. Between 2014 and 2018 our donations were spent on their Centenary Woods project in the UK.

To find out more about our authors and books visit **www.ospreypublishing.com**. Here you will find extracts, author interviews, details of forthcoming events and the option to sign up for our newsletter.

CONTENTS

ACKNOWLEDGMENTS

Numerous individuals deserve great thanks for providing crucial support during the writing of this book. First and foremost, thank you to my loving family, my wife Lesa, daughter Caitlyn and sons Patrick and Ryan, for tolerating my ceaseless words of enthusiasm and providing encouragement and support for this project. Thank you also to David Pfeiffer (Civil Records Archivist), Nate Patch (Military Records Archivist) and the staff of the Textual Reference Branch of the US National Archives and Record Administration (NARA) at College Park, Maryland. Thanks to Holly Reed and the staff of the Still Pictures Branch of the US NARA at College Park, Maryland. In addition, thanks to Archie DiFante and Tammy T. Horton of the Air Force Historical Research Agency (AFHRA) at Maxwell AFB, Alabama, for providing additional research assistance and materials. Finally, thank you to Kate Igoe, Rights Management Archivist, National Air and Space Museum, Smithsonian Institution, Washington, D.C., Greg Goebel, John Mounce, Donald Nijboer, Steve Ozel, Richard Reinsch, Arjun Sarup, Dean Shaw, Richard Vandervord, and Edward M. Young, and everyone who has provided photographic support.

This Ki-43-II, also from the 1st Sentai's 3rd Chutai, was flight tested by USAAF pilots at Liuchow in 1944, prior to being shipped back to NAS Anacostia for performance, capability and weak spot testing. The fighter was repainted in Chinese Nationalist Air Force camouflage and insignia, although Japanese Hinomaru were briefly applied so that a series of recognition photographs could be taken. A Ki-43-I had also been test flown in China during the spring of 1943. (*Richard Reinsch*)

INTRODUCTION

The first Japanese military aircraft to be test flown in the US following the start of the Pacific War was this A6M2, dubbed the "Akutan Zero" by the US Navy personnel seen here who recovered it from a marshy field on the deserted Akutan Island in the Aleutians. It took three attempts to extract this highly prized aircraft from its remote location. *(P233-v110 Alaska State Library Aleutian/Pribilof Project Photo Collection)*

The ill-fated pilot of the "Akutan Zero" was 19-year-old PO1c Tadayoshi Koga, who was killed instantly on June 4, 1942 when his battle-damaged fighter flipped over onto its back after he tried to land with its undercarriage extended on what he mistakenly thought was a grass-covered field. The pilot's body was found strapped into the cockpit when the aircraft was examined by the first salvage team to be flown in from Dutch Harbor – Koga's target – on July 11, 1942. The IJNAF aviator was extricated from the Zero-sen and given a Christian burial in a nearby knoll. (*Wikipedia Commons/ public domain*)

During and immediately following the surprise attack on US military installations and ships at Pearl Harbor, America was overwhelmed by Japan's surprising superiority and strength in the air. The dominance of the Japanese Mitsubishi A6M Zero-sen in the Pacific skies during the early stages of World War II made American war planners and military aeronautics officials desperate to obtain an intact version of this Pacific phenomenon. Then, on June 4, 1942, luck befell the United States when PO1c Tadayoshi Koga, flying from the carrier *Ryujo*, attempted a wheels down emergency landing in his battle-damaged A6M2 Zero-sen in a marshy field on deserted Akutan Island, in the Aleutians, following an attack on Dutch Harbor, some 25 miles to the east on Unalaska Island. The aircraft flipped upon landing, killing Koga in the process. The Zero-sen remained virtually intact, with the dead pilot still strapped in the cockpit, and it was eventually spotted on July 10 by a US Navy PBY-5A Catalina flying boat while on patrol. The crew of the latter radioed the position of their important find back to American forces in

A6M2 construction number 4593 was freed from the mud on the third attempt and hauled overland to a waiting barge. The Zero-sen is seen here – minus its engine – at Dutch Harbor, on Amaknak Island, immediately after being carefully lifted off the barge. (*NARA*)

A mobile crane was used to right the fighter once it was pier-side; this photograph clearly shows the purpose-built wooden jig that had been built for its transport to Dutch Harbor. The Zero-sen, which had been delivered to the IJNAF on February 19, 1942, was returned to the jig for onward shipment to Seattle on board the transport vessel USS *St. Mihiel* (AP-32). *(NARA)*

Two civilian dock workers scrape mud out of the cockpit of the "Akutan Zero" prior to it being lowered back onto its jig ready for shipping south. (NARA)

OPPOSITE Looking like an American naval fighter after being repainted in the standard US Navy colors of the day (Blue-Gray over Light Gull-Gray), the "Akutan Zero" sits on the ramp at NACA's LMAL facility in Virginia on March 8, 1943 shortly after it had completed a series of tests in the full-scale wind tunnel on site. The areas examined by the Langley engineers included wake surveys to determine the drag of aircraft components, sideslip tests, and tunnel scale measurements to gauge lift, drag and control effectiveness at varying speeds and angles of attack. (JHM collection)

the vicinity, and the Japanese fighter was successfully retrieved shortly thereafter and shipped back to the US mainland.

Once in America, the captured Zero-sen was extensively tested, both in flight and in the National Advisory Committee for Aeronautics' (NACA) Full-Scale Wind Tunnel at the Langley Memorial Aeronautical Laboratory (LMAL) in Hampton, Virginia. The secrets of this aerial legend of the Pacific were gradually revealed. Armed with data from the flight tests and wind-tunnel research, both the US Navy and the US Army Air Force (USAAF) were able to alter the training of their fighter pilots in order to exploit the weaknesses of the Zero-sen in aerial combat.

For the remainder of World War II, Japanese aircraft manufacturers continued to impress with their increasingly sophisticated fighter and bomber designs. However, many of these examples were produced in too little quantity and appeared too late in the war to make a difference to the outcome of the conflict. As Allied forces, led by the United States,

advanced across the Pacific and retook islands and liberated countries, they captured numerous Japanese war prizes in the form of advanced military aircraft and aerial weapons. Flight testing and evaluation of captured Japanese aircraft by Allied Technical Air Intelligence Units (ATAIU) abroad provided Allied war planners with invaluable insight into the enemy's aircraft and aerial weapon design philosophy, as well as how best to combat these threats during World War II. This evaluation process also provided the Allies with an up-to-date assessment of the state of the aviation industry in Japan in respect to its technological capabilities.

This richly illustrated volume documents the flight testing and evaluation of captured Japanese aircraft during and immediately after World War II.

The A6M2 was transported by barge from Seattle to San Diego, where it was offloaded at NAS North Island on August 12. The Zero-sen's damaged vertical stabilizer, rudder, wing tips, flaps and canopy were repaired here, as was the landing gear – its three-bladed Sumitomo propeller was also replaced. The A6M2 made its first flight in American hands – with Lt Cdr Eddie R. Sanders at the controls – on September 26. This photograph was one in a series that was taken during a flight from NAS North Island on October 15, 1942. The aircraft was captured on film from all possible angles, and these shots were then widely disseminated amongst front-line units to aid in the visual recognition of the IJNAF's iconic fighter. (*NARA*)

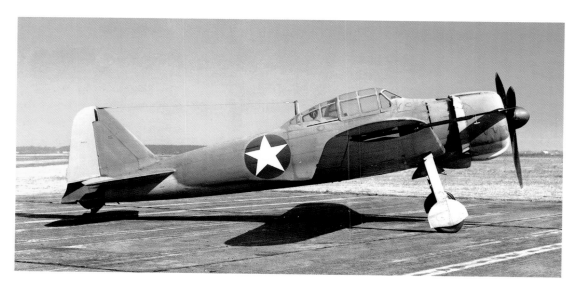

CHAPTER 1

THE ALLIED TECHNICAL AIR INTELLIGENCE UNITS

Technical Air Intelligence Center officers (both US Navy and USAAF) at NAS Anacostia come together for a group photograph in front of Saipan A6M5 construction number 4340 in December 1944. The aircraft, which was designated TAIC 7, is missing part of its engine cowling. Following flight testing and evaluation at NAS Anacostia, TAIC 7 was transferred to Wright Field for use by the USAAF. (*Richard Reinsch*)

In 1944, the US War Department, the USAAF, the US Navy, and Britain's Royal Air Force (RAF) felt it imperative to obtain better technical air intelligence (TAI) regarding both the Imperial Japanese Naval Air Force (IJNAF) and Imperial Japanese Army Air Force (IJAAF) through enhanced coordination and integration of the Allied military services' TAI efforts in the Pacific. Consequently, the US Division of Naval Intelligence was charged with the assignment of final evaluation of technical air information and the dissemination of results. The aforementioned Allied military services also reached concurrence that the US Division of Naval Intelligence was to be supported in its important TAI mission by Allied personnel and facilities.

As the war in the Pacific progressed, the Allies found that TAI results yielded crucial data regarding performance, vulnerability, fields of fire, aircraft recognition, and enemy tactics. Therefore, according to Allied war planners, this heavily influenced "planning, Allied air tactics,

US TAI played a vital role in providing US Naval Intelligence model aircraft makers with technical information that allowed them to build accurate scale replicas of Japanese aircraft, which were in turn used to aid US military personnel in enemy aircraft identification during World War II. Here, a US sailor puts the final touches on a model of an IJAAF Ki-21 "Sally" heavy bomber. (US Navy, Naval History and Heritage Command)

economic warfare, target information, and domestic design."[1] The "vital importance of TAI" was quickly recognized by top US and British military services war planners, who agreed:

> The centralizing of responsibility for this important activity in a single agency, staffed with experienced technical air intelligence personnel of the Allied military services, will provide the military services and government agencies interested in scientific development, or in assessing the war economy of the enemy, with more accurate and complete data on:

> 1. Performance and characteristics of Japanese air equipment.
> 2. Design and construction of Japanese air equipment.
> 3. Quality of workmanship in Japanese air equipment.
> 4. Raw material situation as related to Japanese air equipment.
> 5. Recognition features of Japanese aircraft.
> 6. Japanese Air Force maintenance and supply facilities.[2]

In mid-1944 the Secretary of the Navy, James V. Forrestal, decided to create the Technical Air Intelligence Center (TAIC) at Naval Air Station (NAS) Anacostia, in Washington, D.C., to support a broad and comprehensive final evaluation of technical air information as well as the quick dissemination of TAI results. The TAIC would accomplish these goals through its provision of organizational structure and special facilities. The official duties of the TAIC included:

This fighter was the subject of an early Allied TAIU recovery of a Japanese aircraft. Indeed, A6M3 "EB-201" was the first enemy machine to be flown by the recently formed Technical Air Intelligence Unit-South West Pacific (TAIU-SWPA) after restoration in Hangar No. 7 at Eagle Farm near Brisbane, Queensland. Seen here during a test flight from Wright Field following its shipment to the US in late September 1943, the Zero-sen had been rebuilt using parts from five different airframes captured at Buna, in New Guinea, on December 27, 1942. (*NARA*)

1. To receive, evaluate, and analyze all intelligence reports, dispatches, photographs, etc., relating to enemy air equipment.
2. To determine Japanese aircraft and engine performance data.
3. To prepare master drawings, silhouettes, sketches, and models for use in recognition training, and in the development of performance data.
4. To receive, catalog, examine, overhaul and rebuild captured aircraft, engines, and air equipment as necessary, and to arrange for or conduct required tests.
5. To train personnel for technical air intelligence duties in the field, including salvage, repair, and re-construction of aircraft and the erection and installation of equipment and facilities.
6. To produce and issue timely and useful technical air intelligence summaries and reports for dissemination to the Allied military services and government agencies.[3]

The TAIC comprised five primary sections consisting of USAAF and US Navy personnel, and some RAF personnel. As stated in an official Division of Naval Intelligence report:

The sections perform the following functions:

Aircraft Data Section – Evaluates and analyzes all intelligence reports, dispatches, photos, etc., having to do with enemy and Allied aircraft, and sees that pertinent technical intelligence on Japanese aircraft is disseminated without delay to all concerned.

Development Section – Makes up master drawings, models, and photographs for use in developing recognition material and performance data.

Performance Section – Analyzes all intelligence reports, dispatches, photos, etc., relating to Japanese aircraft and engines for the purpose of developing accurate performance data.

Engine and Equipment Section – Evaluates and analyzes all intelligence reports, dispatches, etc., having to do with enemy and Allied engines and equipment, and sees that pertinent technical intelligence on Japanese engines and equipment is disseminated without delay to all concerned.

Captured Equipment Section – Receives and catalogs captured air equipment, and when necessary for test or display purposes, rebuilds or overhauls such equipment. Makes up reports on captured air equipment and sees that the information is disseminated without delay to all concerned. Coordinates test program of Army, Navy, and British.[4]

TAIC personnel pose with a Ki-46-II "Dinah" parked in front of Hangar 152 at NAS Anacostia in the summer of 1945. Captured at Hollandia, in New Guinea, in April 1944 and made airworthy there five months later, the "Dinah" was eventually shipped to NAS Anacostia for further flight testing and evaluation. This photograph is one of a number in the collection of Capt Richard Paul Reinsch, who can be seen here sitting in the front row, fifth from left. (*Richard Reinsch*)

By mid-1944, US Navy TAIU personnel had been transferred to NAS Anacostia to establish the TAIC, the primary mission of which was to serve as the hub for the coordination of evaluation reports emanating from various test centers in the US and in the front-line theaters of war. Shortly thereafter, all TAIU-SWPA personnel were posted from Eagle Farm to NAS Anacostia to help staff the TAIC. Following the successful invasion of the Philippines in October 1944, a reformed TAIU-SWPA was formed and flown out to the theater in early 1945.

The advances made by the Japanese in aeronautical technology soon became readily apparent to the evaluation teams, who retrieved numerous advanced (as well as some more established) IJNAF and IJAAF aircraft destined to help counter and repel the anticipated Allied invasion of Japan. These types included fighters like the A6M5, Mitsubishi J2M3 "Jack," Ki-45 KAIc "Nick," Ki-61 "Tony," Kawanishi N1K1-J "George," Nakajima Ki-44-II "Tojo," Nakajima Ki-84-I Ko "Frank" and the Nakajima J1N1-S "Irving" nightfighter; torpedo-bombers such as the Nakajima B5N2 "Kate" and Nakajima B6N2 "Jill"; the Yokosuka D4Y3 "Judy" dive-bomber and Mitsubishi G4M2 "Betty" level bomber; transports such as the Showa L2D3 "Tabby" and Tachikawa Ki-54C "Hickory"; and the Mitsubishi Ki-46-III "Dinah" reconnaissance aircraft.

In late 1943 the TAIU for Southeast Asia, a joint RAF/USAAF TAI team, was established in Calcutta, India. It was subsequently dissolved in Singapore three years later. Two additional units were also formed, TAIU for the Pacific Ocean Area (TAIU-POA), consisting of US Navy personnel who conducted operations in the Pacific Islands, and TAIU for China (TAIU-CHINA), a unit directed by the Nationalist forces of the Chiang Kai-shek regime.

OPPOSITE A P1Y1 "Frances" was also amongst the IJNAF types found at Clark Field, and like the "Jill," it too was pored over by TAIU-SWPA personnel. The fast bomber could be fitted with a flexible 20mm Type 99 Model 1 cannon in the nose, and this photograph reveals details of the hydraulic mounting to which the weapon would have been attached. The cannon could be rotated a full 360 degrees thanks to the geared teeth that can be seen running around the inner edge of the mounting. The motor that provided power for the mounting's drive mechanism is fitted to the left side of the nose. Note also the two footrests for the gunner. (*NARA*)

CENTER This annotated photograph of a "Baka" captured at Yontan airfield, on Okinawa, in April 1945 was included in the TAIC report on the weapon. More than ten examples were duly shipped back to the US, where they underwent detailed technical evaluation at various sites, including NAS Anacostia. (*NARA*)

BELOW TAIU teams visited a number of Japanese aircraft factories in the weeks and months after VJ Day, including the bomb-damaged Nakajima factory at Koizumi in Gunma Prefecture, northwest of Tokyo, in early October 1945. Here, they found a handful of advanced types in various states of construction, including sub-assemblies for the G8N "Rita" bomber – these are wing sections for the four-engined long-range land-based heavy bomber. (*NARA*)

RIGHT This illustrated page was taken from a detailed TAIC report on the Yokosuka MXY-7 "Baka" rocket-powered, manned flying bomb that was air-launched from a G4M2e Model 24J "Betty" during the final months of the war in the Pacific. The purpose of these diagrams was to illustrate the weapon's areas of vulnerability to fighter aircraft and ships' anti-aircraft gunners alike. Fortunately for the Allies, the MXY-7, christened the Ohka by the IJNAF, enjoyed only limited success. (*NARA*)

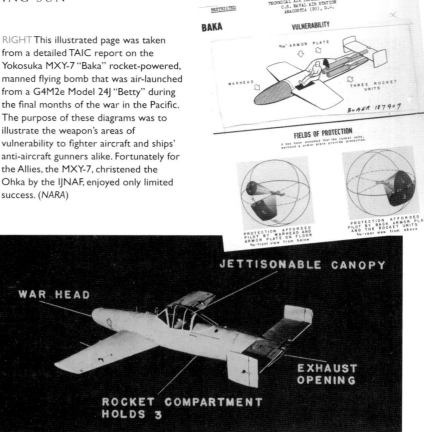

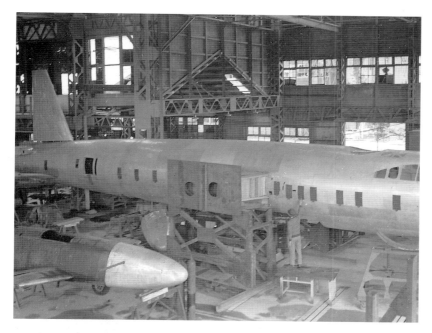

TOP Aside from several "Rita" fuselages, TAIU personnel also discovered as many as 23 Kikka jet fighters under construction in the main factory building at Koizumi. Some of these were subsequently shipped to the US for evaluation. (*NARA*)

CENTER More familiar types were also found at Koizumi, including dozens of engineless A6M6cs and A6M7 Zero-sens, seen here crammed into one of the final assembly buildings on site. Production of both models had been assigned to Nakajima by the IJNAF in early 1945, although delivery of aircraft to front-line units was badly delayed by a shortage of water-methanol boosted Sakae 31 engines. (*NARA*)

BOTTOM An exotic variety of IJNAF and IJAAF fighter, reconnaissance, and dive-bomber types (45 in total) have been lashed down to the flightdeck of the escort carrier USS *Barnes* (CVE-20) in Yokosuka harbor in November 1945, bound for the US. Easily the most unusual type visible – at bottom left – is the twin-engined Nakajima J5N1 Tenrai ("Heavenly Thunder") single-seat interceptor, of which only six prototypes were built. The type never entered series production. (*Aviation History Collection / Alamy Stock Photo*)

BELOW All the aircraft sent by carrier to the US were sprayed with an anti-corrosion coating to protect them from the salt-laden environment that they would be exposed to during their shipment across the Pacific. Four examples of each available type that had not previously been evaluated were chosen for transportation (one each for the USAAF, US Navy and RAF, and one as a source of spare parts). (*Aviation History Collection / Alamy Stock Photo*)

TAIUs remained operational post war. Following the cessation of hostilities, USAAF Commanding General Henry H. "Hap" Arnold requested that four of each type of Japanese aircraft be preserved – one each for the USAAF, US Navy, RAF and a planned national aviation museum in the US. The aircraft were assembled at Yokosuka naval base's Oppama airfield, 40 miles south of Tokyo, in late 1945. A total of 115 IJAAF and IJNAF aircraft were shipped to America, and 73 were supplied to the USAAF and 42 to the US Navy. Just six were restored to a flyable state, test-flown and evaluated by the USAAF, and two by the US Navy. Only 46 Japanese aircraft found their way to aviation museums and the remainder were scrapped.[12] At the beginning of 1946, ATAIU-SEA, based in Singapore, managed to retrieve a total of 64 IJAAF and IJNAF aircraft for shipment to Britain. Unfortunately, only four of them actually made it to England, where they were eventually displayed in aviation museums.[13]

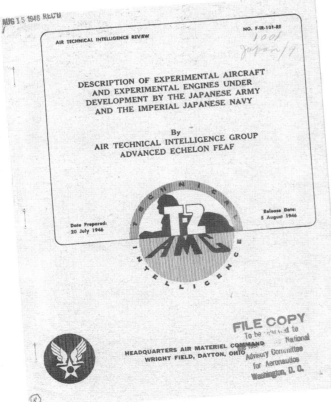

The RAF's ATAIU-SEA flew a radar-equipped G4M2a fitted with ASV radar from the former IJNAF airfield at Tebrau, on the Malayan mainland, in early 1946. Appropriately marked with RAF roundels, this "Betty" was one of nine IJNAF and IJAAF types displayed for the benefit of the press and visiting VIPs. Interestingly, these aircraft were flown by Japanese pilots, and most of the IJNAF types had actually been based at Tebrau during the conflict. (© *IWM CF 897*)

The Air Technical Intelligence Group (which was part of the USAAF's Headquarters Air Materiel Command) produced a series of reports and reviews during 1946, providing expert summaries on the various Japanese aircraft, engines, and weaponry its staff had evaluated both in the US and Japan since the end of the war. This was the cover page to Review No. F-IR-101-RE, published on August 5, 1946. (*NARA*)

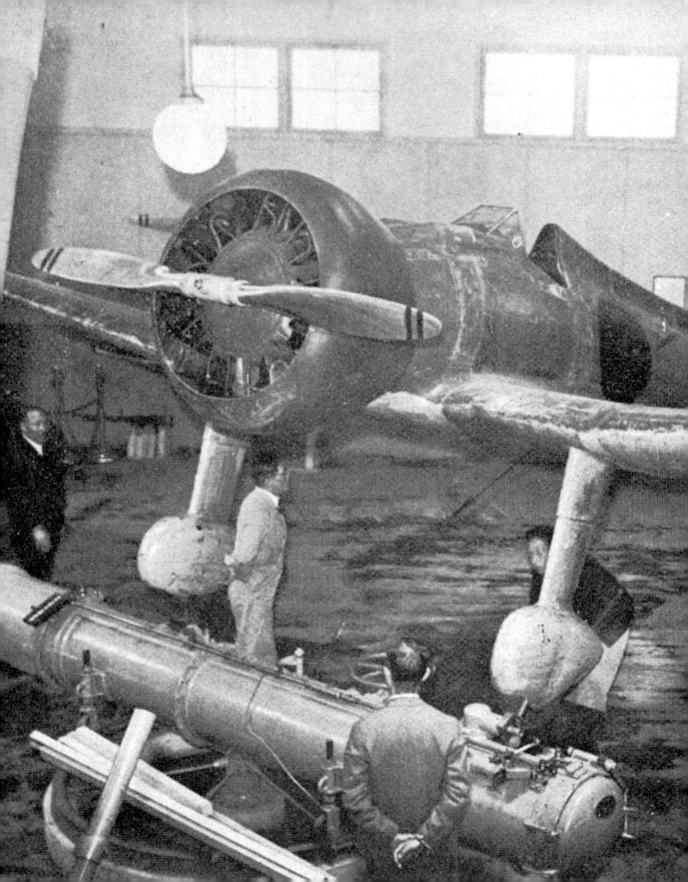

CHAPTER 2

EVALUATING FIGHTERS

One of at least three A5M4 "Claudes" that fell to anti-aircraft fire between September 1937 and February 1938 during the Second Sino-Japanese War. These aircraft were from the 12th and 13th Kokutais. A well-aimed shell had taken off a large section of the aircraft's outer port wing. The "Claude" was part of a public display staged in Nanchang, Jiangxi, China, in December 1937. This A5M4 was almost certainly one of three examples that were transported to the USSR for technical evaluation; the Scientific Research Institute of the Air Force duly returned one to airworthiness. (*NARA*)

The flight testing and evaluation of captured Japanese World War II fighters quickly revealed the strengths and weaknesses of the design philosophy adopted by manufacturers such as Mitsubishi and Nakajima. Japanese designers were encouraged by the IJNAF and IJAAF to emphasize speed and maneuverability in their aircraft at the expense of self-sealing fuel tanks and armor protection for the pilot. The emphasis on speed and maneuverability also meant that Japanese fighter designs had to be as light as possible. Therefore, unlike the aircraft of their Allied foes, the A6M and Ki-43, for example, were not equipped with gun cameras for recording aerial and ground attack combat successes.

Toward the end of World War II, however, Japanese fighter design philosophy changed. Excellent aircraft such as the IJAAF's Nakajima Ki-84 "Frank" and the IJNAF's Kawanishi N1K1/2-J "George" featured more powerful engines, increased firepower, enhanced armor protection for the pilot and self-sealing fuel tanks. Allied aircrew began to encounter these superb fighters in aerial combat following the invasion of the Philippines in October 1944. Unfortunately for Japan, they were "too little too late" to have a significant impact on the outcome of the war.

United States Intelligence services began noticing the change in Japanese aircraft design and development toward the end of the war. As stated in a US Navy Technical Air Intelligence Summary written in July 1944:

> Very recent documentary evidence has indicated clearly that both the Japanese Navy and Army are engaging in extensive experimental work in new models of aircraft. This development program seems to embrace both new designs and improvements of existing types. Constant allusions by PoWs to new fighters tie in very closely with the captured documents and lead to the belief that Japan is exerting every effort to modernize her entire Air Force.
>
> The recent withdrawal of the Japanese Air Force from forward areas and avoidance of individual combat does not necessarily denote an overall weakness but rather a predetermined plan to reform and regroup their squadrons with available new metals.[1]

TAI learned of Japanese enhanced fighter aircraft powerplants in 1944, as stated in the following report:

> The largest engine referred to as being fitted to a new plane is rated 2500 hp. This is not at all unreasonable in view of BuAer's assessment of the potentialities of the recently captured Kasei 25 and Namomiu II engines – both of which will soon undergo power tests. Frequent

mention is made of engine ratings, varying between 1800 and 2200 hp, and the Jap tendency is to sharply increase the size of powerplants in all their new planes.

Captured engines that have been examined show excellent design and workmanship and readily lend themselves to continued improvements. This factor will place many new series enemy aircraft in the 400 mph class which in the past they have been unable to attain.[2]

TAI also began to notice a trend toward enhanced firepower in Japanese fighter aircraft in 1944: "Consistent reports from documents and PoWs stress the fact that the Japs are becoming increasingly aware of the inadequacy of their armament. References to 25mm, 80mm, 30mm and 40mm guns have appeared."[3]

By 1944, TAI learned that the Japanese were now producing fighter aircraft with improved armor protection for the pilot, as stated in a 1944 TAI Summary:

> Harsh lessons have forced the Japs to revise their original concept of armor protection. No definite pattern of armor plating has been found so far, but more planes are being found with increasingly heavy plate. The protection does not seem to be incorporated as part of the basic design, but rather improvised after manufacture. As larger engines become operationally available it is expected that heavier armor with more comprehensive arrangement will be adapted.[4]

TAI experts also noted that in the past, the Japanese, particularly the IJAAF, had made only "half-hearted" attempts to add self-sealing fuel tanks to their fighter designs. By 1944, it became clear that the Japanese had changed this kind of thinking in new designs.

SINGLE-ENGINED FIGHTERS

Mitsubishi A5M4 "Claude"

On December 9, 1937, during the Second Sino-Japanese War, an IJNAF Mitsubishi A5M4 "Claude" was flying over Nanchang, in China's Jiangxi province, when half of its port wing was blown off by anti-aircraft fire. In a testament to its solid structural design, the "Claude" remained aloft long enough for its pilot to make an emergency landing. He and his aircraft were captured by the Chinese, and the "Claude" was put on public display. The aircraft was later repaired and restored to flying condition, being test-flown and studied to assess the state of Japanese aeronautical technological progress. The fighter was eventually turned over to the Soviet Union, where it undertook further flight testing.

Nakajima Ki-27 "Nate"

On April 25, 1942, Chinese troops managed to capture an IJAAF Nakajima Ki-27 "Nate" fighter. Subsequent test flying and evaluation at Kweilin revealed that the aircraft suffered from the same deficiencies as the A5M4 "Claude" – light armament, lack of adequate armor protection for the pilot, and no self-sealing fuel tanks. In aerial combat in 1941–42, IJAAF "Nates" had proven vulnerable to American Volunteer Group (AVG) Curtiss Tomahawk IIBs, although Japanese pilots had previously enjoyed considerable success against inferior and obsolescent Chinese and Soviet biplane and monoplane fighters.

A Ki-27 of the 54th Sentai shortly after its capture by Chinese troops at Kweilin airfield in China on April 25, 1942. The pilot, Sgt Maj Kazuka Kobayashi, was obliged to force-land with engine trouble while performing a reconnaissance sortie over the airfield. The 2nd Chutai leader, Capt Toshio Dozono, landed in an abortive attempt to rescue Kobayashi, but he too was immediately taken prisoner. It appears that Sgt Maj Kobayashi was killed shortly after he landed at Kweilin. (NARA)

A head-on view of the captured Ki-27, showing the fighter's elegant lines and relatively long wingspan. Given the code P-5015, the aircraft was thoroughly flight tested by both Chinese and American pilots. Brig Gen Claire Lee Chennault, who led the AVG in China, sent performance data for the "Nate" to the Pentagon following flight trials that included mock dogfights with the Tomahawk I. This information was reportedly lost, however. (NARA)

Sgt Maj Kazuka Kobayashi's Ki-27 was repainted in Chinese Nationalist Air Force colors and insignia, its engine repaired and the fighter test flown. Here, it is being examined with interest by pilots from the AVG, which was also based at Kweilin. (*NARA*)

Mitsubishi A6M2 Model 21 Zero-sen

The first A6M2 Model 21 Zero-sen fell into Allied hands in China on November 26, 1941. On a reinforcement mission (to serve as escorts for G4M1 "Betty" bombers operating against the British forces in Burma and Malaya) from the IJNAF airfield at Tainan, in Taiwan, to Saigon, two A6M2s of the Tainan Kokutai strayed from their formation and encountered fog at low altitude. Zero-sen construction number 3372 (tail code V-172) was flown by PO1c Shimezoh Inoue, while the other fighter (tail code V-174) had FPO2c Taka-aki Shimohigashi at the controls.

En route to Hainan Island to refuel, the two Zero-sen pilots had drifted apart from the primary formation and now found themselves in quite a predicament as they were running out of fuel and their aircraft lacked radios in an attempt to boost the A6Ms' range. Relying solely on their compasses for guidance, Inoue and Shimohigashi pressed on until

Captured Tainan Kokutai A6M2 construction number 3372 (tail code V-172) was the very first Zero-sen to fall into Allied hands, on November 26, 1941. Sister-aircraft V-174 was badly damaged, when both fighters force-landed on a Chinese beach and it was cut into transportable pieces but V-172 was recovered virtually intact. Both aircraft then took several months to be moved from Leichou to Liuchow, where, by late summer 1942, V-172 had been reconstructed by Chineese engineers and mechanics. (*NARA*)

大道之行天下為公

ABOVE Chinese officials pose with a USAAF officer, believed to be Col Nathan F. Twining, in front of V-172. In the foreground is one of the severed wings from V-174. During re-assembly of the fighter it was found that V-172's fuselage panels aft of the cowling had been lost in transit whilst being moved north to Liuchow – they are clearly missing in this photograph. Chinese mechanics quickly fashioned substitute panels with uncharacteristic louvered vents as replacements. (NARA)

ABOVE RIGHT V-172 was checked over by USAAF mechanic Gerhard Neumann, who had traveled to Liuchow with SSgt George L. Mackie to get the fighter ready for a flight to Kweilin. Painted in Chinese Nationalist Air Force colors and markings, and given the serial P 5016, the fighter is seen here at Kweilin in the fall of 1942. (NARA)

the dense fog lifted, whereupon they spotted a lengthy beach near a town that appeared to be suitable for an emergency landing. Within minutes they had both landed on the beach on the Leichou coastline, where the pilots and their aircraft were captured by Chinese troops. Although Inoue's fighter was virtually unscathed, Shimohigashi's Zero-sen had suffered extensive damage upon landing and had to be written off. Inoue's A6M2 was later repaired by US engineers at Kunming airfield, in China, with a section of the forward fuselage just aft of the engine cowling boasting a new improvised covering that featured specially designed ventilation/cooling slits. The aircraft was also repainted in Republic of China Air Force colors, consisting of dark green with light blue underside camouflage, and adorned with Chinese national insignia.

During 1942 Inoue's Zero-sen was rigorously flight tested, undertaking a series of dogfights against Curtiss P-40E/K Warhawks and Republic P-43A-1 Lancers of the USAAF's 23rd Fighter Group. During

the mock combats it was found that the Zero-sen was considerably more maneuverable than any of the American fighters it was pitted against. Like most Japanese aircraft of the period, the A6M2 was found to possess virtually no armor protection. In comparative fly-offs with the P-40E, the Zero-sen exhibited a superior rate of climb above 10,000ft.[5] Meanwhile, the P-43A-1 boasted a superior rate of climb at altitudes in excess of 12,500ft.[6] The Zero-sen's US opponents also proved to be faster at all altitudes. In mock aerial combat, American test pilots stated:

The P-40 can effectively fight the Zero without necessarily diving away. This is accomplished by proceeding away from the Zero on the initial pass at high speed until approximately one-and-one-half miles away, at which time a maximum turn is begun back into the path of the pursuing Zero. This turn can be completed just in time for the P-40 to pass through the path of the Zero and barely miss a collision. If the Zero does not dodge from his own attack, the P-40 can fire a very effective head on burst in this manner. Of course, the Zero can take evasive action, but he cannot maneuver into such a position as to get effective fire into the P-40 without also getting return fire.

With the P-43, the same tactics can be used, but head-on runs are not advisable with this airplane due to lack of both

All five members of "The Zero Club" pose for a photograph at Kweilin in December 1942. They are, in the top row from left to right, Col Clinton D. "Casey" Vincent (Operations Officer, China Air Task Force, six victories), Lt Col John R. Alison (CO of the 75th FS/23rd FG, six victories), and Col Bruce K Holloway (CO of the 23rd FG, 13 victories), and in the foreground, from left to right, Lt Cols Albert J. "Ajax" Baumler (CO of the 76th FS, nine victories) and Grattan "Grant" Mahony (CO of the 76th FS, five victories). (USAF)

ABOVE P 5016 sits at Kweilin alongside P-40K "115" of the 76th FS, assigned to six-victory ace 1Lt Marvin Lubner. The Warhawk, complete with an AVG "Flying Tiger" decal on its fuselage, was flown in mock aerial combat against the A6M2, with a member of "The Zero Club" at the controls of the latter. The IJNAF fighter was found to be more maneuverable than the P-40K. (NARA)

RIGHT The Zero-sen also engaged a P-43A Lancer in the skies of Kweilin. The Lancer was one of a handful acquired on loan by the 23rd FG from the Chinese Nationalist Air Force for reconnaissance work, and it too was easily out-flown by the A6M2. (NARA)

fire power and protection. It is believed that the best tactics for engaging the Zero in individual combat with the P-43 is to climb away from the Zero and attempt to gain an advantageous position for a diving attack. The P-43 has a slight advantage in rate of climb and has a considerably higher best climbing speed.[7]

The Model 21 Zero-sen was loved by its pilots, and the fighter fared well in combat against Allied aerial opposition during the early stages of the Pacific War.

Perhaps the most significant Zero-sen captured during World War II, and the one that contributed most to Allied victory in the Pacific, was the A6M2 Model 21 known as "Koga's Zero." The aircraft's history is particularly intriguing. In accordance with the IJN's Midway offensive, it launched an attack on the Aleutian Islands, located in the southern coastal region of Alaska, in June 1942. The Japanese task force responsible

for the strike was under the command of Rear Admiral Kakuji Kakuta, and his carrier-based aerial strike force bombed Dutch Harbor, located on Unalaska Island, twice on June 3–4.

Assigned to the second of these strikes, 19-year-old PO1c Tadayoshi Koga took off in his A6M2 (construction number 4593) from the carrier *Ryujo* during the afternoon of June 4. Flying in a formation consisting of three Zero-sens, Koga was accompanied by wingmen CPO Makoto Endo and PO Tsuguo Shikada. The three pilots strafed Dutch Harbor and downed the US Navy PBY-5A Catalina flown by Lt Bud Mitchell. Koga's aircraft, however, subsequently sustained damage from American ground fire. With the return oil line of his fighter having been damaged, resulting in the Zero-sen trailing oil in its wake, Koga pulled back on the throttle in an attempt to keep the engine running long enough for him to reach Akutan Island, 25 miles to the east of Dutch Harbor. The IJNAF pilots had previously decided that Akutan was to be used as an emergency landing site should any of their aircraft be badly damaged, downed aviators then being rescued by IJN I-Boats (submarines) that were patrolling in the waters off the island.

Upon overflying a grassy area of Akutan, near Broad Bight, Shikada wrongly believed that there was solid ground beneath the grass. He communicated this to Koga, who attempted a conventional, gear down, landing. His aircraft flipped over as soon as its undercarriage came into contact with the marshy ground. While the Zero-sen received little further damage, Koga suffered a broken neck when the fighter came to rest

In early 1943 P 5016 was flown to Karachi, India, from Kunming, China, for shipment on to the US. The Zero-sen was provided with an escort of 23rd FG P-40Ks for the long flight, and one by one all the Warhawks aborted their mission with a series of mechanical failures, leaving the Zero-sen to arrive in Karachi alone. There, Gerhard Neumann supervised the crating of the fighter, which was duly transported to America for further testing. The aircraft was damaged in transit to such an extent that it had to be rebuilt by Curtiss before being delivered to Wright Field in July 1943. This photograph was almost certainly taken there, as the background has been blanked out by the wartime censor. (NARA)

TOP Given the USAAF Evaluation Branch code EB-2 once at Wright Field, the A6M2 was photographed internally and externally. This photograph shows the left side of the cockpit. Amongst the various controls visible is the chain-driven elevator trim tab control wheel immediately above the bomb release levers. Below the levers is the fuselage/wing tank switching cock and the wing tanks selector lever. Above the rectangular switchboard are the throttle lever, propeller pitch adjustment lever, and mixture control lever. Various Kanji characters can be seen on the instrumentation. (NARA)

CENTER EB-2's central instrumentation panel was also photographed, "framed" by the brake pedals at the bottom of the shot and the empty gun mountings partially visible at the top of the image. The hole on the left-hand side of the panel should have been filled by a radio direction indicator, but it is possible that this had yet to be installed when the fighter came down on the beach at Leichou. (NARA)

BOTTOM EB-2 is seen in flight above Wright Field on October 1, 1943. In 1944 the Zero-sen embarked upon a War Bond tour that took it as far west as California. Its final mention in official records appears on March 10, 1946, when EB-2 was noted on a list of aircraft available for release to industry. The final fate of this well-traveled Zero-sen remains unrecorded. (NARA)

inverted, killing him instantly. All fighter pilots had been ordered to destroy any Zero-sen that made an emergency landing in Allied-held areas to prevent the aircraft from falling into enemy hands. Endo and Shikada believed that Koga had survived the emergency landing, however, and they chose not to strafe the fighter prior to departing the area.

The aircraft remained preserved at the crash site for more than a month. Then, on July 10, a US Navy PBY Catalina, with Lt William "Bill" Thies at the controls, made visual contact with Koga's overturned Zero-sen – the wreckage had first been spotted by PBY crewman Machinist's Mate Albert Knack. After circling the downed Zero-sen several times and confirming and recording the position of the wreck, the PBY flew back to Dutch Harbor. The following day, a recovery team was flown by Thies out to the crash site to assess the aircraft. After removing Koga's corpse from the cockpit and hastily burying it close to the wreckage, Thies determined that the Zero-sen was recoverable and reported this to his commander at Dutch Harbor. On July 13 Lt Robert Kirmse led a recovery effort on Akutan. After providing Koga with a Christian burial near to the crash site, Kirmse and his men began the aircraft recovery process. After bringing in heavy lift equipment, the Zero-sen was extricated from the mud and moved via land transport to a barge, which shipped it to Dutch Harbor. Once the fighter had reached the port the preservation process was initiated.

Koga's Zero was subsequently loaded on board the transport vessel USS *St. Mihiel* (AP-32) and shipped southeast to Seattle, Washington. The aircraft was then transported by barge to NAS North Island, arriving on August 12. Here, the fighter's damaged vertical stabilizer, rudder, wingtips, flaps and canopy were repaired, as was the landing gear and the Zero-sen's three-bladed Sumitomo propeller.[8] The aircraft was then repainted in standard US Navy colors of the day (Blue-Gray over Light

PO1c Tadayoshi Koga's overturned Mitsubishi A6M2 as it appeared to US Navy recovery crews in a marshy field on deserted Akutan Island in the Aleutians on July 11, 1942. The Zero-sen was virtually intact, and subsequent flight testing and evaluation of the restored machine provided American aircraft designers with critical data needed to develop US fighters that could outperform the A6M. (NARA)

ABOVE The preservation process of Koga's Zero-sen commenced at Dutch Harbor upon its careful removal from the barge that had transported it from Akutan Island. A mobile crane was used to lift the fighter, minus its engine, from the vessel and turn it the right way up, before lowering it back onto its purpose-built shipping jig on the dock. The fighter's wing flaps had also been removed prior to it being moved to Dutch Harbor. (NARA)

OPPOSITE This view of the cockpit of Koga's Zero-sen was taken shortly after the fighter had been righted on the dock at Dutch Harbor. The vacant spaces on either side of the artificial horizon and the turn-and-bank indicator, just above the main flight instrument panel, had previously been filled by a pair of 7.7mm Type 97 machine guns. (NARA)

RIGHT A close-up view of the engine/propeller/spinner assembly from the Akutan Zero-sen on the dock at Dutch Harbor shortly after it had been craned off the barge. The compact, and ultra-reliable, Nakajima Sakae-12 radial engine, with a single-stage supercharger, was rated at a modest 950hp. Koga had lost power from this engine after its return oil line was damaged by American ground fire during his strafing attack on Dutch Harbor on June 4, 1942. (NARA)

LOWER RIGHT One of two 20mm Type 99-1 wing cannon removed from Koga's A6M2 when the fighter was recovered from Akutan Island. Cleaned up at NAS North Island, the weapons were then placed on a white cloth and photographed for intelligence purposes. A single 20mm cannon was mounted in each wing just outboard of the propeller arc, the weapons being fed by an angular and circular ammunition canister. The cannon had a relatively slow maximum cyclic rate of fire of 490 rounds per minute, which meant that most aerial victories credited to A6M2 pilots were achieved using the quicker firing Type 97 machine guns, which had a maximum cyclic, and quite fast, rate of fire of 900 rounds per minute. It was commonplace for more aggressive Zero-sen pilots to return from combat with empty machine gun magazines, whilst they rarely used all the cannon ordnance, even during strafing runs. (NARA)

Gull-Gray) and adorned with US national insignia. Closely guarded by military police, the A6M2 made its first flight in American hands – with Lt Cdr Eddie R. Sanders at the controls – on September 26.

Preliminary data obtained from ground study and evaluations of Koga's Zero-sen were relayed to both the Bureau of Aeronautics and Grumman, and it was the latter company's Leroy Grumman and his design team that benefited most from this information. They were able to subtly modify their new F6F Hellcat prior to it entering widespread

armor to protect the pilot and had no self-sealing fuel tanks. The American pilots described the cockpit arrangement as "fair," although legroom was inadequate for a man of normal size. They also found that the brakes could not be applied when the rudder was fully extended.[11]

The final fate of this aircraft remains unrecorded, the fighter almost certainly being summarily scrapped immediately post war.

Mitsubishi A6M3 Model 22 "Hamp"

In late 1942, the Allies began to encounter yet another Zero-sen variant in aerial combat in the form of the A6M3 Model 22. It was hoped that this aircraft would rectify the shortcomings of the A6M3 Model 32 by providing it with folding wingtips and a new wing design with increased fuel tank capacity – what had been the inner wing fuel tanks in the Model 32 were moved to the outer wing. In addition, provision was made for the fitting of a single 330 l (87 US gal) external fuel tank under each wing. The increased fuel capacity and the new wing design led to an overall enhancement of the aircraft's long-range mission capability.[12]

Following the surrender of Japanese forces on Bougainville on September 1, 1945, Royal New Zealand Air Force (RNZAF) Intelligence operatives learned of the existence of a virtually intact Zero-sen at nearby Kara airstrip. The subject aircraft (construction number 3844, tail code 2-152) had almost certainly been assigned to the 582nd Kokutai at Rabaul in 1943. Having been flown to Bougainville, it was caught on the ground there and seriously damaged in the bombing raids that accompanied the Allied landings in November 1943. The A6M3 was hidden at Kara airstrip for 18 months until a decision was made to

Hastily painted in a one-off surrender scheme (including green underwing crosses) of predominantly white, but with the area immediately forward of the cockpit still in IJAAF dark green, A6M3 construction number 3844 is seen here shortly after arriving at Piva Yoke airfield from Kara airstrip on September 15, 1945. The officer wearing the peaked cap peering into the cockpit is almost certainly Air Commodore G. N. Roberts, Commander of the New Zealand Air Task Force in the Solomons. (*Tony Holmes collection*)

OPPOSITE EB201 basks in the sunshine between flights at a P-38 OTU airfield in 1944. The bulk of the Lightning training was conducted by the Fourth Air Force at its airfields in California, specifically March Field, Riverside, and Hamilton Field, so it would seem likely that one of these sites is the location for this photograph. The fighters parked behind the Zero-sen are P-38Hs. (*NARA*)

The Kara Zero-sen was shipped to Auckland, New Zealand, in October 1945 and then sent by barge to RNZAF Station Hobsonville. Here, the fighter was stripped of its temporary surrender scheme and briefly flown by the base commander, Wg Cdr A. E. Willis. The Zero-sen was photographed sharing the ramp with PB2B-1 Catalinas of No. 5 Sqn RNZAF during 1946. (*Tony Holmes collection*)

return it to airworthy condition as a morale-boosting exercise for the 60 to 70 Japanese personnel that remained based in the area. During the rebuild the aircraft received a new tail section, scavenged from another Zero-sen that was derelict on the airfield.

With the aircraft airworthy by July 1945, PO Sekizen Shibayama was flown over from Rabaul in an Aichi E13A1 "Jake" floatplane to test-fly the Zero-sen and ferry it back to Rabaul. The fighter remained firmly grounded, however, owing to overwhelming Allied air superiority in the Bougainville area – the only Japanese aircraft seen in the air since March 1944 were floatplanes like the "Jake" undertaking clandestine courier flights. On September 15, 1945 Wg Cdr Bill Kofoed and Engineering Officer C. D. Kingsford were dispatched from Piva Yoke airfield in a Wirraway from No. 5 Sqn RAAF to Kara airstrip to evaluate the status of the Zero-sen. Upon their arrival, Kofoed received flight instructions from the Japanese regarding the fighter and proceeded to fly it back to Piva, with its undercarriage locked down for the entire 32-minute flight. Kofoed had in fact been ordered not to fly the aircraft by the Allied Surrender Commission, who saw no official reason to salvage the Zero-

sen. Once at Piva, the aircraft was thoroughly examined by RNZAF personnel, with one of the first to sit in the cockpit being Air Commodore G. N. Roberts, Commander of the New Zealand Air Task Force in the Solomons. He later recalled: "Kofoed had to be 'matted' for disobeying orders, but with that formality over I took him to my quarters, gave him a couple of whiskies and congratulated him for being so bloody stupid."

Although the fighter's engine was run at Piva, it never flew again. The Zero-sen was eventually loaded onto the ferry steamer *Wahine*, which had been chartered to repatriate RNZAF personnel from the Pacific back to New Zealand, and shipped to Auckland (arriving here on October 20, 1945). It was then sent by barge on to RNZAF Station Hobsonville. In early December, the base commander, Wg Cdr A. E. Willis, carried out taxiing trials and, on or around December 12, authorized himself to make a ten-minute flight in the Zero-sen. He subsequently noted "the aircraft was quite pleasant to fly, being rather like a Harvard. It appeared to have no unusual traits in the ten minutes I was flying." On December 18 Air Commodore S. G. Wallingford, Air Member for Supply, reported to the Minister of Defence: "The Zero is

A6M3 construction number 3844 is carefully pushed back into a hangar at RNZAF Station Hobsonville. The fighter was kept in storage here for more than a decade until it was transferred to the Auckland War Memorial Museum in 1959. Eventually restored by Aircraft Component Engineering in 1995–97, the Zero-sen has been on display within the Museum's "Scars on the Heart" exhibition for more than 20 years. (*Tony Holmes collection*)

now serviceable and will be flight tested within two or three days. It is proposed to allot the aircraft to the Central Fighter Establishment at Ardmore, where it will be used for tactical training of fighter pilots."

No test flying was ever authorized, however, and a subsequent proposal to allot the Zero-sen to the Central Flying School at Wigram (in Christchurch) also came to nothing. The aircraft was then designated to serve as a training aid with No 1 Technical Training School, also at Hobsonville, in February 1947. Never actually used in this role, the fighter remained in storage for more than a decade until it was transferred to the Auckland War Memorial Museum in 1959. The Zero-sen was eventually restored by Aircraft Component Engineering in 1995–97 and was then put on display within the Museum's "Scars on the Heart" exhibition.

The Kara A6M3 was not the only Japanese aircraft surrendered to the New Zealanders, for on September 18, 1945 (three days after Kofoed's flight) four machines flown by Japanese pilots and escorted by RNZAF Corsairs were flown into the base at Jacquinot Bay, on New Britain. Three of the aircraft were A6M5 Model 52s (including construction numbers 3479 and 4043), while the fourth was Ki-46-II "Dinah" construction number 2783, which suffered damage to its undercarriage on landing. The fighters remained flyable, however, with two of them being presented to the RAAF and the third occasionally flown by RNZAF pilots. An E13A1 "Jake" floatplane also alighted in Jacquinot Bay on October 14 and remained moored in the harbor until a leak developed in one of its floats and the aircraft sank. The airworthy

"Zeke" and the damaged "Dinah" were subsequently abandoned where they were parked when the RNZAF pulled out of Jacquinot Bay shortly thereafter, and they could be seen there for many years after the war.

Mitsubishi A6M5 Model 52 "Zeke"

From the fall of 1942, Allied units in the Pacific began to encounter the improved A6M5 Model 52 Zero-sen in aerial combat. This variant featured shorter wings than previous models, with heavier-gauge skin and redesigned non-folding rounded wingtips in an attempt to improve the Zero-sen's diving speed. Its ailerons were also modified and strengthened. Model 52 Zero-sens were initially built by Mitsubishi, although Nakajima subsequently took over production. The Model 52 was powered by the same Sakae 21 seen in the A6M3, although the engine featured new individual exhaust stacks that provided some thrust augmentation. This meant that although the A6M5 was 416lb heavier than the A6M3, the new model was 13mph faster. As with previous Zero-sens, the A6M5 and 5a retained the same armament consisting of two 7.7mm Type 97 machine guns in the upper fuselage decking and

BELOW LEFT Firmly secured to a wheeled trailer with rope, an engineless A6M5 is carefully transported through rubble-strewn Aslito Field toward the nearby dock area for loading on board *Copahee*. A number of Sakae 21 engines were also shipped back to the US to act as spares sources for airworthy Zero-sens. Although lacking a motor and its port wing flap, this aircraft is fitted with underwing bomb racks that could carry up to ten 70lb aerial burst bombs. (*NARA*)

BELOW Several dozen A6M5 Zero-sens were found in various states of disrepair at Aslito Field, on Saipan, following the base's seizure by the US Army's 27th Infantry Division in a bloody battle on June 18, 1944. Most of the aircraft, including these examples, belonged to the 261st Kokutai. No fewer than 12 A6M5s from the unit were shipped back to the US on board the escort carrier *Copahee* shortly after they had been captured. (*NARA*)

USAAF groundcrew tinker with an A6M5 discovered at Aslito Field (renamed Isley Field No. I shortly after its capture). The aircraft was almost certainly undergoing rectification work on its undercarriage when the base fell to the 27th Infantry Division. All of the A6M5s on Saipan were Nakajima-built aircraft that had been completed in the early spring of 1944 and supplied as attrition replacements to the 261st Kokutai at Aslito Field. (NARA)

two wing-mounted 20mm Type 99 cannon. However, the A6M5b had one of its Type 97 weapons replaced with a 13.2mm Type 3 machine gun, while the 5c had only a solitary Type 3 in the upper fuselage decking and two more in the wings, along with a pair of Type 99 cannon.

On June 18, 1944, the US Army's 27th Infantry Division captured Aslito Field, on Saipan, and seized a cache of 12 Model 52s from the 261st Kokutai. The aircraft were shipped back to the US on board the *Copahee* the following month, arriving in San Diego on July 16. A6M5 construction number 5357 (tail code 61-120), built by Nakajima, was made airworthy at NAS North Island and completed its first flight from here on August 5. Subsequently designated TAIC 5, the fighter was ferried to NAS Anacostia on August 22 and then on to NAS Patuxent River, in Maryland, for thorough evaluation. Here, test pilots racked up many hours flying the Zero-sen. While at "Pax River," aviation pioneer Charles Lindbergh was also checked out in the A6M5, flying it on October 23.

Between August and November 1944, TAIC 5 was test-flown in mock aerial combat against the F4U-1D Corsair, F6F-5 Hellcat, and FM-2 Wildcat. The pilots (both military and civilian, the latter from aircraft manufacturers Grumman, Chance-Vought, and Bell) participating in the flight evaluations followed a rotated aircraft assignment regime. As noted in the flight-test report:

The Zeke 52 tested was powered by a Nakajima Sakae 31A engine [this must be a mistake, as the 31 did not enter production until late 1944], not equipped with water injection. The cockpit arrangement was quite good, with the exception of the landing gear and flap controls. The airplane was easy to fly, except for excessively high control forces at high speeds. At speeds around 160 knots the controls tightened, and at speeds over 200 knots the control forces became objectionably heavy, especially in the ailerons.

There was a very marked stall warning, the tail stalling about ten knots before the wings, causing a noticeable buffet.

The airplane was considered to be quite stable.

The steep angle of climb of the Zeke 52 gives it the appearance of a very high rate of climb, but its relatively slow climbing speed brings its actual rate below the expected value.

A slightly better turn to the left than to the right was noted at all altitudes.

Excessive vibrations were noted in dives at speeds above 250 knots.[13]

The Model 52 Zero-sen was found to be much slower than its US Navy fighter adversaries at all altitudes. This disparity was quite evident in the comparison flight-test evaluations with the F4U-1D:

This cutaway drawing of the A6M5, codenamed "Zeke 52" by the Allies, was included in a detailed report on the aircraft released in June 1945 by the TAIC following exhaustive evaluation of the Saipan fighters. The aircraft's areas of vulnerability were highlighted by the artist on direct instruction from TAIC personnel. Its engine was erroneously labelled as a "Sakae 31" – the A6M5 was fitted with the earlier Sakae 21 like the A6M3 before it. (NARA)

ZEKE 52 CARRIER BASED FIGHTER

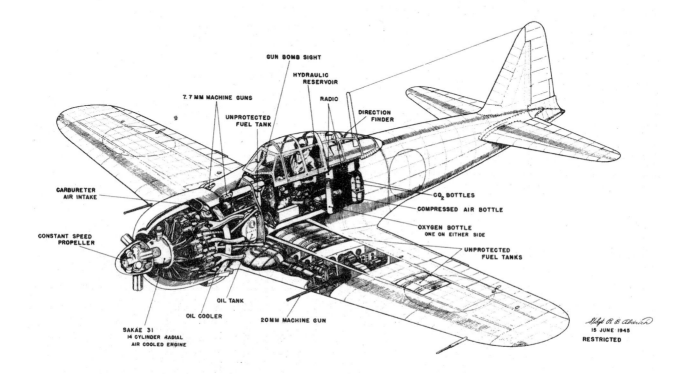

At sea-level the F4U-1D was 48mph faster than the Zeke 52.
At 5,000ft the F4U-1D was 42mph faster than the Zeke 52.
At 10,000ft the F4U-1D was 58mph faster than the Zeke 52.
At 15,000ft the F4U-1D was 70mph faster than the Zeke 52.
At 20,000ft the F4U-1D was 78mph faster than the Zeke 52.
At 25,000ft the F4U-1D was 80mph faster than the Zeke 52.
At 30,000ft the F4U-1D was 74mph faster than the Zeke 52.
Top speeds attained were 413mph at 20,400ft for the F4U-1D and
335mph at 18,000ft for the Zeke 52.[14]

It was found that at speeds below 200 knots, the Model 52 Zero-sen and
F4U-1D had a similar rate of roll, but at speeds in excess of 200 knots,
the Model 52 Zero-sen was "inferior" owing to its high control forces.
Once again, at slower speeds, the Model 52 Zero-sen easily out-
performed the F4U-1D in turns at both low and medium altitudes.
However, at an altitude of 30,000ft, the Model 52 Zero-sen only just
beat the Corsair in respect to its rate of turn. The F4U-1D proved to be
vastly superior in a dive, however.

A6M5c/7 ZERO-SEN COCKPIT

Artwork by Jim Laurier, © Osprey Publishing

1. Type 98 reflector gunsight
2. Artificial horizon
3. Turn and bank indicator
4. Type 3 13.2mm machine gun
5. High-altitude automatic mixture control
6. Exhaust temperature gauge
7. Clock
8. Airspeed indicator
9. Magnetic compass
10. Rate of climb indicator
11. Fuel and oil pressure gauge
12. Tachometer
13. Emergency fuel pump lever
14. Direction finder control unit
15. Emergency power boost
16. Radio direction indicator
17. Magneto switch
18. Altimeter
19. Control column
20. Manifold pressure gauge
21. Oil temperature gauge
22. Cylinder head temperature gauge
23. Cockpit light
24. Throttle quadrant/20mm cannon firing lever
25. Primer
26. Oxygen supply gauge
27. Hydraulic pressure gauge
28. 20mm cannon master switch
29. Oil cooler shutter control
30. Cowl flap control
31. Radio control unit
32. Elevator trimming tab control
33. Circuit breakers
34. Rudder pedals
35. Wing tanks cooling air intake control
36. Emergency undercarriage down lever
37. Loop antenna handle
38. Seat up/down lever
39. Fuel tank jettison handle
40. Fuselage tank fuel gauge
41. Wing tanks fuel gauge
42. Emergency fuel jettison lever
43. Fuselage/wing tanks switching cock
44. Wings tank selector lever
45. Bomb release lever
46. Seat
47. Arresting hook winding wheel
48. Wing tank fuel switching cock

A6M5 construction number 5357 (tail code 61-120) was offloaded from *Copahee* in San Diego on July 16, 1944 and made airworthy in less than three weeks by sailors at NAS North Island, the fighter completing its first flight from there on August 5. Subsequently designated TAIC 5, the Zero-sen was ferried to NAS Anacostia on August 22 and then on to NAS Patuxent River for thorough evaluation. It was photographed at "Pax River" shortly thereafter. (*NARA*)

The test pilots found vision from the cockpit of the Model 52 Zero-sen to be superior to that in the Corsair primarily because of the excellent rear vision in the A6M5 (which featured a bubble canopy and no armor plating behind the pilot). In terms of maneuverability, the Model 52 Zero-sen was vastly superior to the Corsair at speeds up to 175 knots. High control forces at higher speeds, however, degrade the fighter's maneuverability to the point where the Corsair held the edge at speeds in excess of 200 knots.

With the evaluation of TAIC 5 completed, the following tactics were recommended to Corsair pilots when encountering a Model 52 Zero-sen:

Do not dogfight with the Zeke 52.

Do not try to follow a loop or half roll with pull-through.

When attacking, use your superior power and high-speed performance to engage at the most favorable moment.

To evade a Zeke 52 on your tail, roll and dive away into a high-speed turn.[15]

In comparative flight-test evaluations with an F6F-5 Hellcat, it was found that the Model 52 Zero-sen had a superior rate of climb of 600ft per minute up to 9,000ft. However, at an altitude of 14,000ft, the two aircraft were equal in their rate of climb, and at altitudes exceeding 14,000ft the Hellcat held the advantage. The top speed achieved by the Hellcat in a climb was 130 knots, while the Model 52 Zero-sen managed just 105 knots.

In terms of overall speed, it was quite evident that the Hellcat was superior to the Model 52 Zero-sen at all altitudes. As revealed in the flight-test report:

At sea-level the F6F-5 was 41mph faster than the Zeke 52.

At 5,000ft the F6F-5 was 25mph faster than the Zeke 52.

At 10,000ft the F6F-5 was 45mph faster than the Zeke 52.
At 15,000ft the F6F-5 was 62mph faster than the Zeke 52.
At 20,000ft the F6F-5 was 69mph faster than the Zeke 52.
At 25,000ft the F6F-5 was 75mph faster than the Zeke 52.
At 30,000ft the F6F-5 was 66mph faster than the Zeke 52.
Top speeds attained were 409mph at 21,600ft for the F6F-5 and 335mph at 18,000ft for the Zeke 52.[16]

The comparative performance characteristics of the F6F-5 Hellcat and the Model 52 Zero-sen were identical to those of the F4U-1D and the Model 52 Zero-sen in terms of their rates of roll and turn, speed and handling when in a dive, maneuverability and vision from the cockpit. This meant that Hellcat pilots were encouraged to employ the same tactics when engaging the A6M5 in combat as their counterparts flying Corsairs.

The Model 52 Zero-sen proved to be more than a match for the FM-2 Wildcat in the comparative performance flight evaluations, however. The former enjoyed a superior rate of climb at lower altitudes, but was "slightly inferior" at heights in excess of 13,000ft. The Model 52 Zero-sen also proved to be faster than the FM-2 at most altitudes. As stated in the flight-test report:

The Zeke 52 was progressively faster than the FM-2 above 5,000ft.
At sea-level the FM-2 was 6mph faster than the Zeke 52.
At 5,000ft the FM-2 was 4mph slower than the Zeke 52.
At 10,000ft the FM-2 was 12mph slower than the Zeke 52.
At 15,000ft the FM-2 was 8mph slower than the Zeke 52.
At 20,000ft the FM-2 was 19mph slower than the Zeke 52.
At 25,000ft the FM-2 was 22mph slower than the Zeke 52.
At 30,000ft the FM-2 was 26mph slower than the Zeke 52.
Top speeds attained were 321mph at 13,000ft for the FM-2 and 335mph at 18,000ft for the Zeke 52.[17]

The Model 52 Zero-sen exhibited similar roll capability to that of the FM-2, particularly at speeds below 160 knots. The FM-2 proved to be a better performer in terms of roll capability at speeds in excess of 160 knots, however, owing to the A6M5's high control forces. The Zero-sen held the advantage over the FM-2 with respect to its rate of turn, the Japanese fighter also being faster in a dive, possessing superior vision from the cockpit and being more maneuverable below 200 knots, but not at speeds in excess of this figure. The following tactics were recommended to FM-2 pilots when encountering a Model 52 Zero-sen in combat:

After helping to prepare US Navy fighter pilots bound for the Pacific war zone, TAIC 5 had logged more than 190 flying hours by the time it was declared surplus to requirements at NAS Alameda on September 30, 1945. The aircraft was eventually purchased as scrap by pioneer warbird collector Ed Maloney in 1951 and exhibited in The Air Museum (later renamed Planes of Fame) from 1957. (*Stocktrek Images, Inc. / Alamy Stock Photo*)

Do not dogfight with the Zeke 52.

Maintain any altitude advantage you have.

To evade a Zeke 52 on your tail, roll and dive away into a high-speed turn.[18]

This rear view of TAIC 7 at a snowy Wright Field was taken on February 20, 1945. The aircraft bears the nickname *TOKYO ROSE* in small lettering on the port-side of its engine cowling. Note also the construction number 4340 just forward of the tailplane. TAIC 7 had returned from the warmer climes of Eglin Field shortly before this photograph was taken, having undertaken comparative performance evaluations with a P-38J, a P-47D and N, and a P-51D while in Florida. (*NARA*)

With its fighter trials over, TAIC 5 was returned to NAS North Island to help with the training of US Navy fighter pilots about to be posted to the Pacific war zone. By the end of September 1945 the aircraft had logged more than 190 flying hours in US hands. On the last day of that month it was flown to NAS Alameda, near San Francisco, and subsequently declared surplus to requirements. The Zero-sen was eventually purchased as scrap by pioneer warbird collector Ed Maloney in 1951 and exhibited in The Air Museum (later renamed Planes of Fame) in Claremont, California, from 1957. In 1973 work began on restoring the fighter to airworthy status, the Zero-sen returning to the sky in June 1978. Currently the only airworthy A6M5 equipped with an authentic Sakae engine, the Zero-sen remains a prized exhibit within the Planes of Fame Museum in Chino, California.

A6M5 construction number 4340 (tail code 61-108) was amongst the Zero-sen captured at Aslito Field in June 1944, this aircraft being assigned the code TAIC 7 upon its arrival in San Diego. Made airworthy as NAS Anacostia in September 1944, the fighter was transported to Wright Field for flight testing and evaluation by the USAAF – it had the nickname *TOKYO ROSE* applied to its cowling while here. In early January 1945, TAIC 7 was transferred to Eglin Field, Florida, where it undertook comparative performance evaluations with a P-38J, a P-47D and N and a P-51D. During the trials the Zero-sen was flown by a test pilot, while combat-experienced aviators were at the controls of the USAAF fighters.

In the comparative performance flights, it was found that the P-51D-15, P-38J-25 and P-47D-30 were vastly superior to the Model 52 Zero-sen in terms of top speed at altitudes of 10,000ft and 25,000ft. As stated in an official TAIC report,

A6M5 construction number 4340 (tail code 61-108) was the second Saipan Zero-sen to fly in the US. Allocated the code TAIC 7 upon its arrival in San Diego, the fighter was restored to airworthiness at NAS Anacostia in September 1944. Totally devoid of paint, bar a thin anti-glare stripe forward of the cockpit, and with mixed American and Japanese insignia, the fighter is seen here coming in to land at Wright Field after a test flight in January 1945. (NARA)

> Due to advantages in speed, acceleration and high-speed climb, all three AAF fighters were able to maintain the offensive in individual combat with the Zeke 52, and to break off combat at will. The Zeke 52 is greatly superior to all three AAF fighters in radius of turn and general maneuverability at low speeds.[19]

As a result of these flight tests, the USAAF also developed tactics for combating the A6M5. As recommended in the flight-test report:

> The pilots of AAF fighter aircraft (P-38, P-51 and P-47 types) should take advantage of high speed performance superiority when engaging the Zeke 52 in combat; speed should be kept well above 200 knots indicated air speed (IAS) during all combat: "hit and run" tactics should be used whenever possible, and following the Zeke through any continued turning maneuvers must be strictly avoided.[20]

Other interesting Type 52 Zero traits were also revealed through the comparative performance flight tests:

> Dogfight comparisons with each AAF fighter were made under three different initial conditions. In the first condition, combat was begun from an approach or parallel course 500ft apart. The other two combat comparisons were begun with either airplane 2,000ft above and behind

Declared surplus to requirements in early 1946, TAIC 7 spent many years in storage following its acquisition by the NASM. It was eventually restored in 1974–75 for exhibition in the new NASM building on the national Mall, the fighter being painted in the camouflage and markings it wore while assigned to the 261st Kokutai in 1944. This Zero-sen has been on permanent display in Washington, D.C. for more than 40 years. (*Arjun Sarup*)

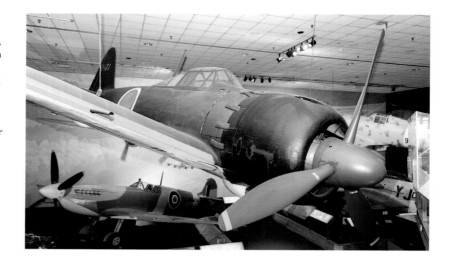

the other. In every case, the Zeke was forced on the defensive after combat started. All three AAF fighters could break away from the initial condition by shallow dives and high-speed climbs out of range. After the first disengagement, AAF fighters could re-engage combat from an altitude advantage, and could make passes at will, breaking away as before. The Zeke was sufficiently maneuverable to turn into every pass and take a snap shot at the attacking aircraft. Only when the AAF fighters slowed down or turned after a pass could the Zeke get in a shot (other than head on defensive shooting). The Zeke could easily get in firing position and stay on the tail of AAF fighters through all low-speed maneuvers.[21]

A6M5 construction number 2193 was also part of the Saipan haul, and it was given the code TAIC 8. The fighter performed a dedicated aerial recognition photo-flight from Bakersfield Municipal Airport, California, in April 1945 while assigned to the 412th FG. Undertaking mock combat with the unit's P-59 Airacomet and P-80 Shooting Star jet fighters, TAIC 8 was eventually scrapped the following year. (*NARA*)

TAIC 7 was ultimately obtained by the National Air and Space Museum (NASM) and restored to pristine condition in 1976, becoming the very first Japanese airplane to be refurbished by the organization. The aircraft has been displayed in the NASM's World War II gallery for many years.

Nakajima Ki-43 "Oscar"

In development from December 1937 and introduced into service in 1940, the Ki-43 was, broadly speaking, the IJAAF's equivalent of the IJNAF's Zero-sen. Codenamed "Oscar" by the Allies, the fighter was built as a replacement for Nakajima's highly successful, but now obsolescent, Ki-27 "Nate." The lightweight Ki-43-I featured a Nakajima Ha-25 radial engine and two-bladed, variable-pitch metal propeller. Like the Ki-27, the Ki-43 was highly maneuverable, but later suffered during the war from a lack of adequate armor to protect the pilot and an absence of self-sealing fuel tanks. The airplane was also very lightly armed, initially boasting just a pair of 7.7mm Type 89 machine guns. Nevertheless, the "Oscar" managed to down more Allied aircraft than any other IJAAF fighter, and it was the mount of many Japanese aces. A total of 5,919 Ki-43s had been produced by war's end.

Two "Oscars" (a Ki-43-Ib and a Ki-43-II) captured in New Guinea were restored to flying condition by TAIC maintainers in Hangar No. 7 at Eagle Farm airfield in Brisbane in 1943–44 and then test-flown against Allied fighter aircraft in Australian skies.

In early 1945, an intact Ki-43-II "Oscar" from an unknown IJAAF unit was captured at Clark Field on Luzon, in the Philippines, by US Army personnel. The aircraft was soon restored to flying condition and eventually test-flown by pilots from the TAIU-SWPA, which had reformed following the American victory in the Philippines. The USAAF evaluation pilots found the Ki-43-II to be extremely maneuverable and to possess an excellent rate of climb. The aircraft's enhanced performance was determined to have been achieved through the fitting of a water injection system to its Nakajima Ha-115 engine. The fighter was armed with two 12.7mm Type 1 (Ho-103) machine guns in the engine cowling.

Ki-43-I "Oscar" XJ002 has its Nakajima Ha-25 radial engine run up at Eagle Farm in March 1944. The aircraft had been found abandoned by Australian troops at Lae airfield, New Guinea, on September 16, 1943. The "Oscar's" first post-restoration flight was made on March 17, 1944, with Capt William O. Farrior at the controls – he is almost certainly the pilot sat in the cockpit in this photograph. (*Australian War Memorial*)

TAIU-CHINA gained access to a number of Ki-43s during World War II, several of which were restored to airworthiness. One such example was this Ki-43-II of the 1st Sentai's 3rd Chutai, which was stripped down and rebuilt at Liuchow airfield during 1944. (*Richard Reinsch*)

KI-43-II "OSCAR" COCKPIT

Artwork by Jim Laurier, © Osprey Publishing

1. Army Type 100 reflector gunsight
2. Airspeed indicator
3. Turn and bank indicator
4. Rate of climb indicator
5. Manifold pressure gauge
6. Compass
7. Altimeter
8. Tachometer
9. Fuel pressure gauge
10. Oil pressure gauge
11. Oil temperature gauge
12. Undercarriage warning lights
13. 12.7mm guns
14. Guarded switch cover
15. Engine primer fuel pump
16. Cocking handle
17. Cabin lamp
18. Elevator trimming
19. Chronometer
20. Radio tuner
21. Radio dial
22. Cylinder temperature
23. Exhaust temperature
24. Control column
25. Canopy winding mechanism
26. Combat flap control buttons
27. Main switches
28. Oxygen control
29. Oxygen flow meter
30. Fuel gauge (main tanks)
31. Fuel gauge (auxiliary tanks)
32. Right and left auxiliary tank selector
33. Right and left main tank selector
34. Pilot's seat
35. Hydrostatic plunger for main tanks
36. Hydrostatic plunger for auxiliary tanks
37. Hydraulic brake pedals
38. Rudder pedals
39. P.4 compass
40. Emergency hydraulics hand pump
41. Magneto switch
42. Throttle lever
43. Mixture control
44. Propeller pitch control
45. Friction adjuster
46. Control handle valve (use unknown)
47. Internal tanks cock
48. Main fuel cock
49. Undercarriage emergency operation
50. Cam manipulation
51. Undercarriage selector
52. Flap selector
53. Compressed air bottle

ABOVE The Liuchow Ki-43-II was also adorned with 16 stylised "stars and and bars" beneath the cockpit on the starboard side of the fuselage. The significance of these markings – applied in decal form – has been lost over the intervening 75 years since this photograph was taken. (*Richard Reinsch*)

RIGHT TAIU personnel inspect and remove 12.7mm ammunition from the two Ho-103 Type 1 machine guns installed in Ki-43-II construction number 5653, which had force-landed on Long Island, New Guinea on January 22, 1944. This aircraft was almost certainly from the 59th Sentai. According to the TAIU report on the fighter, "Only combat damage noted was one bullet strike through the right barrel cover that nicked the barrel and then severed the oil line." (*Richard Reinsch*)

The American evaluators also discovered that 12mm armor plating had been installed behind the pilot and rubber-lined fuel tanks were fitted in this "Oscar" variant. The aircraft was found to be limited to a speed of just 372mph when in a dive.

Post war, the captured Ki-43-II was placed atop a pole near the entrance to Base Operations at Clark Air Force Base (AFB). It remained on display into the 1960s, when the base commander ordered its disposal. The fighter was summarily scrapped shortly thereafter.

A second intact Ki-43-II, belonging to the IJAAF's 1st Sentai, was also captured in the China Theater of Operations during 1944 and it too was restored to airworthy status and test-flown from Liuchow airfield. The aircraft's final fate remains unknown.

Kawasaki Ki-61-Ia "Tony"

From April 1943, Allied units in New Guinea began to encounter an all-new IJAAF fighter that was vastly superior to the Ki-43 with respect to its speed and firepower. The aircraft, the Ki-61 "Tony," had been created in 1940 in answer to an IJAAF request for a fighter that could achieve aerial supremacy at low and medium altitudes. The Ki-61-Ia was equipped with two fuselage-mounted 12.7mm Type 1 (Ho-103) machine guns and a pair of wing-mounted 7.7mm Type 89 machine guns – later models boasted two fuselage-mounted Ho-5 20mm cannon and two Ho-103 machine guns in the wings. The aircraft was also capable of carrying either two 50-gallon fuel tanks or two 220lb bombs on underwing racks.

Undoubtedly the "Tony's" most distinctive feature was its Kawasaki Ha-40 inline, liquid-cooled engine, this 1,175hp powerplant being a license-built version of the Daimler-Benz DB 601A motor fitted to the Messerschmitt Bf 109E. Unlike most other Japanese fighters of its time,

This Nakajima-built Ki-43-II (construction number unknown) was one of several "Oscars" abandoned by the 59th Sentai at Cyclops airfield in northern New Guinea in late April 1944. Found by troops from the US Army's 41st Infantry Division, the aircraft was moved to nearby Hollandia airfield, where it was examined by TAIU personnel (as well as the curious RAAF pilots seen in this photograph) and assigned the tail code XJ004. The aircraft was made airworthy by groundcrew from the 8th FS/49th FG and TAIU personnel from Eagle Farm. Shipped to Brisbane during the summer of 1944, its ultimate fate is unknown. (PF-(sdasm3) / Alamy Stock Photo)

RIGHT This Ki-43-II KAI was captured intact at Clark Field in February 1945. Its unit allocation is unknown, as both the 31st and 71st Sentais flew from Clark in 1944–45. Although examined by the TAIU-SWPA, it appears that the fighter was never flown by the unit due to the "Oscar's" obsolescence by this late stage in the Pacific War. (NARA)

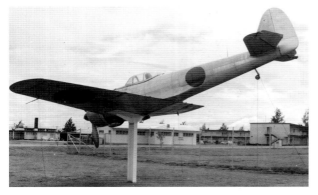

ABOVE Devoid of any distinguishing markings, this anonymous Ki-43-II was displayed at Clark Air Force Base for almost 20 years from 1948. Unsubstantiated reports claim that it was found intact in the nearby jungle by a lieutenant serving on-base shortly after the war had ended. The Ki-43 was eventually scrapped in the late 1960s on the orders of a new base commander who apparently had a "hatred of all things Japanese." (Courtesy of the San Diego Air & Space Museum)

the Ki-61 had a self-sealing fuel tank positioned behind the cockpit and armor protection for the pilot. The final series production version of the "Tony," the Ki-61-II KAI, was equipped with the more powerful 1,500hp Ha-140 engine.

The following excerpt from an early ATAIU report reveals the impressions of American Air Intelligence experts with respect to the "Tony":

Just when TONY appeared on the scene is open to conjecture. The Tokyo raiders and combat reports, dating back to February 1942, reported the use of in-line engine fighters by the Japs. Some were thought to be Messerschmitts, some Heinkels. The in-line engine fighters, however, were seen too seldom for positive identification. TONY is designated "Type 3" by the Japs and, if there is any consistency in the Jap system of nomenclature, TONY could not have gone into production until 1943.

In several important ways, TONY is a distinct departure from previous Jap practice. While TONY's engine shows definite German inspiration, the aircraft is essentially Japanese in design. Perhaps the reason for this is that Kawasaki designed TONY while all other Jap SSFs [single-seat fighters] are either Mitsubishis or Nakajimas. TONY has built-in-armor-plate for the pilot and an attempt at fuel tank protection. Although TONY has been shot down in flames, it does not show the tendency to explode that is common with ZEKE or OSCAR. Externally, aside from the use of an in-line engine, TONY varies most noticeably from other Jap SSFs in the cockpit enclosure, which fairs into the fuselage instead of assuming the characteristic Jap blister.

From a structural standpoint, TONY is the first Jap fighter that shows any consideration for mass production design. Large skin panels are used, and while flush riveting is employed, the skin is lapped, not butt-jointed. The spars are built up, without extrusions, and extend through the fuselage in the familiar Jap one-piece wing. The internal structure of the wing, however, appears to be much less complicated than on other Jap aircraft. Combat reports indicate that TONY is faster than HAMP, ZEKE or OSCAR and has a faster dive, but does not climb quite as fast and is not quite as maneuverable. P-38s have clocked TONY at better than 400mph in shallow dives, but there are indications that steep dives are avoided, even when considerable advantage is to be gained through such a maneuver. Armament includes 1 x 7.7mm or 1 x 12.7mm in each wing and two synchronized 12.7mm in fuselage. The recognition features of TONY have been covered previously in BuAer Confidential Bulletin No. 2-43.[22]

Built by Kawasaki at the Kagamigahara factory during April 1943, Ki-61-Ia construction number 263 of the 68th Sentai's 2nd Chutai was found abandoned but intact at Tuluvu airfield, Cape Gloucester, by the US Marine Corps on December 30, 1943. Almost certainly assigned to chutai commander Capt Shogo Takeuchi, the "Tony" had been grounded due to mechanical problems. Dubbed the "Cape Gloucester Ki-61," the aircraft was dismantled, transferred to Hangar No. 7 at Eagle Farm, and rebuilt by TAIU-SWPA personnel. (NARA)

Flown just three times in Australia before suffering an engine failure, the Ki-61 was shipped from Brisbane to NAS Anacostia in June 1944, where it was made airworthy once again. It is seen here at the latter location shortly after being repaired, with traces of its TAIU-SWPA XJ003 code just visible on the rudder to the right of the TAIC 9 identifier that had been applied. (NARA)

The "Tony" proved to be superior to the USAAF P-40 Warhawk in aerial combat and, later in the war, was an exceptional B-29 Superfortress bomber interceptor. More than 3,000 Ki-61s were produced during World War II.

On December 30, 1943, the US Marine Corps found the discarded 68th Sentai Ki-61-Ia construction number 263, equipped with a "Ko" armament configuration (two 12.7mm Ho-103 cannon in the forward fuselage and two 7.7mm Type 89 machine guns in the wings) when they

KI-61-IB HIEN COCKPIT

Artwork by Jim Laurier, © Osprey Publishing

1. Army Type 100 reflector gunsight
2. Turn and bank indicator
3. Compass
4. Rate of climb indicator
5. Airspeed indicator
6. Clock
7. Altimeter
8. Ho-103 12.7mm machine guns
9. Coolant temperature gauge
10. Oil temperature gauge
11. Oil pressure gauge
12. Fuel pressure gauge
13. Coolant shutter indicator
14. Oxygen flow meter
15. Fuel gauge
16. Engine fuel primer pump
17. Fuel tank changeover cock
18. Fuel injection pump
19. Landing gear indicator lights
20. Type 99 No. 3 wireless receiver
21. Rudder pedals
22. Hand-operated fuel pump
23. Wing-mounted gun cocking handles
24. Emergency landing gear release handle
25. Oil pressure pump handle
26. Emergency oil pressure changeover lever
27. Flap lever
28. Fuselage gun cocking lever
29. Radiator flap control lever
30. Undercarriage lock safety lever
31. Undercarriage lever
32. AC lever
33. Trim tab control lever
34. Control column
35. Throttle
36. Propeller pitch control
37. Fuel tank changeover cock
38. Tachometer
39. Manifold pressure gauge
40. Engine magneto switch
41. Outside air temperature gauge
42. Cockpit lights
43. Seat
44. Electric control panel
45. Oxygen control lever
46. Machine gun trigger
47. Seat adjustment lever
48. Oil pressure gauge

ABOVE The "Cape Gloucester Ki-61" was later repainted in overall mid-brown/green in order to make it more representative of front-line IJAAF types being encountered in combat. The aircraft was thoroughly flight tested by both USAAF and US Navy test pilots, with the latter noting that it possessed "pleasant" flight characteristics. The "Tony's" enhanced fuel and pilot protection constituted a significant advancement in Japanese fighter aircraft design. (NARA)

captured Cape Gloucester airstrip on New Britain. The fighter had been assigned to Capt Shogo Takeuchi, CO of the 68th Sentai, who had perished while flying a different "Tony" over Hansa Bay. Dubbed the "Cape Gloucester Ki-61," the fighter was dismantled and loaded on board a US Navy LST for shipment to Brisbane. Once in Queensland, it was transferred to Hangar No. 7 at Eagle Farm airfield and rebuilt by TAIU-SWPA personnel. All of the aircraft's original camouflage and markings were removed during this period, replaced with US national insignia and the tail code XJ003.

Once restored to airworthiness, the Ki-61 completed three flights in June–July 1944 with Sqn Ldr D. R. Cuming from the RAAF's No. 1 Aircraft Performance Unit at the controls – he had flown up specially to make these flights from RAAF Base Laverton. Cuming had also recently

BELOW Once camouflaged, the "Cape Gloucester Ki-61" was photographed on the ground at "Pax River" from every possible angle. The fighter's widely splayed undercarriage is shown to advantage here. (*NARA*)

carried out flight trials of the Ki-43-I rebuilt at Eagle Farm. It had been hoped to fly the Ki-61 in a series of tactical trials against the P-38, P-40, P-47 and Spitfire VIII, but this had to be canceled after bearing metal was found in the engine oil filter following the third flight.

The "Cape Gloucester Ki-61" was transported from Brisbane to NAS Anacostia shortly thereafter, where it was made airworthy once again. The fighter duly undertook additional flight testing, impressing US Navy pilots with its "pleasant" handling characteristics. However, they also noted maintenance difficulties with the aircraft. Advanced elements of the design, including enhanced fuel and pilot protection, were closely analyzed, as they marked a significant improvement in Japanese fighter aircraft design. Indeed, the aircraft's armor protection for the pilot, in the form of 10.3mm steel plating, underwent special evaluation at the US Army's Aberdeen Proving Ground, in Maryland, where it was found that the plating was penetrable by 0.50-cal and 0.30-cal machine-gun shells.

Further flight testing of the "Tony" was carried out by the NATC at "Pax River" until July 2, 1945 when the fighter suffered an engine failure during a ferry flight from "Pax River" to Eglin Field. Its pilot, Lt John A. Thomas, belly landed at Yanceyville, North Carolina, writing off the Ki-61 in the process.

Nakajima Ki-44 "Tojo"

Shortly after Nakajima was instructed to proceed with the design of the Ki-43, it was also asked by the IJAAF to create an interceptor, the speed and rate of climb of which were to take precedence over maneuverability – the most important trait in all Japanese fighters up to then. Designated the Ki-44, the prototype commenced flight testing in August 1940 and pre-production examples were sent to front-line units for service evaluation in the fall of the following year. Given the Allied codename "Tojo," the Ki-44 was indeed less maneuverable than the "Oscar." However, it was faster, had a rate of climb/dive that equaled Allied fighters of the same time period and was more heavily armed than the Ki-43. The base armament configuration of the "Tojo" was two 12.7mm machine guns in the wings and two more in the forward fuselage. However, these weapons could be partly or fully replaced by the 20mm Ho-3 cannon, while a small number of Ki-44-IIb/cs had two wing-mounted 40mm Ho-301 cannon.

Thanks to this armament, its good rate of climb and high-altitude performance, the Ki-44 proved to be a useful B-29 interceptor in 1944–45. The "Tojo" was powered by a 1,250hp Nakajima Ha-41 14-cylinder double-row radial engine and capable of a maximum speed of up to 376mph at an altitude of 17,000ft. The aircraft was also equipped with butterfly flaps similar to those found on the Ki-43 for enhanced maneuverability.

The following excerpt from an early ATAIU report reveals what American Air Intelligence experts thought of the "Tojo" after wreckage of several examples had been examined in China in 1942–43:

This aircraft was one of two serviceable Ki-44-IIs (from the 29th and 246th Sentais) captured by the US Army when Clark Field was liberated in early February 1945. This particular example was from the 29th Sentai, and it bore the construction number 2068. It was equipped with drop tanks, which were carried inboard of the undercarriage. The character 木 "ki" (wood) was stencilled onto the front of each tank to indicate their plywood construction. An intact Ki-45 "Nick" can be seen in the background. (NARA)

✳✳✳

TOJO is the new Army, Ki-44 Type 2 SSF. Two marks of TOJO are known to exist. Mark I, powered with a 1250 H.P. engine, has never, as far as is known, been encountered. This summary, therefore, deals exclusively with the Mark II version. Recently operational in China, TOJO is expected to appear, shortly, in other Japanese theaters. This plane, the smallest fighter thus far encountered, carries the most powerful engine ever found in a Jap SSF. Manufactured by Nakajima, who also makes the aircraft, it is a 14-cylinder, two-row radial of, as yet, unknown designation. With a displacement of 2290 cu. In. and a two-speed, 12-inch diameter supercharger, this engine is expected to deliver approximately 1450 H.P. at its rated altitude of 8600ft.

In general, TOJO follows the accepted Jap philosophy of fighter design. Construction is light, no protection is provided for the pilot, engine, or fuel tanks, and the armament is inadequate by American standards. Two synchronized 7.7mm guns are fixed in the fuselage and one 12.7mm is fixed in each wing, firing from just outside the

Ki-44-II COCKPIT

Artwork by Jim Laurier, © Osprey Publishing

1. Army Type 100 reflector gunsight
2. Airspeed indicator
3. Turn and bank indicator
4. Rate of climb indicator
5. Manifold pressure gauge
6. Compass
7. Altimeter
8. Tachometer
9. Fuel pressure gauge
10. Oil pressure gauge
11. Oil temperature gauge
12. Landing gear indicator lights
13. Ho-103 12.7mm machine guns
14. Cabin lamps
15. Elevator trim control
16. Hydraulic pressure gauge
17. Radio tuner
18. Cylinder temperature gauge
19. Exhaust temperature gauge
20. Control column
21. Canopy winding mechanism
22. "Butterfly" flaps control buttons
23. Main switches
24. Oxygen control
25. Oxygen flow meter
26. Fuel gauge (main tanks)
27. Fuel gauge (auxiliary tanks)
28. Left and right auxiliary tank selector
29. Left and right main tank selector
30. Pilot's seat
31. Hydrostatic plunger for main tanks
32. Hydrostatic plunger for auxiliary tank
33. Hydraulic brake pedals
34. Rudder pedals
35. P.4 compass
36. Emergency hydraulic hand pump
37. Magneto switch
38. Throttle lever
39. Mixture control
40. Propeller pitch control
41. Friction adjuster
42. Internal tanks cock
43. Main fuel cock
44. Undercarriage emergency operation
45. Cam manipulation
46. Undercarriage selector
47. Flap selector
48. Compressed air bottle
49. Clock
50. Flap position indicator
51. Hydraulic brake pressure gauge

propeller arc. As might be expected, TOJO is fast, maneuverable, and has a high rate of climb. A number have been shot down over China and at least three of the crashes were investigated by Naval Technical Air Intelligence Officers. These planes were practically demolished, but sufficient data was recovered to assure reasonable recognition drawings and performance estimates. Both are provisional and will be revised as new material becomes available.

The wing is almost identical, in plan, with the Thunderbolt's. Construction is unique in that it is the only Jap SSF with detachable outer panels. The joint is located just outboard of the wing gun and inboard of the aileron. Dihedral is slight. The landing gear retracts up and inward, into the wing. The tail wheel is fully retractable.

The fuselage has a heavy, round nose-section which tapers to an oval section and then down to a full-length rudder, giving TOJO a stubby, compact appearance. The rudder is very similar to OSCAR's in shape, but the horizontal tail surfaces are set unusually far forward, making an excellent recognition feature. The pilot sits about midway between the leading and trailing edges, enclosed in a typical Jap blister green-house. The engine cowling, too is typically Jap. From the front, it is circular, broken by an air scoop at the bottom and two small machine gun blast-tubes at the top. The oil radiator is located in line with the air scoop, directly aft of the full gill-cowl. Construction is stressed-skin, flush-rivetted, semi-monocoque, except for fabric-covered movable surfaces. Workmanship and finish are up to the usual Jap standards.

The 40mm Ho-301 wing cannon armament of abandoned Ki-44-II Otsu construction number 1747 is seen here in close-up. This photograph was taken at Clark Field by an ATAIU team sent to inspect the fighter. (NARA)

The fact that TOJO is powered by an engine of at least 1450 H.P., and that engines of similar horsepower have been appearing on some of the late Jap medium bombers, leads to the assumption that existing SSFs will soon be modified to take the more powerful engines. PoW examinations have tended to support this assumption. There exists a further possibility that the Japs may be willing to use a little of the 1450 H.P. to carry protection for the crew and fuel tanks.[23]

***

A subsequent ATAIU assessment report on the "Tojo's" 40mm cannon read as follows:

***

A preliminary report on a crashed TOJO states that a 40mm cannon was installed in each wing and 2 x 12.7mm guns were mounted in the fuselage. This is the first confirmed instance wherein a cannon larger than 20mm has been fitted in the wings of any Japanese aircraft.

An early TOJO document showed that 2 x 40mm cannon was the projected armament, but no previous crash ever revealed a gun larger than 12.7mm. A study of Table 1 listed below would indicate that this particular TOJO was one of a small production group which may have been intended for ground attack.

Airframe No.	Armament Modifications (from document)	
	Wing	Fuselage
1355 & earlier	2 x 12.7mm Ho 103	2 x 7.7mm
1356 to 1749	2 x 40mm Ho 301	2 x 12.7mm
1750 & later	2 x 12.7mm Ho 103	2 x 12.7mm

One of two cowling-mounted Ho-103 12.7mm machine guns installed in Ki-44-II Otsu construction number 1747 found at Clark Field. Rate of fire for the 12.7mm weapon was 800rpm. (*NARA*)

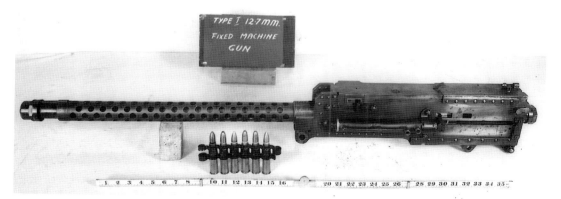

All of these installations have now been confirmed by actual crash examination. One additional armament combination was found in the early part of 1944, which consisted of 1 x 12.7mm in each wing, 1 x 7.7mm outboard of each 12.7mm and no fuselage mounts.

The recovered 40mm Ho 301 automatic cannon has the following characteristics:

Rate of fire – 400 rounds per minute (from document)
Weight – 120 pounds
Overall Length – 58 1/2 inches
Ammo Capacity – 10 rounds/gun (found in recovered TOJO)

This Oerlikon-type cannon is a very light weapon for its caliber. Magazine feed is used, but exact details of the arrangement are unknown. It is fired electrically by two solenoids mounted in tandem under the receiver. Charging is manual and is believed to be accomplished on the ground before takeoff. The wall thickness of the rifled barrel is uniform from muzzle to breech.

The ammunition is very unusual for this type of weapon, the propelling charge being contained in the rear portion of the projectile and no cartridge case used. The round contains an explosive charge of TNT and is fitted with a centrifugally-armed nose impact fuze. The propelling charge appears to be the standard flake type used in small arms ammunition and is ignited by the usual type of primer. Twelve exhaust ports in the base plate permit the expanding gases to escape and drive the projectile forward. A copper rotating band acts as a gas seal.

The 40mm Ho-301 wing cannon armament from abandoned Ki-44-II Otsu construction number 1747 was also removed for examination in close up by the ATAIU team. It was photographed in uncocked or fired condition. When cocked, the whole exterior frame forward of the receiver was drawn back to expose the barrel, the tip of which can be seen here. The Ho-301 fired unique caseless ammunition from a ten-round box magazine. *(NARA)*

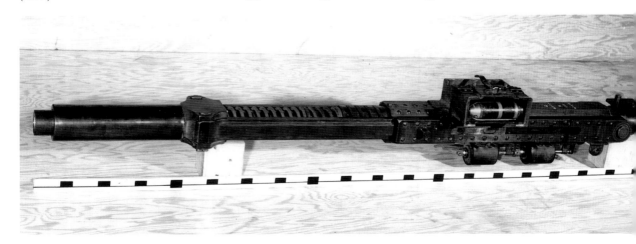

A Ho-301 40mm round showing the perforated holes in the base of the projectile that allowed the charge to propel it, thus eliminating the need for loose cartridge cases to be ejected from the cannon. Primarily an anti-bomber weapon, the low muzzle velocity of the Ho-301 required the Ki-44 to approach close to its target – a near-suicidal tactic in daylight. In fighter-versus-fighter combat, the Ho-301 was often removed or replaced by the 12.7mm Ho-103 machine gun. (*NARA*)

The small amount of propellant indicates that this weapon will have a very low muzzle velocity and a short range. The presence of this cannon may explain the large flashes at the leading edge of TOJO's wings which have been mentioned in combat reports.[24]

✳✳✳

Two Ki-44-IIs (from the 29th and 246th Sentais) were captured by the US Army when Clark Field was finally liberated in early February 1945 following a bloody week-long battle. One of these aircraft (possibly the 29th Sentai machine, which bore the construction number 2068) was restored to airworthy status and flight tested by the TAIU-SWPA. The "Tojo" was stripped of all paint, marked with US insignia and given the fin code "S11," along with red, white and blue rudder markings as seen

One of the pair of airworthy Ki-44-IIs captured at Clark Field was stripped of its well-worn camouflage, adorned with US insignia and given the fin code "S11," along with red, white and blue rudder markings as seen on other Japanese aircraft flown by the TAIU-SWPA from the base at this time. (*NARA*)

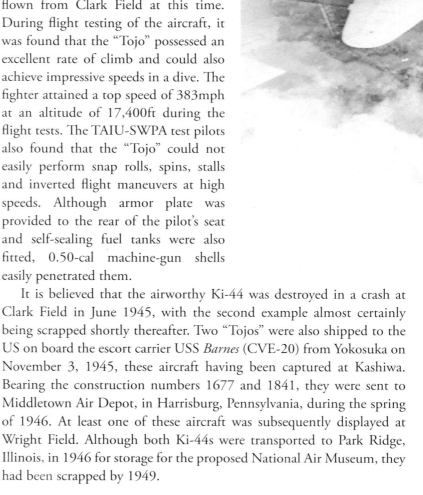

ABOVE Two "Tojos" captured at Kashiwa were shipped to the US in 1945. At least one was later displayed at Wright Field: the last surviving Ki-44 was photographed there. It is identified as a "Nakajima Tojo 2," highly polished and with a spurious emblem on the tail. (NARA)

RIGHT The Ki-44-II Hei (possibly construction number 2068 of the 29th Sentai) was flown extensively by TAIU-SWPA pilots in mock combat with Allied fighter types in the skies above the Philippines. Pilots found it possessed an excellent rate of climb and could achieve impressive speeds in a dive. (US Navy)

on other airworthy Japanese aircraft flown from Clark Field at this time. During flight testing of the aircraft, it was found that the "Tojo" possessed an excellent rate of climb and could also achieve impressive speeds in a dive. The fighter attained a top speed of 383mph at an altitude of 17,400ft during the flight tests. The TAIU-SWPA test pilots also found that the "Tojo" could not easily perform snap rolls, spins, stalls and inverted flight maneuvers at high speeds. Although armor plate was provided to the rear of the pilot's seat and self-sealing fuel tanks were also fitted, 0.50-cal machine-gun shells easily penetrated them.

It is believed that the airworthy Ki-44 was destroyed in a crash at Clark Field in June 1945, with the second example almost certainly being scrapped shortly thereafter. Two "Tojos" were also shipped to the US on board the escort carrier USS *Barnes* (CVE-20) from Yokosuka on November 3, 1945, these aircraft having been captured at Kashiwa. Bearing the construction numbers 1677 and 1841, they were sent to Middletown Air Depot, in Harrisburg, Pennsylvania, during the spring of 1946. At least one of these aircraft was subsequently displayed at Wright Field. Although both Ki-44s were transported to Park Ridge, Illinois, in 1946 for storage for the proposed National Air Museum, they had been scrapped by 1949.

Nakajima Ki-84 "Frank"

One of the finest Japanese fighters of World War II, the Nakajima Ki-84 "Frank" was designed in early 1942, just weeks after the Ki-43 had seen combat for the first time. Undertaking flight trials from April 1943, the Ki-84 featured protection for the pilot, a heavy armament, an impressive top speed and the trademark agility associated with previous IJAAF fighters. The Allies first encountered the Ki-84 in aerial combat in China in the late summer of 1944, and in the fall of that year the aircraft began appearing in increasing numbers in the Philippines following the US invasion in October.

This 11th Sentai Ki-84-I was also captured by the US Army at Clark Field in February 1945, the fighter being substantially intact bar a missing leading edge section from its left wing. The aircraft's camouflage paint was quickly stripped away, and US insignia and standard TAIU-SWPA markings were applied. (NARA)

The aircraft soon proved to be more than a match for Allied fighters thanks to its powerful armament (two fuselage-mounted 12.7mm Ho-103 machine guns and two wing-mounted 20mm Ho-5 cannon in the Ki-84-Ia, four Ho-5s in the Ki-84-Ib and two Ho-5s and a pair of 30mm Ho-105s in the Ki-84-Ic) and impressive 1,900hp Nakajima Ha-45 18-cylinder radial engine. The "Frank's" outstanding performance qualities were negated somewhat during the last year of the war owing to substandard manufacturing practices, reliability and servicing issues with the engine, weak landing gear and a shortage of experienced IJAAF pilots. Nevertheless, the aircraft proved to be the fastest fighter built in quantity by the Japanese during the conflict, with a top speed of 392mph at 20,080ft.

The following excerpt from an early intelligence report drawn up before a "Frank" had knowingly been engaged in combat clearly reveals that the USAAF was rightly concerned about the Ki-84's potential:

Rather complete documentary data has been obtained on the Ki 84 and its approximately 2000HP engine. By making aerodynamic assumptions in view of the similarity of its airframe to USAAF aircraft types, the Ki 84 is provisionally assessed to have a top speed of 482mph at 21,000ft, and a deck rate of climb at 3,780ft per minute. This is the highest speed and climb combination ever attributed to a Jap plane and is a clue to their present type of thinking. It should be pointed out clearly that not one of these new "Ki" aircraft has ever been knowingly sighted, photographed or examined but they constitute a serious threat if the Japanese are able to put them into mass production.[25]

More than 3,500 Ki-84s were produced during World War II.

In February 1945 US Army troops captured a number of Ki-84-Is at Clark Field, at least two of which were subsequently test-flown from here. Construction number 1446 from the 11th Sentai was one of these aircraft, and like all other captured Japanese types made airworthy at Clark Field; its original camouflage paint was stripped off and American insignia applied (as well as the TAIU-SWPA's distinctive rudder colors). The fighter was test-flown by several pilots while still in the Philippines, including 1Lt Arthur Murray, and detailed excerpts from his official USAAF Memorandum Report regarding the handling characteristics of the aircraft are recounted as follows:

***

FACTUAL DATA

1. INTRODUCTION

The Frank I is a single-place, single-engine, low wing, Japanese Army fighter with hydraulically retracted alighting gear and a glass-enclosed sliding greenhouse type canopy. All metal stressed skin construction is used throughout, with the exception of the fabric-covered movable control surfaces.

Power is supplied by a Nakajima HA-45 Homare Model 21, twin row, radial, air-cooled, 18-cylinder engine developing 1,970 brake horsepower at sea level with 3,000 RPM.

The propeller is a four bladed, constant speed, non-feathering, automatic or manually operated model, similar to the United States' Curtiss Electric Type.

A total of 11 1/2 hours was flown on the aircraft by Flight Test pilots to determine its handling characteristics and to obtain pilots' comments.

The program was hampered by repeated failures of the exhaust stacks due to poor material, welding and method of suspension.

In general the pilots agree that the maneuverability of the Frank I is slightly inferior to that of the Zeke 52, while level flight speeds are much higher with less vibration at comparable velocities. Control forces are lighter than those of most American aircraft even though elevator forces on the Frank I are heavier than those of the Zeke 52.

2. FLIGHT CHARACTERISTICS
a. Cockpit Layout

Entrance to the cockpit is from the left wing root walkway and is facilitated by presence of a retractable step and a push-in type hand hold at the wing trailing edge and a retractable step just below

The 11th Sentai's red lightning bolt adorned the tail of the Ki-84-I seen in the previous photograph, and that marking is clearly visible from this angle. (*NARA*)

Ki-84 COCKPIT

Artwork by Jim Laurier, © Osprey Publishing

1. Wing-mounted Ho-5 20mm cannon arming cock
2. Exhaust temperature gauge
3. Cylinder temperature gauge
4. Overboost control lever
5. Model 1 ignition switch
6. Landing gear position indicator
7. Propeller speed control
8. Type 1 oil temperature gauge
9. Type 100 tachometer
10. Type 2 boost pressure gauge
11. Type 3 speed indicator
12. Type 98 compass
13. Type 98 turn indicator
14. Artificial horizon cock
15. Type 98 artificial horizon
16. Cockpit airflow control lever
17. Army Type 3 reflector gunsight
18. Main instrument panel
19. Type 97 vertical speed indicator
20. Type 97 altimeter
21. Type 100 aeronautic clock
22. Oxygen flow gauge
23. Type 95 fuel gauge
24. Data table
25. Type 1 fuel gauge
26. Two-speed compressor oil pressure gauge
27. Tank pressurization fuel pressure gauge
28. Turn indicator adjustment
29. Oil gauge selector
30. Airspeed indicator rain remover
31. Tank pressurization selector
32. Electrics box
33. Type 95 oil gauge
34. Ho-103 12.7mm machine gun arming cock
35. Rudder peddle position adjustment handle
36. "Hi" Mk 3 wireless receiver
37. Type 94 oil pressure gauge
38. Rudder pedals
39. Ultraviolet cockpit light
40. Cannon firing switch
41. Main power switch
42. Starter switch
43. Oil cooler shutter control
44. Cowl flap control lever
45. Seat light
46. Dust filter control lever
47. Air warmer control lever
48. Five-way cock control lever
49. Manual oil pressure pump lever
50. Control column
51. Three-way cock control lever
52. Seat
53. Elevator trim tab control
54. Canopy open lever
55. Throttle lever
56. Manual propeller pitch control lever
57. Radio remote control
58. Supercharger zero-speed selector lever
59. Supercharger automatic high-altitude valve selector lever
60. Supercharger two-speed selector lever
61. High altitude valve adjustment lever
62. Flap control
63. Landing gear control
64. Tail wheel lock control
65. Ho-103 12.7mm machine guns
66. Seat height adjustment lever

In pulling out of a dive at high speed, the force of acceleration must be less than 4Gs.

In executing special maneuvers, it is necessary to maintain speed and altitude, always keeping in mind special characteristics of the plane.

To save wear and tear on the engine, flight drill should be performed at an engine speed of 2,600rpm.

The elevator trim tabs are left at cruising position except when diving (vertically).

The spin characteristics are good. The plane will not go into an inadvertent spin. When the plane has been put into a spin, the various control surfaces should be neutralized.

Execute loops with starting speed of 250mph.

An Immelmann is executed with a starting speed of approximately 250mph. The altitude gained in an Immelmann should be about 2,500ft.

Execute the Chandelle by climbing at an initial speed of approximately 220mph and at an angle of 80°. Open the throttle until manifold pressure reaches +100 mm (34 Hg). When the speed drops to 95–100mph, follow standard procedure to complete maneuver.

CAUTION: The first phase of a Chandelle must be executed slowly, with full force of acceleration not exceeding 3Gs.

To perform a split-S, set the pitch lever at 2,600rpm. During level flight, speed should be approximately 170mph. Carry out the standard procedure for a half-snap-roll or half-slow-roll split-S. Loss of altitude will be approximately 3,000ft. Speed, upon regaining level flight, will be approximately 250mph.

The slow roll is executed at 2,600rpm and 200mph. Standard procedure applies.

Sharp turns should be executed with an engine speed of 2,600–2,900rpm, manifold pressure of 35–40in. Hg, and initial speed of approximately 250mph. In a left turn the plane tends to nose downward because of torque. In a right turn the plane will tend to nose upward.

In executing a dive do not overcontrol the trim tabs. Even though the controls become heavy, the elevator trim tabs should not be lowered over 50° except in extreme cases. When executing dives, allow a sufficient margin of altitude and successively increase the speed, extending it to the permissible limit (464mph).

OVERLEAF At least four more Ki-84s (two for the US Navy and two for the USAAF) joined construction number 1446 in the US post war, being shipped across the Pacific as deck cargo on board the escort carrier Barnes following their capture at Utsunomiya South airfield. Construction numbers 2366 and 3060 were handed over to the USAAF on December 7, 1945, and both "Franks" were returned to airworthiness at Middletown during the spring of 1946. This particular aircraft is construction number 3060, which was given the code FE-302 prior to being flown in a series of mock combat sorties against a P-47N and P-51H from Wright Field. (NARA)

OVERLEAF INSET Like the Clark Field Ki-84, both of the USAAF "Franks" flown from Wright Field were earmarked for inclusion in the planned National Air Museum, although unlike construction number 1446 they were eventually scrapped after spending time in storage at Park Ridge. (NARA)

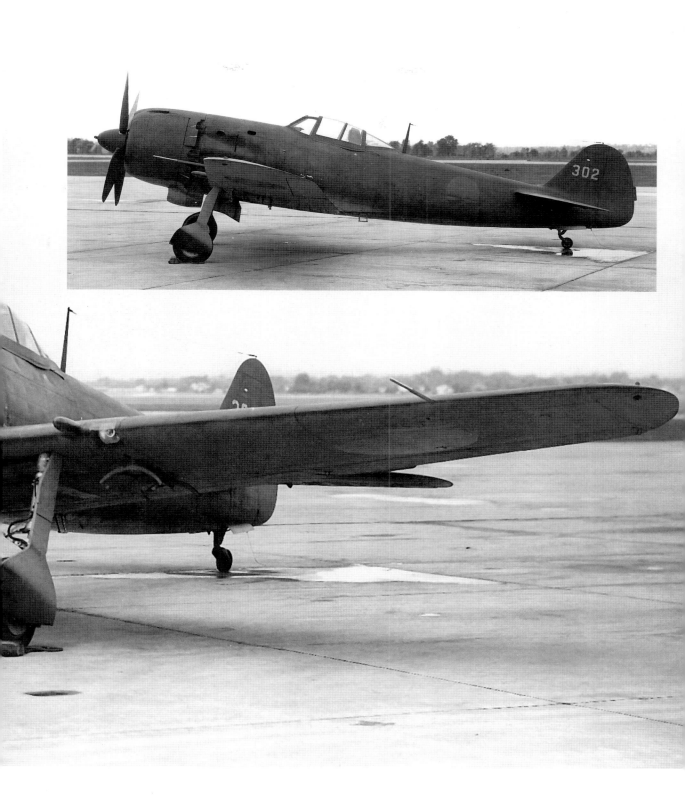

A typical set of conditions for diving follows.

1. With altitude of 16,500ft, rpm of 2,900, manifold pressure of 26in. Hg and at a speed of 220mph execute half-roll and put nose down.

2. During dive, open throttle until manifold pressure is 40in. Hg.

3. On pulling out of the dive, altitude will be approximately 4,300ft.

4. Precautions.

   a. Do not exceed the permissible rpm (3,200rpm for 30 seconds with manifold pressure at 20in. Hg, otherwise 2,900rpm).

   b. At time of pull-out, close throttle halfway.

   c. Pilot should check elevator tabs before entering plane, when diving is contemplated.

   d. If plane should vibrate during a dive, close throttle, then slowly reopen.

   e. Extra care is necessary in vertical dives because the increase in speed and loss of altitude when pulling out is much greater than in normal diving.[27]

✳✳✳
———

The handbook also provided insight into the "Frank's" dive-bombing capability:

———

BOMBING

This plane is best suited for dive-bombing. The following is an outline of dive-bombing procedure.

Start dive at an altitude of approximately 5,000ft, an airspeed of approximately 130mph, and an angle of 55°.

Use the machine gun sight; sight the target just within the 300km ring.

Release bombs when plane has a speed of approximately 360mph and an altitude of approximately 2,000ft.

When bombs are away, pull out of dive quickly. The loss of altitude will be approximately 1,000ft.

There is an electrical bomb-release button on the throttle and a manual release control on the left side of the cockpit floor.[28]

***
———

Following World War II, several Ki-84s were evaluated by the Allies. Two of these were test-flown by the TAIU-SWPA from Clark Field, these aircraft being stripped to bare metal, adorned with US insignia and given the codes S10 and S17 in black. They also had the unit's rudder markings. S10 was soon written off in a crash during a test flight, but S17 (construction number 1446) survived to be shipped

The Clark Field Ki-84, construction number 1446, was declared surplus to requirements in 1952 and sold to Ed Maloney's Air Museum. The world's sole surviving Ki-84 was restored to airworthiness in 1963, and is now on display at the Tokko Heiwa Kinen-kan Museum in Kagoshima Prefecture. (*Arjun Sarup*)

back to the US on board the escort carrier USS *Long Island* (CVE-1). Initially flown from NAS Anacostia, the fighter was sent to Park Ridge in July 1946 for storage for the proposed National Air Museum. Declared surplus to requirements in 1952, the "Frank" was sold to Ed Maloney's Ontario Air Museum in Claremont, California. Eventually restored to airworthiness by the AiResearch Aircraft Company at Los Angeles Airport in April–June 1963, the Ki-84 made a handful of flights prior to being returned to Maloney's collection at Chino. The "Frank" was eventually sold to the Arashiyama Museum in Kyoto in 1973 and it is presently displayed at the Tokko Heiwa Kinen-kan Museum in Kagoshima Prefecture.

At least four more Ki-84s (two for the US Navy and two for the USAAF) were also shipped to the US on board the escort carrier *Barnes* post war after being captured at Utsunomiya South airfield in Japan's Tochigi Prefecture. Construction numbers 2366 and 3060 were handed over to the USAAF on December 7, both "Franks" being returned to airworthiness at Middletown Air Depot in Harrisburg, Pennsylvania, during the spring of 1946. They were given the codes FE-301 and FE-302 at this time, with the latter aircraft being evaluated at Wright Field against a P-47N and a P-51H. Although its performance compared favorably with both fighters, the "Frank's" short range and lack of armor was criticized in the flight-test report. It was also noted that the flight-test program had been hampered by persistent failures of the engine exhaust stubs owing to their construction from poor material. They had also been badly welded and incorrectly fitted at the factory. Like the Clark Field Ki-84, both "Franks" were earmarked for inclusion in the planned National Air Museum, although they were eventually scrapped after spending time in storage at Park Ridge.

A similar fate befell the two unidentified Ki-84s from Utsunomiya South that were sent to "Pax River" for evaluation by the US Navy, these aircraft eventually being scrapped in 1947.

Kawasaki Ki-100 Goshikisen

From March 9, 1945, American forces began to encounter yet another late war IJAAF fighter in the form of the Kawasaki Ki-100 Goshikisen. Essentially an improved version of the Ki-61, the Ki-100 featured the more reliable Mitsubishi Ha-112-II radial engine in place of the troublesome Ha-140 (a more powerful development of the Ha-40 fitted in the "Tony"). Indeed, the stockpiling of engineless Ki-61-II KAI airframes at Kawasaki's Kagamigahara factory was the primary driver behind the hasty adoption of the Ha-112-II. Having studied the engine mounting of an imported Focke-Wulf Fw 190A, Kawasaki engineers managed successfully to fit the powerplant (which had a diameter of four feet) with the slim "Tony" fuselage (only 2ft 9in in width). The resulting Ki-100 prototype performed its maiden flight in February 1945, the radial-engined machine proving to be lighter than the Ha-140-powered Ki-61-II KAI. This in turn meant that the "new" fighter was also more maneuverable thanks to lower wing and power loadings. The Ki-100 was slightly slower, however, because of the larger frontal drag associated with the Ha-112-II. The reliability of the latter more than made up for

Equally as rare as the Clark Field Ki-84 is the world's only surviving Ki-100-Ib, seen here on display in the shadow of Avro Lincoln B 2 RF398 at RAF Museum Cosford. It was found at Tan Son Nhut airfield in Saigon by the ATAIU-SEA in August 1945 and test flown by an IJAAF pilot, before being ferried to nearby Bien Hoa on November 26, 1945. The fighter was eventually shipped to Britain in June 1946. (*Richard Vandervord*)

effective during taxiing and no tailwheel lock is fitted. Takeoff is normal, with little tendency to swing, but the tail does not come up readily owing to the small elevators. When the tail is raised, forward vision is good. Takeoff run is short and the aircraft leaves the ground readily at 100mph. There is practically no change in trim with gear retraction. Climb angle is steep and the rate of climb rapid, and the cooling of engine and oil appears to be excellent. Handling and control are good at all speeds from the stall up to 325mph, although the ailerons are heavy at normal cruise speeds, and become exceptionally so above 325mph. The elevators are on the light side at all speeds up to 325mph. The rudder is satisfactory at all speeds.

Rudder and elevator trim tabs are controlled by parallel wheels in longitudinal plane on the port side of the cockpit, and the rudder control tab is ineffective, but little change in rudder trim is required. The elevator tab is adequate and very effective, but it works in reverse of Allied procedure (i.e., rolling the wheel backwards makes the aircraft nose heavy). The aircraft is dynamically and statically stable longitudinally and directionally, and neutrally stable laterally. In short, stability is excellent. The uneven use of fuel from either port or starboard wing tank quickly results in the aircraft becoming markedly wing heavy.

The aircraft was stalled clean and dirty, and stalling characteristics are excellent except for a lack of stall warning. The nose drops gently, either straight ahead or on either wing, and recovery is very rapid, with little loss of altitude. The oil and engine cowl flaps have no noticeable effect on stalling speed, and there is no tendency to spin. Rolls, Immelmanns and turns are executed with ease at normal speeds, although ailerons are heavy at all operating speeds and the aircraft cannot be rolled as rapidly as a P-51. Maneuver flaps of Fowler type are fitted, and are controlled by a safety switch and a trigger on the stick. These are extended only when the trigger is depressed, and retract immediately the trigger is released, and their operation is superior to any used on our aircraft. The elevators are too light at normal and high speeds, and it is felt that the aircraft may be easily damaged by rough handling of the elevators.

The engine was rough at cruising rpm in automatic mixture setting. This roughness was reduced as soon as the mixture was leaned out, but this caused the exhaust temperature to go above the limits. Vibration is not excessive, but the canopy fitted on this particular aircraft vibrates and makes considerable noise. For a normal-sized pilot the aircraft is comfortable. There is ample headroom and body room, and the cockpit enclosure is wide, permitting freedom of movement of the head, and this improves vision. The ventilation system, which comprises forward and aft ventilators, is superior to any fitted to our fighters. The rigging of the stick and rudder is satisfactory, and all controls are readily accessible. The cockpit layout is, in general, very satisfactory, and the engine and flight instruments are well grouped, although the airspeed indicator is too far from the rev counter and manifold pressure gauge (this is especially noticeable during the takeoff run). Intermittent noise is the only real objection to comfort. Ground observers state that the noise emitted by the cooling fan is very noticeable, but that it is not heard in the cockpit. Vision in climb, level flight and for landing is good, although rather poor for takeoff until the tail comes up. Aft vision is good if the rear transparency panels are kept clean, but the metal framing of the windscreen tends to obstruct forward vision.

The powerplant is generally satisfactory. It is very easy to start, hot or cold, but, as already mentioned, runs roughly at cruising revs. Airscrew operation is satisfactory at normal revs but hunts at higher revs at about 10,000ft, although it should be noted that airscrew control on this particular aircraft had been changed from hydraulic to electric, so is non-standard. Oil and engine cooling are exceptionally good, and gave the impression that they would over-cool in cold weather. It was noted that there is considerable vibration for a short period when the engine is put into high blower at 12,000ft pressure altitude.

In conclusion, it may be said that the favorable features of this fighter are: (1) good stability; (2) good stalling characteristics; (3) comfort; (4) good takeoff and landing qualities; (5) good performance; (6) maneuver flaps. Its poor features are: (1) brakes and rudder brake action; (2) heavy ailerons and lack of maneuverability at high speed; (3) low mechanical reliability; (4) short range.[29]

***
—––—

A J2M2 and a J2M3 were test-flown from Clark Field, these aircraft having been captured on Dewey Boulevard, in downtown Manila, by liberating US troops in mid-February 1945. Dewey Boulevard had been used by the IJNAF as an emergency airstrip during the final weeks of the

ill-fated defense of the Philippines, both "Jacks" having served with the 381st Kokutai. Following their capture, the aircraft had been trucked to Clark Field, where they were stripped of their camouflage and given US insignia and the TAIU-SWPA striped rudder. J2M3 construction number 3008 (TAIU tail code S12) managed just two flights, totalling 3hr 20min, before the engine seized when the main oil delivery hose failed. The pilot of the fighter managed to make a successful deadstick landing – almost certainly the last of many in the J2M. During the test flights, the J2M2 (the identity of which is unknown) had attained a top

As with Ki-84 S17 (see page 101), J2M3 S12 was joined in flight by a Fleet Air Arm Seafire III and a US Navy F6F-5 during a photo sortie from Clark Field. The USAAF P-51D seen aloft with S17 was also airborne at the same time, but it does not appear in this shot. (NARA)

Two ex-381st Kokutai J2M3s were returned to airworthiness by the RAF, with the help of Japanese personnel, in early 1946. They were then flown by IJNAF pilots working with the ATAIU-SEA at Tebrau, on the Malayan mainland. These flights were for the benefit of the press or visiting VIPs, and five different Japanese types were flown during this period. Here, IJNAF pilots and groundcrew, under armed guard, observe flight operations at Tebrau in front of "Jack" BI-02. (© IWM, CF 894)

Of the five "Jacks" – three J2M3s and two J2M5s – shipped back to the US, only this example, J2M3 construction number 3014, survived scrapping. The world's only surviving J2M, it is currently displayed in the Planes of Fame Museum at Chino. (*Dean Shaw*)

speed of 407mph at an altitude of 17,400ft, while the J2M3 attained a top speed of 417mph at 16,600ft.[30] The J2M2 was subsequently written off when a B-25 taxied into it on the ground at Clark Field.

Two ex-381st Kokutai J2M3s were also returned to airworthiness by the RAF, with the help of Japanese personnel, in early 1946. They were then flown by IJNAF pilots working with the ATAIU-SEA from the former IJNAF airfield at Tebrau, just across the Johore Straits from Singapore. These flights were for the benefit of the press or visiting VIPs, and there is no evidence to suggest that any performance measurements or equipment evaluations were made. The ATAIU-SEA flew five different IJNAF and IJAAF types during this period.

No fewer than five "Jacks" – three J2M3s and two J2M5s – were shipped back to the US for evaluation after the war following their capture at Atsugi naval airfield. The J2M5 variant was fitted with the MK4U-4 Kasai 26a engine that boasted a mechanically-driven three-stage supercharger and an enlarged intake manifold. Capable of speeds up to 375mph at 26,250ft, just 34 J2M5s had been built by war's end owing to delays with production of the Kasai 26a engine. It appears that none of these fighters was ever flown in the US, and four of the "Jacks" had ended up at Middletown Air Depot by August 1946. Three of the fighters were scrapped here shortly thereafter, while the fourth (a J2M3) was noted at Park Ridge in 1949, awaiting inclusion in the National Air Museum – it too was scrapped, however, in 1950. The fifth J2M3, construction number 3014, was eventually discarded by the USAF and ended up as a playground attraction in a Los Angeles park. Rescued by Ed Maloney for his growing Air Museum and restored to airworthy condition (although never flown) in the 1970s, the "Jack" has been on display in the Planes of Fame Museum at Chino for a number of years. It is the world's only surviving J2M.

Kawanishi N1K1-J and N1K2-J "George"

Privately developed by Kawanishi from its single-seat N1K1 "Rex" floatplane fighter of 1943, the N1K1-J "George" retained the former's basic airframe in combination with a retractable wheeled undercarriage. Aside from the fitting of the latter, the primary change made centered on a switch of radial powerplants from the Mitsubishi MK4C Kasai 13/15 to the Nakajima NK9H Homare 21. The retention of the "Rex's" mid-mounted wing would later cause many problems with the aircraft's overly long (and weak) undercarriage legs and their complex retraction system. Like the "Rex," the "George" had two 7.7mm Type 97 machine guns in the nose and a pair of 20mm Type 99 cannon in the wings – an additional pair of cannon could be carried in underwing gondolas.

Initial flight trials of the N1K1-J revealed not only undercarriage problems, but also that the fighter was some 45mph slower than anticipated owing to the 1,990hp Homare engine failing to deliver its promised levels of power. Pilots also complained of restricted visibility due to the positioning of the wing mid-fuselage. Despite these failings, the N1K1-J was still a vast improvement on the IJNAF's venerable A6M and temperamental J2M, and when the first "Georges" saw combat over the Philippines in October 1944, Allied pilots soon learned to respect their fighting capabilities. Aside from the N1K1-J/Ja fighter variants, the

A small number of N1K1-J "George" fighters from the 341st Kokutai were discovered at Marcott, one of Clark Field's surrounding satellite sites. Although none of these aircraft were more than a few months old, some, like this example, had suffered heavy weathering in the tropical conditions of Luzon and Formosa. Wearing the code 341-S23 when captured on January 30, 1945, this fighter was subsequently stripped of its flaking camouflage and marked up as TAIU-SWPA S9. (NARA)

fighter-bomber optimised N1K1-Jb/Jc also saw action in the ill-fated home defense campaign of 1945.

In February 1945, US Army ground forces found a handful of N1K1-Js that had been abandoned by retreating Japanese troops at Clark Field. At least two of these aircraft were restored to airworthiness by the TAIU-SWPA and briefly test-flown. Both examples were stripped of their camouflage and marked with US insignia, as well as the striped rudder synonymous with the TAIU-SWPA. One of the fighters was given the tail code S7, and it was damaged beyond repair when the undercarriage collapsed at the end of the "George's" first flight. According to the official flight-test report:

✱✱✱

GEORGE was flown by an Allied field officer after it had been assembled and repaired by the Technical Air Intelligence Unit at Clark Field. One flight was made for a total of one hour and forty-five minutes. The main purpose of the flight was to make the initial check and get the airplane in mechanical condition for tactical trials. The airplane was in excellent shape mechanically, except for the brakes, but was slightly left wing heavy. The right oleo leg collapsed at the end of the landing roll, and the aircraft was badly damaged. In connection with this, it is of interest that a PoW stated there has been considerable difficulty with the landing gear in particular, and that this may have been the result of trying to convert GEORGE from a floatplane into a land plane.

Conclusions: Excellent takeoff, climb, high speed and good vision, but does not impress the pilot with that feeling of confidence which one normally gets in a good, substantial airplane.

Its favourable features are: (1) good vision; (2) good stability; (3) good takeoff qualities; (4) good performance; (5) good instrument layout; (6) automatic propeller throttle control; (7) high diving speed; (8) improved rudder and elevator control on approach and landing.

Its unfavourable features are: (1) poor stalling and accelerated stalling characteristics; (2) brakes and rudder brake action; (3) weak landing gear; (4) complicated gear and flap system; (5) poorly balanced controls; (6) heavy ailerons at high speed.

Main Conclusion: Though GEORGE appears to function satisfactorily in the air, it is apparently difficult to maintain in operation because of its weak landing gear.

An interrogation of a PoW reveals that he heard it was a very difficult plane for the pilots to handle and they didn't like it. It was

particularly tricky in landing and taking off, and there were accidents and crack-ups in almost every landing. There had been particular difficulty with the landing gear, and this had held up production a great deal. The gear would simply crumble under any kind of a strain at all. These difficulties may have been the result of trying to convert GEORGE from what was originally a floatplane to a land-based plane.

Other PoWs, as well as the Allied test pilot who flew the rebuilt GEORGE stated that a grass runway was absolutely essential, and that the brakes must be used only when necessary. Of some 60 GEORGEs found in Luzon, at least two-thirds had been destroyed or damaged in crashes resulting from landing gear failure. This condition would seem to preclude GEORGE 11 appearing in large numbers operationally. However, a later low-wing version (GEORGE 21) which has been reported will probably be fitted with stronger gear than the stop-gap design of GEORGE 11.[31]

✳✳✳
———

GEORGE 11
TECHNICAL

(MODIFIED) – NAVAL LAND BASED FIGHTER – SPAN 39'-4¼" LENGTH 29'-6¼"

AIR INTELLIGENCE CENTER

NAVAL AIR STATION, ANACOSTIA, D. C.

RESTRICTED

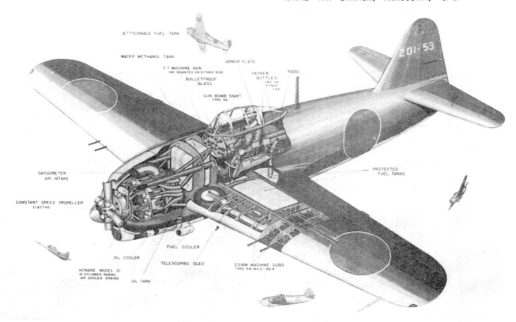

TAIC artist SSgt R. B. Aldrich also completed a "George 11" cutaway in March 1945, and the artwork was included in the intelligence report on the N1K1-J supplied to front-line units in the Pacific Theater. (NARA)

When American forces occupied Omura in southern Kyushu on September 14, 1945, they found 80 N1K2-J Shiden-Kais of the 343rd Kokutai. The following month, six of the fighters were restored to airworthiness and flown by former IJNAF pilots (including Lt Cdr Yoshio Shiga, seen here standing next to the cockpit) to test their suitability for shipping to the US for further evaluation. (*Tony Holmes collection*)

The second aircraft to be flown, which had belonged to the 341st Kokutai (having carried the tail code 341-S23), was marked up as S9 and completed a handful of flights. While being tested at Clark Field in April 1945, its underwing gun gondolas and machine guns in the nose were removed in order to give the N1K1-J a similar performance to the more advanced N1K2-J variant. This aircraft was eventually scrapped at Clark Field.

Acknowledging the faults of the N1K1-J even before the latter had entered series production, Kawanishi commenced work on the improved

N1K2-J in mid-1943. To eradicate the undercarriage problems, the wing on the Shiden-Kai was lowered. Other improvements saw the engine moved forward and the fuselage slightly lengthened to cure a centre of gravity problem, redesigned tail surfaces, and a revised cowling shape. The construction of the fighter was also simplified, allowing building man hours to be reduced and the overall weight of the aircraft to be lightened by 500lb.

Deliveries of aircraft to the front line commenced in July 1944, and although eight factories were tooled up for mass-production of the N1K1-2, B-29 raids severely hampered overall output to the extent that just 428 had been built by VJ Day – one factory actually failed to produce a single completed fighter.

The Shiden-Kai was easily the best IJNAF fighter of the war, and it could more than hold its own against any Allied foe thanks to its

Three examples deemed to be in the best mechanical condition were sent to Yokosuka on October 16, 1945 – two of those aircraft are seen here. Flown by IJNAF pilots, the "Georges" were escorted by four FG-1D Corsairs from VMF-113. Devoid of ammunition and running on high octane American aviation fuel, the N1K2-Js easily outpaced the escorting Corsairs, the pilots of which had orders to shoot the Japanese fighters down if they deviated from straight and level flight. (*Tony Holmes collection*)

All six of the "Georges" made airworthy were hastily marked with US insignia prior to them undertaking a series of check flights between October 13–15, 1945. The pilot of this well-weathered example is keeping a close eye on the mechanic pulling away the wheel chocks in front of the starboard gear leg. (*Tony Holmes collection*)

This N1K2-J was found in the Showa factory at Shinonoi in late 1945, having been sent to the facility by Kawanishi to serve as an instructional aid. Showa had been contracted to build Shiden-Kais for the IJNAF, but none were completed at this location prior to VJ Day. Behind it is the fuselage of an L2D4-1 "Tabby" cargo transport aircraft. The final fate of the Showa N1K2-J is unknown. (*Richard Reinsch*)

impressive top speed and excellent maneuverability, making it more than a match for its American fighter opposition. The aircraft proved to be less effective as a B-29 interceptor, however, owing to its poor rate of climb and degraded engine performance at high altitudes. The handful of units that received the N1K2-J were employed almost exclusively on home defense operations or as kamikaze escorts during attacks on Allied ships off Okinawa.

It would appear that as many as six N1K2-Jas were shipped back to the US following VJ Day, the bulk of these aircraft being ex-343rd Kokutai aircraft found at Omura in September 1945. The following month three of these machines were flown by IJNAF pilots to Yokosuka, where they were sprayed with an anti-corrosion coating (to protect the aircraft from seawater) and loaded on board the escort carrier *Barnes*. Once in America, the aircraft were split evenly between the US Navy and the USAAF and briefly test-flown. The fighter was found to possess "excellent" performance qualities, specifically for aerial dogfighting.

NIK2-Ja construction number 5341 is seen at NAS Norfolk, Virginia, with an NIKI "Rex" parked behind it, during the summer of 1946. Both aircraft were destined to escape the scrap man's blow torch and have survived to this day. (*Smithsonian National Air and Space Museum (NASM 72-3983)*.)

Although all three "Georges" assigned to the US Navy were destroyed as targets at the Naval Proving Ground (NPG) Dahlgren Junction, Virginia, in late 1946, the remaining three USAF fighters survived to become museum exhibits. The "George" displayed in the National Museum of the US Air Force in Dayton, Ohio, is believed to be construction number 5312. After being declared surplus to requirements in the late summer of 1946, the aircraft somehow ended up under the control of the City of San Diego. Donated to the USAF in 1959, it was displayed within the USAF Museum at Dayton until removed in 1998 to undergo a ten-year restoration using parts sourced from wrecks found in Japan immediately post war and then kept in long-term storage.

Construction number 5341 was initially sent to the Naval Aircraft Factory in Philadelphia, Pennsylvania, following its arrival from Japan in late 1945. The following year, the "George" was transferred to "Pax River" before being sent to NAS Willow Grove, Pennsylvania, in

Construction number 5341 was photographed on static display at NAS Willow Grove, Pennsylvania in 1958, by which point it had been stripped to bare metal. The fighter would be resident here from December 1946 until it was moved to the NASM's storage facility at "Silver Hill" in 1983. Note that the fighter's flying surfaces have visible holes in them after being subjected to the elements for more than a decade. (*Author collection*)

December 1946. Here, it was placed on outdoor static display with other Japanese and German aircraft. In 1983 the now weather-beaten fighter was obtained by the Smithsonian Institution and put in storage at the NASM's Paul E. Garber Preservation, Restoration and Storage Facility in Suitland, Maryland. The "George" was loaned to the Champlin Fighter Museum in Mesa, Arizona, in December 1991, where it was restored over a three-year period. Eventually returned to the NASM in 2003, it has been on display at the museum's Steven F. Udvar-Hazy Center for a number of years.

The N1K2-Ja (construction number 5128) displayed in the National Naval Aviation Museum (NNAM) in Pensacola, Florida, had been passed on to the US Navy by the USAAF and then shipped to the Naval Research Laboratory in Washington, D.C. in 1946. Left to become derelict in a nearby children's playground after it was declared surplus to requirements by the US Navy, the aircraft was eventually placed in storage at NAS Norfolk, Virginia, in 1957. The "George" was subsequently loaned to the New England Air Museum of Windsor Lock, Connecticut, in 1975. Restored by Georgia Metal Shaping in 1994–95, it was handed back to the US Navy in 1998 and subsequently put on display in the NNAM.

Mitsubishi A7M "Sam"

When US troops occupied Japan following VJ Day, they discovered a handful of examples of an advanced single-engined IJNAF fighter that had been developed by Mitsubishi to replace its venerable A6M Zero-sen. Work on what would become the A7M Reppu ("Strong Gale"), given the Allied codename "Sam," had commenced as early as 1940 with the issuing of the 16-Shi specification for a new carrier-based fighter. However, a shortage of design staff at Mitsubishi and continual

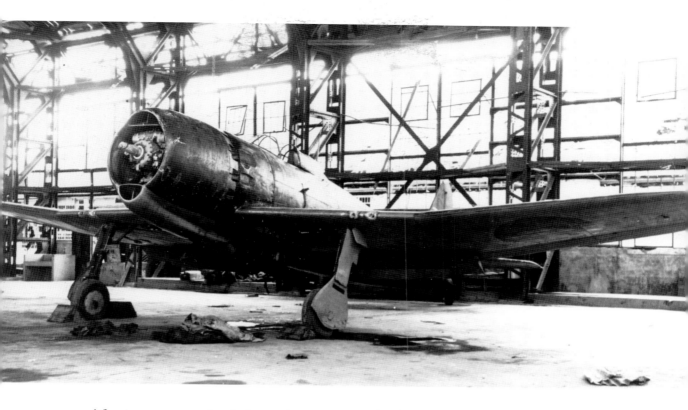

modifications to types already in production meant that little progress was made on the 16-Shi. Indeed, the specification was eventually withdrawn.

The project was revived in April 1942 when Mitsubishi was instructed by the IJNAF to design the M-50 Reppu fighter to the 17-Shi specification. Zero-sen designer Jiro Horikoshi insisted that the Mitsubishi MK9A/B 18-cylinder air-cooled radial engine then under development be fitted to the new machine, which was expected to enter service in 1945. The IJNAF disagreed, however, choosing the lower-powered Nakajima NK9K Homare 22 instead. Fitted with self-sealing tanks, a bullet-proof windscreen and armor plating behind the pilot's seat, the first prototype Reppu, now designated the A7M1, was eventually completed in April 1944 after Mitsubishi had had to give priority to newer variants of the A6M and rectifying problems with the J2M. The Reppu was a large aircraft, featuring a wingspan of 45ft 11in and a wing area of 332.173 sq ft – almost half as much again as that of the A6M5.

On May 6, 1944 the first of two A7M1s completed its maiden flight. Three weeks later the aircraft was handed over to the IJNAF for service trials. The new fighter was praised for its stability and handling

A three-quarter head-on view of a gull-winged A7M Reppu found by US troops in the badly damaged Mitsubishi factory in Nagoya shortly after the occupation of Japan. Given the Allied codename "Sam," the A7M was the much-delayed advanced fighter developed to replace the venerable A6M Zero-sen in IJNAF service. (*US Navy, Naval History and Heritage Command*)

ABOVE A side-on view of the same A7M seen in the previous photograph. Although the "Sam" was highly regarded by the IJNAF, the US Naval Intelligence team that examined this aircraft post war along with the surviving fourth, sixth, and seventh prototypes did not deem the fighter worthy of shipment to the US for further analysis. (US Navy, Naval History and Heritage Command)

RIGHT The Reppu was a large aircraft, with a wingspan of 45ft 11in and a wing area of 332.173 sq ft – almost one-and-a-half times that of the A6M5. Mitsubishi had to make the outer wing panels hydraulically foldable in order to allow the fighter to fit below deck when embarked in IJN aircraft carriers. No A7Ms ever undertook sea trials, however. (US Navy, Naval History and Heritage Command)

characteristics, and, thanks to its unique combat flaps, the A7M1 was as maneuverable as the "Zeke." However, the fighter was slower than had been hoped for owing to the Homare engine developing only 1,300hp at 19,600ft (it was rated at 2,200hp on takeoff). The "Sam's" top speed was only 357mph and it took up to 11 minutes to reach 20,000ft – the 17-Shi specification had called for a time of six minutes or less. The IJNAF duly suspended further flight trials in July 1944, shortly after which Jiro Hirokoshi succeeded in getting official clearance to fit the MK9A engine as he had originally requested.

Installation of the new powerplant meant a complete redesign of the forward fuselage of the re-designated A7M2 because the Mitsubishi engine had a larger diameter than the Homare. When flight trials recommenced in October 1944, the fighter's top speed at 21,600ft had increased to 390mph thanks to the MK9A generating 1,800hp at that altitude. Plans were immediately drawn up to put the aircraft into production in Mitsubishi's Nagoya and Osaka factories, the operational A7M2 being fitted with either four 20mm Type 99 Model 2 cannon in the wings or two of the latter and two fuselage-mounted 13.2mm Type 3 machine guns. The IJNAF at last appeared to have a fighter that could wrest back aerial supremacy from the F6F Hellcats and F4U Corsairs that had dominated the skies in the Pacific since late 1943.

With the A7M2 now seemingly on the cusp of front-line service, production of the fighter suffered a series of setbacks, including a massive earthquake in the Nagoya area that all but destroyed the Oe Airframe Works, followed by a largescale B-29 raid on the Daiko engine plant where the MK9A was to be built. These events so badly affected Mitsubishi that only a single production aircraft had been built by war's end. A US Naval Intelligence team examined this aircraft, along with the surviving fourth, sixth and seventh prototypes, post war, although none of these aircraft was deemed worthy of shipment to the US for further analysis.

Kyushu J7W1 Shinden

On August 3, 1945, a truly unique IJNAF single-engined fighter took to the skies above Japan. Built by Kyushu, the J7W1 Shinden ("Magnificent Lightning") featured swept wings (which also supported tall tail surfaces inboard of the ailerons) positioned toward the rear of the fuselage, single horizontal control surfaces with elevators either side of the nose and a "pusher" engine for propulsion. The fighter, intended to serve as a land-based B-29 interceptor, was to be armed with four nose-mounted 30mm Type 5 cannon.

The fighter was the brainchild of Capt Masaoki Tsuruno of the IJNAF's Technical Staff, who from the very start envisaged replacing the J7W1's 2,130hp Mitsubishi MK9D radial engine – which drove a six-bladed propeller – with a turbojet. Three all-wood MXY6 gliders with an identical configuration were designed by the Dai-Ichi Kaigun Koku Gijitsusho (First Naval Air Technical Arsenal) to test the proposed fighter's handling qualities at low speed; they were built by Chigasaki Seizo K.K. in the summer of 1943. Flight trials commenced shortly thereafter, and these proved the feasibility of Tsuruno's design. The IJNAF subsequently instructed Kyushu Hikoki K.K. to design an Otsu (B) Type Interceptor Fighter to meet the 18-Shi specification it had issued to match the "pusher"

ABOVE The second prototype of the canard-pusher Kyushu J7W1 Shinden undergoing technical evaluation at Wright Field in 1946. The aircraft was never test flown due to the lack of a serviceable 2,130hp Mitsubishi MK9D radial engine. (NARA)

RIGHT A rear view of the J7W1 at Wright Field. The Shinden ("Magnificent Lightning") featured swept wings and tall tail surfaces inboard of the ailerons – the tail surfaces are clearly visible, as is the port horizontal control surface, with elevators, attached to the fighter's nose. The aircraft's MK9D radial engine drove a six-bladed propeller, although Kyushu had planned on swapping this for a turbojet engine. (NARA)

created by Tsuruno. Although inexperienced in high-performance aircraft construction, Kyushu was chosen because its design team and production facilities had the capacity to take on the job.

Work on the J7W1 commenced in June 1944, with the prototype being completed within ten months. Desperately short of heavily armed high-performance interceptors with which to defend Japan from high-flying B-29s, the IJNAF ordered the Shinden into production prior to the prototype taking to the air. Problems with engine cooling during ground power runs and shortages of key parts delayed the first flight until August 3, 1945, when Capt Tsuruno took the aircraft aloft from Fukuoka Airport. Two more flights were performed shortly thereafter (on the 6th and 9th), taking the Shinden's total flight time to just 45 minutes by VJ Day. Keeping the landing gear extended on all three flights, Tsuruno had reported that the prototype was highly maneuverable, but that it suffered from a strong torque pull to starboard on takeoff and excessive propeller and drive shaft vibration once airborne.

A second prototype had been completed just prior to the Japanese surrender, although this aircraft was never flown – it was duly found in the Kyushu factory at war's end. The first Shinden prototype was viewed with some astonishment by US Naval Intelligence personnel, who eventually decided to ship the second prototype home on board the escort carrier *Barnes* on November 3, 1945. Once in America, the aircraft was reassembled but it was not flown owing to the lack of a serviceable engine. Sent to Middletown during the summer of 1946, the Shinden was transferred to Park Ridge in September of that same year. In 1960 the USAF donated the prototype to the NASM in Washington, D.C., and it was placed in storage at the Museum's Paul E. Garber Facility, also known as "Silver Hill." In 2016, the forward fuselage/nose section of the aircraft was put on static display at the NASM's Steven F. Udvar-Hazy Center, forming an intriguing component within the latter's World War II aviation exhibition.

In 1960 the USAF donated the Shinden prototype to the NASM. The forward fuselage/nose section of the aircraft is seen here on static display at the museum's Steven F. Udvar-Hazy Center. (*Arjun Sarup*)

TWIN-ENGINED FIGHTERS

Kawasaki Ki-45 "Nick"

Designed in 1937 as the IJAAF's first twin-engined fighter, the Ki-45 Toryu ("Dragon Slayer") proved to be a successful platform for both the ground attack and nightfighting missions, but vulnerable as a day fighter when tested in combat in World War II. The prototype aircraft was initially powered by license-built Bristol Mercury engines, but these had such disappointing performance that they were replaced by 1,050hp Nakajima Ha-25 radials. Kawasaki also thoroughly overhauled the design

On December 30, 1943, the US Marine Corps captured Ki-45 KAIb construction number 1023 at Cape Gloucester airstrip on New Britain. The aircraft had been damaged during an Allied strafing attack in September 1943. Although declared "restorable," the Ki-45 was not recovered. (*NARA*)

at around the same time, the revised fighter, designated Ki-45 KAIa (for *kaizo* – modified), emerging with a remodeled fuselage, new wings and tail, heavier armament and increased fuel capacity.

By October/November 1942 the first production-standard Ki-45 KAIas had made their combat debuts over Burma and China, the aircraft being given the codename "Nick" by the Allies. Employed as a ground-attack platform using a variety of weaponry, the Ki-45 also eventually became a makeshift, "radarless," nightfighter following the shifting of B-24 raids by the USAAF's Fifth Air Force to the hours of darkness. Further specialist cannon and machine gun fits were trialled and approved by the nightfighting Ki-45 sentais, which were in turn adopted by Kawasaki. New 1,080hp Mitsubishi Ha-102 engines were also fitted to the Ki-45 in late 1943, resulting in production of the near-definitive Toryu, the Ki-45 KAIb (and follow-on KAIc and KAId). These variants proved to be formidable opponents for the B-29 when they appeared over Japan in 1945, for they were able to perform interceptions both during the day and at night, at any altitude.

This Ki-45 KAIa was one of 45 "Nicks" that were captured by US Army troops at Clark Field in February 1945. The majority of these aircraft belonged to the 45th Sentai, which had been stationed there. (*NARA*)

"Nicks" were fitted with a variety of weapons depending on their role in front-line service, with a combination of 7.7mm and 12.7mm machine guns and 20mm and 37mm cannon being installed in nose, ventral tunnel and dorsal (oblique) fixed mounts and a 7.7mm or 7.92mm machine gun in a rear-firing flexible mount. The aircraft could also carry bombs on external racks.

On December 30, 1943, the US Marine Corps captured Ki-45 KAI construction number 1023 at Cape Gloucester airstrip on New Britain. The aircraft, which belonged to the Rabaul-based 13th Sentai (which had been in-theater since May 1943), had been damaged on the ground at Cape Gloucester during an Allied air attack in September 1943. Lacking parts to repair the "Nick," the unit had declared it "unserviceable" shortly thereafter. Examined by Allied Intelligence personnel, it was noted that the aircraft was armed with a Type 94 (Ho-203) 37mm cannon in a ventral tunnel on the starboard side of the fuselage, two Type 1 12.7mm machine guns in the nose and a Type 89 7.7mm machine gun on a flexible mounting to the rear for the radio-operator/gunner. Although declared "restorable," this aircraft never flew again.

No fewer than 45 "Nicks" were captured by US Army troops at Clark Field in February 1945, with the majority of these aircraft belonging to the 45th Sentai, which was stationed here. At least two of the Ki-45 KAIcs were flown by the TAIU-SWPA, with both aircraft being stripped to bare metal and adorned with US insignia and the unit's striped rudder markings. One of the fighters, construction number 3303, was later shipped to America and evaluated by the US Navy at NAS Anacostia. It was subsequently scrapped. Two more Ki-45 KAIcs (including construction number 4268) configured as nightfighters were captured at Fujigaya airfield in Chiba Prefecture and shipped to the US on board the escort carrier *Barnes* in November 1945. Handed over to the Flight Test Section at Middletown in April 1946, they were delivered to Freeman Field, Indiana, the following month and flown on a number of occasions until August of that same year. The following notes come from the official USAAF evaluation report compiled following the flight trials at Freeman Field:

***

1. DESCRIPTION

The Nick-II is of typical Japanese design and construction. The general construction is light and creates considerably more vibration than most USAAF aircraft. Care must be taken in high-speed

A Ki-45 KAIc nightfighter, fitted with two obliquely-mounted upward-firing 20mm Ho-5 cannon in the center fuselage, is parked at Clark Field ahead of the Ki-45 KAIa seen in the previous photograph, a Ki-46 "Dinah," and a J1N1-S "Irving." The Ki-45 KAIc had a more pointed nose than other "Nick" variants because it lacked armament in this location, radar being installed instead. (*NARA*)

dives or maneuvers to prevent excessive vibration which may cause undue strain on the wing empennage and fuselage sections. A particularly weak point of this aircraft is the landing gear; extreme care must be exercised during landing and taxiing to prevent accident.

The plane is a conventional twin-engine, two-seated fighter with no outstanding recognition characteristics. The wings and fuselage are of normal design, being all-metal, flush-riveted and of cantilever construction. A point of additional interest is the absence of corrosion preventive finishes. Neither lacquer or anodizing has been applied to the interior surfaces.

The control surfaces of the Nick-II are conventional, being of metal framework covered with fabric. All control surfaces are provided with trim tabs. The elevator and rudder tabs can be adjusted in flight, but the aileron trim tab is the fixed type and must be adjusted on the ground. The wing flaps are the push-pull torque tube system, hinged at the leading edge of the flap to the wing panel. The wing flaps are constructed of sheet metal and covered with metal on the lower surface only. The wing flap extends from the aileron to the junction of the fuselage to the wing.

The canopy is of the hinged type, opening from the left side for both the pilot's and gunner's compartments. There is no emergency exit release.

The main gear is actuated hydraulically and retracts backward into the nacelles. The tail wheel is retracted hydraulically but no doors are provided to cover the wheel well.

The Nick-II is powered by two HA-31 Model 21 Type-1-1050 Mitsubishi radial engines. This is a 14-cylinder, radial air-cooled engine, incorporating a single-stage, two-speed integral supercharger

ABOVE Captured 45th
Sentai Ki-45 KAIc
construction number 3303
was one of at least two
"Nicks" flown by the
TAIU-SWPA; both aircraft
were stripped to bare metal
and adorned with US insignia
and the unit's striped rudder
markings. Given the unit
code S14, the fighter is seen
here, devoid of armament,
between flights at Clark Field
in March 1945. (NARA)

ABOVE LEFT This 37mm
Ho-203 cannon was
removed from a Ki-45 KAIb
found at Clark Field. Derived
from the Year 11 Type
direct-fire infantry gun, the
Ho-203 was installed in the
"Nick" (KAIb, KAIc, and
KAId variants) as an
anti-bomber and anti-ship
weapon. It used a long recoil
artillery-style falling block
action and was fed from a
25-round magazine in flexible
mountings or a 15-round
"birdcage" closed loop
endless belt in fixed
mountings. as seen here The
rate of fire achieved by the
Ho-203 could be adjusted by
changing the recoil buffer
fluid, although 120 rounds
per minute was typical in
front-line service. (NARA)

manually controlled by a selector valve. It is comparable to the
Pratt & Whitney R-1830, the chief difference being the valve-
operating mechanism. This mechanism is so designed that all
valves are operated from one double-track, three-lobe cam ring,
located in a separate section of the engine between the nose section
and the power section. This engine uses 92-octane fuel. The
propellers are similar to the Hamilton Standard, three-bladed,
10ft, constant-speed type. They are non-feathering and are
controlled by governors which maintain constant propeller speed
by regulating the flow of oil from the engine to the propeller hub.
Each propeller is equipped with a spinner.

The Nick-II is fitted with five guns. One is a fixed hydraulically
charged 37mm gun in the nose of the fuselage. Another fixed
37mm gun is located on the lower right side of the fuselage (this
can be replaced by two 20mm guns). It is also hydraulically
charged by the pilot. Both guns are electrically fired by the pilot.
Between the pilot's and the rear gunner's compartment are two
fixed guns of 20mm, hydraulically charged by the rear gunner
and electrically fired by the pilot. In the rear gunner's compartment
there is a flexible 7.9mm gun mounted on a semi-circular track.
Provisions are made for carrying external bombs or droppable
gas tanks. Armor of 13mm is installed behind and ahead of the
37mm magazine and behind the pilot. The Nick-II has very little

remote control or automatic equipment to aid the pilot. The rear gunner or observer has no control over the aircraft. There are very few devices in the Nick-II to provide for the safety of the crew. Fire extinguishers for the engines, or emergency escape means for the pilot and gunner are not provided.

2. FACTUAL DATA

a. Dimensions:

Span	49.5ft	Length	34.7ft
Height	9.7ft	Wing Area	365 sq ft

b. Weight:

Empty	8,335lb
Gross Weight	11,685lb
Overload Fighter	12,349lb

c. Speed at Gross Weight of 12,213lb:

At Sea Level	290mph
10,000ft	330mph
20,000ft	353mph
30,000ft	330mph

d. Rate of Climb at Gross Weight 12,213lb:

Time to 10,000ft military hp	4 min
Time to 20,000ft military hp	8.2 min
Rate of Climb at Sea Level WEP	2,892 ft/min
Rate of Climb at 18,500ft WEP	2,475 ft/min

e. Armament:

Two 37mm fixed guns (or one 37mm and two 20mm guns) Ammunition – approx. 16 rounds per gun (and 100 rounds 20mm if 20mm guns are installed, or 16 rounds of 37mm) Bombs – 2 x 50kg (total 220lb) Bombs carried externally in place of droppable gas tanks

3. FLIGHT-TEST REPORT

The Nick-II is a twin-engine, low mid-wing, single fin and rudder airplane, powered by two Mitsubishi type 1-1050 engines equipped with three-bladed hydromatic constant speed non-feathering props similar to the Hamilton-Standard. The Nick-II was utilized by the

climb about 1,900ft/min. These figures are stated to be actual flight-test results.

Documents gave the original armament as 1 x 20mm and 2 x 7.7mm fixed nose guns, 4 x 7.7mms in two twin-gun remote controlled top turrets and 1 x 7.7mm in the belly. Of the 17 IRVINGs found on Tinian, however, only one had this armament; 15 had 1 x 20mm fixed nose gun, and 4 x 20mm fixed guns in what was formerly the radio operator's compartment. These guns are mounted in pairs, one pair firing forward and up at about 45° and the other firing forward and down at the same angle. Armament on the remaining IRVING was unreported except that there was a single top turret. Some of the Tinian IRVINGs were equipped with radar, while all had wing bomb racks and a small piece of armor plate for the pilot's protection.

IRVING is continuing in production and will probably be met to an increasing extent. Model 11 has not proven an outstanding success but the re-engined Model 12 should be far superior.[33]

✳✳✳

During the US occupation of Japan following VJ Day, approximately 145 IJNAF and IJAAF aircraft were loaded onto three US Navy escort carriers and shipped to America for technical evaluation. Included in this number were four Gekkos that were captured at Atsugi and transported to Yokosuka for shipment across the Pacific Ocean on board the escort carrier *Barnes*. The vessel departed Japan on November 3, 1945 and headed for Virginia,

Stripped of its camouflage, J1N1-S "Irving" construction number 7334 is prepared for flight testing and evaluation at Middletown in June 1946. The aircraft had been shipped to the US on board the escort carrier *Barnes* in November–December 1945 and returned to airworthiness by the Maintenance Division at Middletown. Its engines had been overhauled and the oxygen system, radios, and some flight instruments replaced with American equipment. Mechanics had completed this work by April 9, 1946. Then still assigned to the US Navy, the nightfighter was transferred to the USAAF in early June 1946 and flown on the 15th of that same month for about 35 minutes. (*planecollection / Alamy Stock Photo*)

via the Panama Canal. Once offloaded at Norfolk Naval Yard, J1N1-S construction number 7334 was moved to Langley Field, Virginia, on December 8 and then on to Middletown on January 23, 1946 for restoration to flight-worthy status. During this process some of the aircraft's cockpit gauges and equipment were replaced with American-built items. A USAAF pilot performed the first test flight in the "Irving" on June 15, 1946, remaining airborne for approximately 35 minutes. An additional test flight was undertaken in the aircraft from this location, before it was transferred to Park Ridge in August. By October 4 the nightfighter had been put in museum storage in the vacant Douglas C-54 production plant at this site. The remaining three "Irvings" were scrapped shortly thereafter.

In 1949 the Smithsonian Institution acquired the "Irving" from the USAF and it was eventually moved to the NASM's Paul E. Garber Facility. Restoration of the Gekko commenced in September 1979, with work being completed by December 1983. Subsequently displayed at "Silver Hill" until 2005, the J1N1-S was then moved to the Steven F. Udvar-Hazy Center, where it is exhibited as the last example of its kind in the world.

Kawasaki Ki-102 "Randy"

In August 1942, just as the Ki-45 KAIa was entering front-line service, Kawasaki commenced work on the two-seat Ki-45-II designed around a pair of 1,500hp Mitsubishi Ha-112-II engines – the new aircraft also had a larger and more refined fuselage than the Toryu's. Although initially uninterested in the aircraft, the IJAAF instructed Kawasaki to complete the prototype as a single-seat heavy fighter, which was re-designated the Ki-96 owing to it sharing few components with the Ki-45. Three prototypes were ultimately built, and IJAAF test pilots who flew them

stated that the Ki-96s handled well and had an impressive top speed. However, even before the first example had flown in September 1943, the IJAAF had decided that it had no need for a twin-engined heavy fighter and the Ki-96 was not ordered into production.

Unperturbed, Kawasaki offered a ground attack version of the Ki-96 to IJAAF as a replacement for the Toryu in this role, and in August 1943 the company received official approval for the project under the Ki-102 designation. In order to hasten the aircraft's construction, Kawasaki decided to retain the basic structure and powerplants of the Ki-96 in its original two-seat configuration. Additional armor and petrol tank protection was installed and heavier armament (a nose-mounted 57mm Ho-401 cannon, two fuselage-mounted 20mm Ho-5 cannon and a flexible rear-firing 12.7mm Ho-103 machine gun) fitted. The first of three prototypes was completed and test-flown in March 1944, and only minor changes were required prior to the Ki-102 attaining series production in October of that same year.

Kawasaki intended to develop three versions of the aircraft in the form of the Ki-102a day fighter, Ki-102b ground-attack fighter-bomber and Ki-102c nightfighter. Although most of the 215 Ki-102bs that were subsequently built were kept in reserve in Japan, a small number saw combat during the Okinawa campaign from April 1945. The type was given the Allied codename "Randy" shortly thereafter. A handful of Ki-102bs were also used in the development program for the Igo-1-B air-to-surface guided missile, which the IJAAF hoped to use operationally in response to the seemingly inevitable Allied invasion.

The Ki-102a day fighter was produced following a request from the IJAAF for a high-altitude interceptor with which to combat the B-29 threat. Six pre-production aircraft were duly fitted with Ha-112-II Ru turbosupercharged engines that maintained their rated power of 1,250hp

The well-weathered Ki-102b FE-308/T2-308 (construction number unknown) was one of four "Randy" high-altitude fighters shipped back to the US on board the escort carrier *Barnes* post war – it is seen here at Wright Field between evaluation flights. Although two of the Ki-102s ended up in storage at Park Ridge after being allocated to the proposed National Air Museum, all four examples had been scrapped by 1949. (*USAAF*)

up to 26,900ft – the standard Ha-112-II produced this power up to 19,000ft only. The fighter also featured revised armament that consisted of a 37mm Ho-203 cannon and two fuselage-mounted 20mm Ho-5 cannon, with the rear-firing machine gun omitted. Twenty Ki-102b airframes were modified on the production line into Ki-102as, but these failed to enter front-line service before the Japanese surrender.

Kawasaki was also instructed to build a nightfighter version of the aircraft, which was designated the Ki-102c. Retaining the Ha-112-II Ru turbosupercharged engines, the nightfighter had a lengthened fuselage, a new cockpit, redesigned tail surfaces and a wider wingspan. AI radar was installed and the armament was revised to include two 30mm cannon in the underfuselage and two 20mm cannon obliquely mounted behind the cockpit. The prototype was still undergoing flight trials when the war ended.

Four Ki-102bs were shipped back to the US on board the escort carrier *Barnes* post war, three having been found at Taisho airfield near Osaka and a fourth sourced from Kawasaki's Akashi factory. During flight testing of one of these aircraft it was found that the "Randy" was extremely maneuverable and capable of a top speed of 360mph. Two of the Ki-102s ended up in storage at Park Ridge after being allocated to the proposed National Air Museum, while the other pair was sent to the Atlantic Overseas Air Materiel Center (AOAMC) in Newark, New Jersey. All four had been scrapped by 1949, however.

Mitsubishi Ki-83

In May 1943, Mitsubishi designer Tomio Kubo (who had created the Ki-46 "Dinah," which is detailed in the next chapter) and his team of engineers began development of a new long-range heavy fighter in response to a requirement issued by the IJAAF. Initially, the company

Only four prototypes of the Ki-83 long-range heavy fighter had been built by Mitsubishi prior to VJ Day, and the aircraft was unknown to the Allies until these examples were captured at Matsumotu airfield in Nagano Prefecture. One of the fighters was photographed here after being adorned with US insignia in preparation for its flight to Yokosuka for loading on board a carrier bound for the US. Once at Middletown, it was allocated the serial FE-151/T2-151. (*US Army, http://www.ijaafphotos.com/jbwki831.htm, PD-Japan-oldphoto*)

proposed a single-engined aircraft designated the Ki-73, but delays with its 2,600hp Mitsubishi Ha 203-II 24-cylinder horizontal-H liquid-cooled engine saw the design abandoned before construction had commenced. Kubo instead fell back on his tried and tested Ki-46 layout to create the Ki-83, which proved to be one of the most aerodynamic Japanese fighters of the war.

Four prototypes were built and the first aircraft performed its maiden flight on November 18, 1944. During initial flight testing, the prototype Ki-83 demonstrated excellent maneuverability at high speed, although engine and tail vibrations resulted in modified engine mountings and strengthened horizontal tail surfaces being incorporated into the remaining three aircraft. Capable of attaining 426mph at 26,250ft, the Ki-83 was to have been armed with two 30mm Ho-105 cannon and two Ho-5 20mm cannon grouped together in the nose. The IJNAF was also keen to introduce the aircraft into service, but no production examples had been built by war's end, owing to the IJAAF having to give priority to the construction of single-seat interceptors.

The Ki-83's existence remained a mystery to the Allies until after VJ Day, when all four prototypes were captured at Matsumotu airfield, in Nagano Prefecture. It appears that at least one of these aircraft was briefly flight tested from here, the camouflaged fighter being adorned with US insignia and "gassed up" with high-octane fuel that allowed it to attain a top speed of 473mph at 23,000ft.[34, 35, 36, 37] One of the Ki-83s was also shipped back to the US, being taken to Middletown in February

Armed US troops stand guard in front of the Ki-83 at Matsumotu airfield before its departure for Yokosuka. These men were charged with warding off souvenir hunters and disgruntled former Japanese military personnel alike. (*US Army, http://www.ijaafphotos.com/ jbwki831.htm, PD-Japan-oldphoto*)

A captured IJAAF Mitsubishi Ki-109, with the barrel of its massive Army 75mm Type 88 anti-aircraft cannon clearly visible, heads a line-up of IJAAF Mitsubishi Ki-67 "Peggy" heavy bombers at an airfield in Japan in the autumn of 1945. Just 22 Ki-109 bomber interceptors were built between August 1944 and March 1945. (*Richard Reinsch*)

1946 and then later moved on to Park Ridge after its allocation to the proposed National Air Museum. Still at Park Ridge in 1949, the fighter was scrapped shortly thereafter.

Mitsubishi Ki-109

In an attempt to thwart the USAAF's use of B-29s to bomb the Japanese mainland, the IJAAF's Rikugan Kokugijutsu Kenkyujo (Army Aerotechnical Research Institute) identified the Mitsubishi Ki-67 Hiryu heavy bomber (codenamed "Peggy"), which had been undergoing flight testing since early 1943, as the basis for a hunter-killer aircraft. Designated the Ki-109, two versions were to be built by Mitsubishi – the Ki-109a killer, fitted with two obliquely mounted 37mm Ho-203 cannon in the rear fuselage, and the Ki-109b hunter, equipped with a radar and 40cm searchlight. The cannon were soon replaced by a 75mm Type 88 anti-aircraft cannon in the nose, however, as it was hoped that the weapon's longer range would allow the Ki-109a to remain out of range of the B-29s' defensive field of fire. Just 15 shells were carried for the Type 88, which was hand-loaded by the co-pilot.

Design work on the aircraft commenced in January 1944, with the first prototype being completed eight months later. Aside from the Type 88

cannon in the nose, the Ki-109 looked identical to the Ki-67, retaining the latter's waist gun positions and dorsal and tail turrets. Only the tail turret boasted weaponry, however, in the form of a flexible 12.7mm Type 1 machine gun. This was the aircraft's sole defensive armament.

Flight testing went well enough for the IJAAF to place an initial order for 44 aircraft, with the first 22 powered by two 1,900hp Mitsubishi Ha-104 radial engines. Two prototypes were also fitted with more advanced Ha-104 RU turbosupercharged engines in an attempt to boost the aircraft's performance at the cruising altitude of the B-29, but no production Ki-109s used them. The only front-line unit issued with the Ki-109 was the 107th Sentai, which began to receive examples in early 1945. Despite crews attempting to intercept B-29s on a number of occasions, the Ki-109 never shot a bomber down due to its lack of speed and poor rate of climb.

At least five Ki-67s were shipped to the US post war, three of them on board the escort carrier *Core*. It would appear that one of these aircraft was in fact a Ki-109, which ended up either at Middletown or at the AOAMC in Newark in the summer of 1946, where it was eventually scrapped.

A captured Ki-109 is liberally sprayed with an anti-corrosion coating at Yokosuka, to preserve the bomber interceptor during its shipment to the US on board the escort carrier *Core* in late 1945. Aside from this aircraft, four Ki-67s were also transported across the Pacific to America for evaluation. (*Aviation History Collection / Alamy Stock Photo*)

CHAPTER 3

EVALUATING BOMBERS AND RECONNAISSANCE AIRCRAFT

This bomb-damaged second prototype G8N "Rita" was found in the Nakajima factory at Koizumi, northwest of Tokyo, in October 1945. The "Rita" represented the pinnacle of Japanese multi-engined heavy bomber development in World War II. (*Richard Reinsch*)

The flight testing and evaluation of captured Japanese bombers and reconnaissance aircraft from World War II revealed that they embodied a similar design philosophy to the fighters encountered during the conflict. Of primary importance to both the IJAAF and IJNAF were speed and range, and these attributes were achieved by manufacturers in their early war aircraft at the expense of aircrew protection through the omission of weight-inducing self-sealing fuel tanks and armor protection. Consequently, aircraft such as the G3M "Nell," G4M "Betty," Ki-21 "Sally" and Ki-48 "Lily" quickly caught fire when riddled by gunfire from enemy aircraft.

Toward the latter stages of World War II, however, advanced features such as laminar airfoils, more powerful and better performing engines, self-sealing fuel tanks, enhanced armor protection and improved defensive armament began to appear in Japanese bomber and reconnaissance aircraft designs. US Intelligence services started noticing these changes in early 1944, and they were noted in the following US Navy TAI Summary written in July of that year:

***

GENERAL TRENDS

Very recent documentary evidence has indicated clearly that both the Japanese Navy (JNAF) and Army (JAAF) are engaging in extensive experimental work in new models of aircraft. This development program seems to embrace both new designs and improvements of existing types. Constant allusions by PoWs to new bombers tie in very closely with the captured documents and leads to the belief that Japan is exerting every effort to modernize her entire Air Force.

The recent withdrawal of the Japanese Air Force from forward areas and avoidance of individual combat does not necessarily denote an overall weakness but rather a predetermined plan to reform and regroup their squadrons with available new models.

ARMAMENT

Consistent reports from documents and PoWs stress the fact that the Japs are becoming increasingly aware of the inadequacy of their armament. References to 20mm, 30mm, 40mm and 80mm guns have appeared and PoWs have claimed that 12.7mm and 20mm twin turrets are in existence. The new Model 12 Betty G4M2 is believed to have a top power-operated 20mm turret and the increasing use of electrically operated turrets is to be expected in the future.

ARMOR

Harsh lessons have forced the Japs to revise their original concept of armor protection. No definite pattern of armor plating has been found so far, but more planes are being found with increasingly heavy plate. The protection does not seem to be incorporated as part of the basic design, but rather improvised after manufacture. As larger engines become operationally available it is expected that heavier armor with more comprehensive arrangement will be adopted.

FUEL TANK PROTECTION

Half-hearted efforts have been made to give fuel tanks a form of "self-sealing", particularly by the Army, but it has not proven too satisfactory in the past. Heavy losses have clearly demonstrated to them the necessity of this type of protection and it is reasonable to assume that it will be incorporated in newer models. That the Japs have knowledge and ability to produce a satisfactory protective lining is attested by the well-constructed form of "self-sealing" used on the Navy patrol flying boat/bomber EMILY.

JAPANESE ARMY AIR FORCE (JAAF)

Six new JAAF bombers are shown to be under development and of these, two heavy bombers, Ki-67 and Ki-68, or Ki-82 or Ki-32, and two dive-bombers, Ki-66 and Ki-89, have sufficiently complete specifications to warrant the assignment of new code names. It is not possible at this time to assess the performance characteristics of these planes, but it is quite possible that the Ki-67 and Ki-82 listed as "heavy bombers" may prove to be four-engine types or at least twin-engine aircraft with a markedly increased bomb load. Fragmentary evidence of the new "super heavy bombers" would point to their being four-engine. Additional references were made to other bombers, but no data is available that would permit their present status to be evaluated.

The Army has been making rapid strides in recognizing and modernizing its entire air force. High performance planes of all types seem to be in an advanced stage of experimentation and/or in limited production.

As is the case of the Navy, the crux of the Japanese Air Force threat would appear to be whether they can place new types into heavy production without diminishing existing production. If this can be accomplished, the Jap Air Fleet will become an increasingly serious problem for us near the mainland.[1]

***

US Intelligence also began to learn about how the Japanese use of water injection in its new aircraft engines was leading to significant performance improvements for their bomber fleet, as noted in a US Naval Intelligence Air Operations Memorandum dated April 20, 1944:

> The use of water injection on Japanese aircraft engines, first indicated on Jill (a single-engine torpedo bomber), apparently is becoming an important feature on other aircraft, according to a prisoner-of-war interrogation included in the SoPac Air Combat Intelligence Report. Water injection is now allegedly incorporated in the late versions of Betty (a twin-engine high level and torpedo bomber) and permits operation at 250 knots indicated air speed (283 miles per hour) for periods up to 30 minutes duration.[2]

SINGLE-ENGINED BOMBERS

Aichi D3A "Val"

In mid-1942 Aichi developed a more advanced version of its highly effective D3A1 Type 99 Carrier Attack Bomber Model 11, Allied codename "Val," which had helped sink US Navy warships and destroy military aircraft and facilities at Pearl Harbor during the December 7, 1941 surprise attack. It had then been heavily involved in the damage or sinking of American aircraft carriers during the battles of Coral Sea, Midway and Santa Cruz Islands in 1942, as well as attacks on Allied targets in Australia, New Guinea, Ceylon, the Solomons and the Aleutians. In fact, the "Val" had participated in all major Japanese carrier operations in the first ten months of the war. Heavy losses amongst highly trained crews from Coral Sea onward eventually forced the IJNAF to restrict D3As to employment by land-based units from late 1942.

In June of that year, the improved D3A2 Model 22 had commenced flight testing with Aichi, this aircraft being powered by a Mitsubishi Kinsai

54 14-cylinder radial engine of 1,300hp in place of the Kinsai 44 rated at 1,070hp that had been fitted to most D3A1s. Another change saw the dive-bomber's fuel tankage increased to 1,078 litres. The aircraft's armament of two forward-firing 7.7mm Type 97 machine guns in the upper engine cowling and a flexible 7.7mm Type 92 machine gun for the rear gunner remained unchanged, as did the bombload of one 550lb bomb carried beneath the fuselage and dropped with the aid of a swinging trapeze mechanism and two 130lb bombs mounted on underwing racks.

D3A2s replaced D3A1s from the fall of 1942, and both "Val" variants were subsequently supplanted on board larger carries by the Yokosuka D4Y Suisei (codename "Judy") dive-bomber. Despite their obsolescence, a large number of D3A2s briefly opposed US forces involved in the retaking of the Philippines in October 1944 – the units involved suffered appalling losses to marauding USAAF and US Navy fighters. A large number of D3A1/2s that were being used by training units in Japan were also committed to kamikaze attacks on Allied ships during the final months of the war.

Following the retaking of Guam by US forces in August 1944, an IJNAF D3A2 from the 321st Kokutai was captured intact and evaluated by USAAF TAIU-SWPA personnel. It appears that the aircraft was not flown, however.

This D3A2 "Val" dive-bomber of the 321st Kokutai was captured by US ground forces on Guam in the Mariana Islands in August 1944. Although the aircraft was relatively intact (it had suffered some damage to its starboard wingtip), the investigating TAIU-SWPA team decided the "Val" was not worth recovering for possible flight testing due to the type's obsolescence. (NARA)

Yokosuka D4Y1/3 "Judy"

In late 1938, the design staff of the Dai-Ichi Kaigun Koku Gijitsusho (Naval Air Technical Arsenal) at Yokosuka was instructed by the IJNAF to create a single-engined, carrier-based dive-bomber inspired by the Heinkel He 118V4 that it had acquired production rights for. Created in response to the 13-Shi Carrier Bomber specification, the resulting two-seat D4Y1 Suisei ("Comet") was comparable in size to the A6M2 fighter but the aircraft had the fuel capacity of the much larger D3A2 that it had been designed to replace. Although heavily influenced by the Heinkel dive-bomber, the Suisei was not only lighter and smaller but also vastly superior aerodynamically thanks to its internal bomb-bay – the German aircraft carried its weapons externally.

Production D4Y1s would be powered by the 1,200hp Aichi AE1 Atsuta inline engine, which was a license-built version of the Daimler-Benz DB 601A, although delays in its supply meant that the prototypes had to rely on the 960hp DB 600G – a handful of these had been imported from Germany. The first of nine prototypes took to the air in November 1940, and although the aircraft's performance and flight characteristics exceeded what had been hoped for by the IJNAF, the Suisei experienced wing flutter problems and wing spar cracks when simulated dive-bombing tests were carried out. Despite these issues, the aircraft was cleared for the reconnaissance role as the D4Y1-C.

Production D4Y1s, fitted with AE1A engines, began to reach fleet units in the spring of 1942, where they replaced the appreciably slower B5N2 "Kate." Given the Allied codename "Judy," just 25 examples had been completed by Aichi's Nagoya plant through to the end of April 1943.

US troops seized Tinian from the Japanese in August 1944, and a number of IJNAF aircraft were captured on the island at Ushi Point and Gurguan Point airfields, including this predominantly intact D4Y1 dive-bomber of the 523rd Kokutai. Although the "Judy" was thoroughly evaluated by a TAIU-SWPA team, it was deemed to have been too badly damaged to return to airworthy status. (*NARA*)

By then the fitting of reinforced wing spars and improved electrically operated dive-brakes had allowed the Suisei to finally be accepted into service as a dive-bomber. Armed with two nose-mounted 7.7mm Type 97 machine guns for the pilot and a flexible 7.92mm Type 1 machine gun for the radio operator/rear gunner, the D4Y1 could carry one 1,100lb bomb or two 550lb bombs in an internal bomb-bay and two underwing 70lb bombs or drop tanks. Aichi's production of the dive-bomber increased dramatically from April 1943, with 589 D4Y1s and D4Y1-Cs being built through to March 1944. No fewer than 174 "Judys" were involved in the "Great Marianas Turkey Shoot" in June 1944 when US Navy carrier-based fighters inflicted a terrible toll on IJNAF aircraft flying from nine Japanese carriers during the Battle of the Philippine Sea. Lacking self-sealing tanks and armor plating for the crew, the Suiseis were easy targets for the Hellcats and Wildcats defending the US carriers.

It appears that the IJNAF paid little heed to the slaughter inflicted on its dive-bomber units, for the next production version of the aircraft in the form of the D4Y2 was identical to the original "Judy" variant bar the fitting of 1,400hp Aichi AE1P Atsuta 32 engine and replacement of the 7.9mm machine gun with a 13mm Type weapon. A reconnaissance version of this aircraft (D4Y2-C) was also built, with both types entering service during the battle for the Philippines. Again, losses were horrendous, with a number of Suiseis being used as kamikazes.

Responding to longstanding complaints from front-line units that the Atsuta was difficult to maintain, the IJNAF instructed Aichi to find a replacement air-cooled radial for its troublesome inline engine. Company engineers chose the 1,560hp Mitsubishi MK8P Kinsei 62 14-cylinder radial, which was eventually made to fit the narrow fuselage after considerable modifications had been made to the airframe. A close-fitting

In February 1945, IJNAF Special Attack (Kamikaze) Unit D4Y3 construction number 3957 was one of a number of "Judys" captured by US forces after they had seized Clark Field. Deemed to be the most intact example of a D4Y found by the TAIU-SWPA on Luzon, it was stripped to bare metal and marked with US insignia and the unit's stripped rudder, as well as the code number S16 in black. Rebuilt over a period of several months, the aircraft was eventually flight tested in the Philippines before being scrapped there. (NARA)

Construction number 3957 undertook a series of test flights in the late spring of 1945 following its restoration to airworthiness. During the TAIU evaluation, American pilots found that the D4Y3 boasted better performance characteristics than its principal Allied dive-bombing rival of the day, the brutish SB2C Helldiver. Indeed, testing showed that the radial-engined "Judy" was 81mph faster than the Curtiss aircraft at an altitude of 18,500ft. (*US Navy*)

cowling and smoothly tapered sides to the fuselage forward of the cockpit kept the levels of drag created by the Kinsei 62 to a minimum. Indeed, when the new variant, designated the D4Y3, was flight tested for the first time in May 1944, it had a top speed (357mph at 19,850ft) that was nearly identical to the more aerodynamic D4Y2.

In late 1944 a dedicated kamikaze model in the form of the D4Y4 was created by Aichi, this version dispensing with the radio operator/air gunner and carrying a single 800kg bomb semi-recessed beneath the fuselage. A nightfighter variant of the D4Y2, designated the D4Y2-S and featuring an obliquely upward-firing 20mm cannon fitted in the fuselage in place of the rear-firing gun, and with bomb racks and carrier equipment removed, was also built in small numbers. Although the aircraft lacked AI radar and had a slow rate of climb, some success was achieved by D4Y2s flying at night from bases in central Japan against low-flying B-29s.

The majority of surviving "Judys" were used extensively, and successfully, during the final months of the war in the ill-fated defense of Japan, with aircraft employed both as conventional dive-bombers and as kamikazes. Indeed, a handful of US Navy carriers were badly damaged by Suisei crews that succeeded in hitting their targets – the "Judy's" small size and high speed in a dive made it difficult for anti-aircraft gunners to shoot down if it penetrated the fighter screen.

A handful of D4Y1s were found in various states of disrepair as US forces captured key island strongholds during 1944, but none of these was remotely airworthy. Amongst the more intact examples was a "Judy" from the 523rd Kokutai that was captured on Tinian, in the Mariana Islands. The aircraft was later thoroughly evaluated by a TAIU-SWPA team, but not flown. With the fall of Clark Field to US forces in February 1945, a Special Attack (Kamikaze) Unit D4Y3 (construction number

3957) was captured and quickly restored to flight-worthy status. Stripped to bare metal and marked with US insignia and the TAIU-SWPA's striped rudder, the aircraft was flight tested in the Philippines before eventually being scrapped there. During the TAIU evaluation, the D4Y3 was shown to possess better performance characteristics than Allied dive-bombers of the day, including the Curtiss SB2C Helldiver.[3]

US Intelligence reports written toward the end of the war, but before the D4Y3 had been evaluated at Clark Field, documented the evolution of the "Judy" series as follows:

✳✳✳

JUDY 33 (SUISEI 33) D4Y1-A

During the past two months (January and February 1945), a photograph depicting a successful Judy 33 Kamikaze attack against the US fleet aircraft carrier USS Essex has occasioned considerable conjecture, and [the aircraft] has been variously referred to as GEORGE, JILL, ZEKE, HAMP, KATE and unidentified. It can now be definitely stated that it is the well-known Judy with a radial engine in place of the usual in-line type. Two recent crash examinations in the Philippine area have confirmed it as JUDY 33 (Suisei 33). The D4Y1-A marking that appeared on one fuselage is inconsistent and may be a temporary model/symbol number. (See TAIC Summary No. 18 for JUDY development).

The modification of JUDY into a radial engine aircraft is believed to have been caused either by troubles encountered with the Atsuta

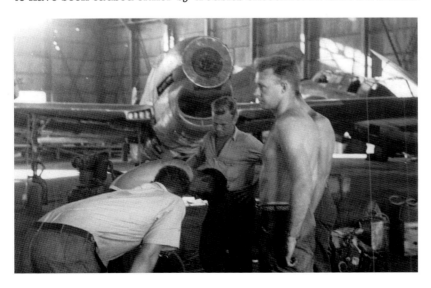

US Navy groundcrew toil away on the restoration of a captured IJNAF D4Y2 at Kisarazu Naval Air Base in October 1945. Note the B7A2 "Grace" parked behind it. A small number of brand new Suiseis were captured at Aichi's Nagoya factory following the occupation of Japan, and two D4Y3s and two D4Y4s were shipped back to the US. At least one early-model "Judy" was also sent to America on board the escort carrier *Barnes*, and it was probably the aircraft seen here. (*Aviation History Collection / Alamy Stock Photo*)

in-line engine, or to the lack of a sufficient quantity of these engines to permit maximum production of JUDY. That the former reason may be more valid is borne out by PoW statements concerning frequent failures of the main bearings of this Japanese version of the DB 601.

At first glance it would appear that another strong reason for the change would be the 200 extra horsepower of the radial engine over the in-line type, but engineering calculations show that this advantage would be almost completely offset by the additional drag of the radial engine cowling.

In addition to the major power plant change, JUDY 33 has the following minor variations from previous JUDY models:

Recognition

Preliminary inspection reports show that this new model is recognitionally similar to JUDY 11 except for:
1. Radial engine and cowling appearance.
2. The tail shape is similar to Judy 12. Due to the radial engine the length may be slightly different from the in-line engine model.

Fuselage

Stencilled "Suisei 33" and of similar construction to Judy 11, except for the engine mount and cowling. The wings were marked "Suisei 11".

Engine

Kinsei 62, 14-cylinder radial engine rated at 1,580 h.p. for takeoff, manufactured by Mitsubishi. Except for a possible change in the reduction gear ratio, this engine is the Navy counterpart of the Army Ha 112.2. The Kinsei Model 62 is noteworthy in that it has a system whereby fuel is injected directly into the cylinder induction ports, and in place of the usual carburettor, this engine is equipped with a throttle body in which are mounted two butterfly valves for air control.

Propeller

3-blade, constant speed Hamilton Type, 9.8ft diameter, has been reported but since this is believed to be incorrect, a re-check has been requested.

Armament

2 x 7.7mm forward firing through cowling at 11 and 1 o'clock positions.

1 x 7.9mm rear cockpit flexible gun.

The use of different guns in the same aircraft which are so close in size as the 7.7mm and the 7.9mm, and yet which require different ammunition appears to be an awkward installation so far as the supply of ammo is concerned.

Bomb Sight

Type 2, Model 1.

Oxygen Bottles

Five oxygen bottles were found in place of six carried in other Judy models.

Performance and Characteristics

The Judy 33 was capable of a top speed of 376mph at an altitude of 18,500ft.[4]

A number of brand new Suiseis were captured at Aichi's Nagoya factory following the occupation of Japan, with two D4Y3s and two D4Y4s being shipped back to the US – at least one D4Y2 was also transported to America on board the escort carrier *Barnes*. Three were sent to "Pax River" for evaluation by the US Navy, and the USAAF retained one at Freeman Field. Two of the aircraft were subsequently transferred to NPG Dahlgren Junction in October 1946 for use as targets and a third ended up at NAS Norfolk, where it was probably scrapped. The USAAF's

D4Y1 construction number 7483 is one of two surviving "Judys," having been built at Yokosuka in February 1944. Sent to Babo airfield in the Dutch East Indies shortly thereafter, its unit assignment remains unknown, as this base was principally home to kokutai equipped with A6M3/5 Zero-sens or G4M1 "Bettys." At some point the aircraft was abandoned while on its landing gear, with the engine having been removed. The "Judy" was acquired by Bruce Fenstermaker in 1991 without an engine – although an Atsuta was also recovered nearby – and exported from Babo airfield to California for the Santa Monica Museum of Flight. The aircraft was later purchased by the Planes of Fame Museum at Chino, and it was restored in 2009–12 as a D4Y3, fitted with an operable Pratt & Whitney R-1830 radial engine that allows the dive-bomber to taxi. (*Edward M. Young*)

D4Y1 construction number 4316 was recovered from Colonia airfield on Yap Island by Nobuhiko Endo in cooperation with the Nippon Television Network in 1972, and has been on display in the Yasukuni Jinja Yushukan shrine in Tokyo since 1988. Parts from three other D4Y2s found at Colonia were incorporated into the "Judy" during its subsequent restoration in Japan. (Edward M. Young)

D4Y4 was sent to Middletown in the summer of 1946 for inclusion in the National Air Museum, but it too was eventually scrapped.

Complete D4Y1s are currently on display in the Yasukuni Jinja Yushukan shrine in Tokyo and in the Planes of Fame Museum in Chino. The aircraft in Tokyo (construction number 4316) was recovered from Yap Island in 1972 and restored in Japan in 1980, while the Chino example (construction number 7483) was acquired by Bruce Fenstermaker in 1991 without an engine – although an Atsuta was also recovered nearby – and exported from Babo Airfield, in Indonesia, to California. This aircraft has been restored as a D4Y3, using a Pratt & Whitney R-1830 radial engine.

Aichi B7A2 "Grace"

In response to the IJNAF's 16-Shi specification for a carrier-borne attack bomber to supplement and then replace the Nakajima B6N "Jill" torpedo-bomber and the Yokosuka D4Y "Judy" dive-bomber, Aichi commenced development of the B7A Ryusei ("Shooting Star"), which was subsequently given the Allied codename "Grace," in 1941. A large aircraft, thanks to its intended operation from a new class of bigger carriers with deck elevators of an increased size, the prototype B7A1 completed its maiden flight in May 1942.

The challenging 16-Shi specification called for an aircraft that could carry more than 1,000lb of bombs or a 1,764lb torpedo at speeds of up to 354mph in excess of 1,000 nautical miles. Furthermore, the aircraft had to be as maneuverable as an A6M. A powerful engine would be needed to give the B7A the required performance desired by the IJNAF, who instructed Aichi to use the Nakajima Homare 18-cylinder radial engine that was then under development. Rated at 1,800hp, the powerplant was still experimental at the time the Ryusei commenced its test program, and teething troubles with the motor delayed progress. Finally, in April 1944, the more reliable Homare 12 became available and the B7A2 commenced production.

The "Grace" could carry two 550lb or six 132lb bombs in an internal bomb-bay, or a 1,764lb Type 91 torpedo mounted externally beneath the fuselage. The aircraft was also armed with two wing-mounted 20mm Type 99 Model 2 cannon and a flexible 7.92mm Type 1 machine gun for the rear gunner – late-production B7A2s replaced the latter weapon with a 13mm Type 2 machine gun. Aside from the "Grace's" size, the aircraft's most distinctive feature was its inverted gull wings, employed by Aichi in order to reduce the length of the undercarriage legs and provide adequate clearance for the 11ft 5in diameter four-blade propeller. The wings were attached mid-fuselage, in order to provide space for the ventral bomb-bay.

Just 105 B7A2s had been built when production ceased following the destruction of Aichi's Funakata plant during the earthquake that struck the Tokei district in May 1945. Two land-based units (Yokosuka and 752nd Kokutais) received "Graces" from late 1944, as the only IJN carriers large enough to accommodate the B7A2 – *Taiho* and *Shinano* – had by then been sunk.

This intact, but propellerless, B7A2 "Grace" attack bomber was found in a wrecked hangar at Kisarazu Naval Air Base. The aircraft had been assigned to the 752nd Kokutai – one of only two land-based units to be issued with the "Grace" prior to war's end. A total of 105 B7A2s had been built by Aichi by the time production was prematurely halted in May 1945 following the destruction of the company's Funakata plant in an earthquake that struck the Tokei district. It is possible that this aircraft was one of the three "Graces" shipped to the US. (NARA)

ABOVE A 752nd Kokutai B7A2 is wheeled out of a hangar at Kisarazu in late September 1945 by US Navy personnel. Despite the gull-winged "Grace's" large size, it possessed the handling and performance qualities of a fighter, being faster and more maneuverable than the A6M5c Zero-sen. (NARA)

RIGHT Two of the three B7A2s transported to the US were assigned to the USAAF, while this example was allocated to the US Navy. Flown on a handful of occasions from "Pax River," the aircraft was sent to Naval Auxiliary Air Station Mustin Field, Pennsylvania in January 1947 and scrapped sometime thereafter. (US Navy)

According to early US Intelligence reports, the Allies were fearful of the "Grace's" combat capabilities:

PART V – POSSIBLE NEW TORPEDO AIRCRAFT

The major threat to our fleet closing in on the mainland is the development by the Japs of new and outstanding torpedo planes. The basic Navy carrier-based planes, KATE and the more modern JILL, have not met with great success and the land-based NELL and BETTY are no longer serious threats as torpedo aircraft. This has left the Japs with an extremely important gap to fill and it seems certain that they have been bending every effort to overcome this situation.

It is quite possible that several types of planes may be adopted for torpedo-dropping including fighters, dive-bombers, land attack and high-speed reconnaissance. Of the present newer types, however, the aircraft listed below has special qualities that could make its use on a large-scale basis a definite threat to our future operations.

GRACE 11 (Ryusei)

GRACE 11 is derived from 16 Experimental carrier-borne attack plane, bears the Model/Type symbol B7A1 and is designed by Aichi. Production information is uncertain, but it is quite possibly in production at present or about ready to go into production. Its specifications indicate it is fitted with an 18-cylinder Homare engine which should markedly increase its performance over that of JILL and other Jap torpedo planes. Up to the present, photographic coverage has not been available and performance computations have not been possible. An attempt will be made, however, in the near future to assess the possibilities of GRACE based on the limited data on hand. That it will be a fast, maneuverable torpedo-bomber with a high rate of climb seems clearly indicated.[5]

Three B7A2s were captured at Kisarazu, in Chiba Prefecture, by US forces following the occupation of Japan and shipped to the US. One was sent to "Pax River" for evaluation by the US Navy and the remaining two were assigned to the USAAF. Flight testing revealed that the "Grace" possessed the handling and performance qualities of a fighter, being faster and more maneuverable than the A6M5c Zero-sen. The "Pax River" aircraft was sent to Naval Auxiliary Air Station Mustin Field, Pennsylvania, in January 1947 and scrapped sometime thereafter. Both of the USAAF B7A2s were at Middletown in May 1946, where one of them was scrapped. The second "Grace" (construction number 816) was sent to Park Ridge four months later and stored until it was eventually passed on to the Smithsonian Institution in 1963. The aircraft was then moved to "Silver Hill," where it remains today.

Nakajima B5N2 "Kate"

In 1935, the IJNAF issued the 10-Shi specification calling for a single-engined monoplane replacement for the Yokosuka B4Y1 biplane torpedo-bomber. The aircraft needed to have a span of less than 52ft 5in, with the ability to fold its wings for storage, armament of one 1,764lb torpedo or equivalent bombload and a 7.7mm machine gun, a top speed of 207mph at 6,560ft, an endurance of seven hours maximum at

B5N2 construction number 2194 from the 931st Kokutai was captured on Saipan's Aslito airfield following the seizure of the island in July 1944 after more than three weeks of bloody fighting. The first intact "Kate" to fall into Allied hands, this aircraft was built in December 1943 and equipped with air-to-surface vessel radar (note the anti-shipping radar antennae arrays at various locations on the aircraft). It is seen here being prepared for shipment back to San Diego on board the escort carrier *Copahee*, along with 13 Zero-sens and 37 Japanese aero engines. Note that one of the propeller blades has been sawn in half to ease the transportation of the aircraft. (*NARA*)

155mph, a crew of three and either a Nakajima Hikari or Mitsubishi Kinsai radial engine. Nakajima's Type K design (designated the B5N1) eventually beat the similar Mitsubishi B5M1 in competitive trials, the prototype having first flown in January 1937. The production variant became known as the Type 97 Carrier Attack Bomber (Allied codename "Kate"). The "Kate's" armament consisted of one 7.7mm Type 92 machine gun for the rear gunner. The aircraft could carry either one Type 91 torpedo or one 1,760lb bomb, or two 550lb bombs, or six 293lb bombs.

Entering front-line service in 1938, the B5N1 had enjoyed success as a level bomber over China during the Second Sino-Japanese War, where its lack of protection for the crew and fuel tank and solitary machine gun went unchallenged because the aircraft was closely escorted by A5M fighters. Nevertheless, in December 1939 Nakajima began test flying the improved B5N2, which featured a more powerful 1,000hp Nakajima Sakae 11 radial engine in place of the 700hp Nakajima Hikari 2 fitted in the B5N1.

By the time the IJNAF launched its surprise attack on Pearl Harbor on December 7, 1941, the B5N2 had replaced the earlier model in all front-line carrier-based units. Playing an important part in that attack, as well as in subsequent carrier clashes at Coral Sea, Midway and Santa Cruz (and raids on Ceylon and Darwin) in 1942, the B5N2 was a key weapon in the Japanese arsenal. Land-based B5N2 units also saw considerable action in the Solomons, and continued to be used as level bombers through to the Philippines campaign in late 1944. When deemed obsolescent for carrier service, a number of "Kates" were modified into anti-submarine warfare (ASW) aircraft, some being fitted with air-to-surface vessel (ASV) radar and others receiving Jikitanchiki magnetic anomaly detectors. B5N2s

LEFT Overhauled, the Saipan B5N2 flew for the first time in US Navy hands on November 16, 1944 from NAS Anacostia. Early test flights evaluated the performance of the aircraft's ASV radar equipment in a series of sorties against US Navy vessels of various sizes sailing off the Delaware coast, the equipment being operated by an experienced radar technician from the Naval Radio Laboratory. (NARA)

LOWER LEFT By October 1945, B5N2 construction number 2194 had been deemed surplus to the TAIC requirements, and the torpedo-bomber, along with an airworthy A6M5, was attached to a unit known as "The Navy's Flying Might." It had been established as a traveling display to take part in Victory Loan promotions across the US. (NARA)

were also flown alongside B5N1-K as advanced training aircraft from airfields in Japan. Finally, a number of "Kates" were used in the kamikaze role from December 1944 through to war's end, with the last example to be shot down falling on August 15, 1945 – the day Japan surrendered to the Allies.

The first intact "Kate" to fall into Allied hands was B5N2 construction number 2194 of the 931st Kokutai that was captured on Saipan's Aslito airfield following the seizure of the island in July 1944 after more than three weeks of bloody fighting. Built in December 1943 and equipped with ASV radar, it was shipped back to San Diego on board the escort carrier *Copahee* along with 13 Zero-sens and 37 Japanese aero engines. Overhauled, the B5N2 flew for the first time in US Navy hands on November 16, 1944 from NAS Anacostia. Early test flights evaluated the performance of the ASV radar equipment during sorties against vessels sailing off the Delaware coast, the equipment being operated by an experienced radar technician from the Naval Radio Laboratory. The US Navy tallied 35.9 hours of test and evaluation flying in the airplane through to the end of April 1945.

Once the TAIC had finished evaluating the "Kate" in October 1945, both it and a surplus A6M5 were attached to a unit known as "The

Navy's Flying Might." It was set up as a traveling display to take part in Victory Loan promotions across the US, and both the "Kate" and "Zeke" had their bare metal fuselages camouflaged in a suitable shade of green and Japanese roundels applied in order to better represent enemy aircraft in the aerial displays that were performed in conjunction with US Navy fighters. The B5N2 served with the unit through to the summer of 1946, after which its final fate remains unrecorded.

Nakajima B6N2 "Jill"

The Imperial Naval Staff had issued a request for a replacement for the B5N as early as 1939 with the release of the 14-Shi specification. This called for a three-seat carrier-borne torpedo-bomber with a top speed of 288mph and a range of 1,150 miles with a 1,764lb bombload. The new airplane, designated the B6N by the IJNAF, was aerodynamically similar to the B5N, but its Nakajima NK7A Mamoru 11 14-cylinder air-cooled radial engine produced 1,870hp – 80 percent more than the Sakae 11 in the "Kate."

Constrained by carrier stowage restrictions, Nakajima's design team was forced to use a wing that was similar to the B5N's in both span and area, despite the new aircraft – called the Tenzan ("Heavenly Mountain") and codenamed "Jill" by the Allies – being considerably heavier than the "Kate." This meant that the B6N would suffer from a high landing speed and wing loading, restricting its fleet use to larger carriers. One of the aircraft's key external features was its forward-swept vertical tail surfaces, which were adopted in order to keep the aircraft's length within the limits imposed by the IJNAF to ensure that the B6N could be accommodated on carrier elevators.

The IJNAF also insisted that the airplane should be powered by the proven Mitsubishi MK4T Kasai 25 engine, rated at 1,850hp, but Nakajima stuck with the new Mamoru 11 because of its lower fuel consumption and room for growth. Flight testing commenced in the spring of 1941, whereupon it was soon found that the design was plagued by serious engineering flaws – including directional stability issues caused by the powerful torque of the airplane's four-bladed propeller. To solve the latter, Nakajima had to move the vertical tail surfaces two degrees to the left. Teething troubles with the Mamoru 11 engine also delayed the test program, which meant that the B6N was not deemed ready for carrier acceptance trials until late 1942. When these eventually took place on board *Ryuho* and *Zuikaku*, the "Jill's" arrestor hook was found to be too weak and several landing mishaps occurred as a result.

The Tenzan was finally accepted for production in February 1943, with the B6N1 introducing a number of modifications to make the airplane suitable for fleet use. These included smaller exhaust stacks, angling down of the torpedo rack, strengthening of the main landing gear attachment and tailplane and fitting of a flexible 7.7mm Type 92 machine gun firing through a ventral tunnel. This weapon doubled the "Jill's" defenses, as a flexible 7.7mm weapon had been installed in the aircraft from the start for the rear gunner.

After completing just 133 B6N1s through to July 1943, Nakajima was instructed by the Ministry of Munitions to cease production of the Mamoru 11 to allow the company to concentrate on building the more widely used Sakae and Homare engines. Fitted with the Mitsubishi MK4T Kasai 25 rated at 1,850hp, the re-engined Tenzan was designated the B6N2. A total of 1,133 B6N2s would be completed by Nakajima between June 1943 and August 1945.

When the B6N finally became operational, in New Guinea, from December 1943, it proved to be largely ineffective owing to the air superiority established by advanced US Navy carrier-borne fighters such as the F6F Hellcat and F4U Corsair. Land-based "Jills" fought in the Marshall and Gilbert islands, in the defense of Truk and in the First Battle of the Philippine Sea. Carrier-based units also participated in the latter action in June 1944, losing a considerable number of aircraft in the "Great Marianas Turkey Shoot." Surviving examples were brought together four months later for the IJN's final carrier action during the Second Battle of the Philippine Sea (also known as the Battle of Leyte

This B6N2 was one of a handful of "Jills" found at Clark Field after the base was liberated by US forces in February 1945. Possibly a survivor from a carrier assigned to the First Mobile Force, which had been decimated during the Battle of Leyte Gulf some four months earlier, the aircraft is riddled with small-caliber bullet holes from its tail to its nose. (*NARA*)

ABOVE Photographed on March 3, 1945, this B6N2 – possibly from the 702nd Kokutai – was chosen by TAIU-SWPA personnel for restoration to airworthy status. There was no shortage of parts available at Clark Field, which was just as well, for the "Jill" has suffered damage to its flying surfaces and cockpit transparencies. After several months of work, the torpedo-bomber finally commenced flight testing from Clark Field. (NARA)

ABOVE RIGHT Looking resplendent in its TAIU-SWPA markings, and wearing the unit code S19, the B6N2 seen in the previous shot holds station off the port side of the camera-ship during a photo sortie near Manila in June 1945. The flight-test team found that although the aircraft had impressive speed for a torpedo-bomber, it still suffered from the same weaknesses and shortcomings as its predecessor, the B5N, namely light defensive armament, ineffective fuel tank protection and no armor for the crew. (NARA)

When viewed from head-on, the B6N2 looked remarkably similar to a late model A6M Zero-sen. The "Jill's" wingspan of just over 48ft was some 12ft greater than the A6M5/7, however. The iconic Japanese fighter was also only ever fitted with a three-bladed propeller. (*NARA*)

Gulf), and again losses for the IJNAF were catastrophic. Formosa-based B6N2 units continued to attack Allied ships until late October 1944, when most remaining "Jills" were sent to the Philippines in an effort to repel invading American forces.

Like the "Kate," many surviving "Jills" were used as kamikaze platforms during the final ten months of the Pacific War. Indeed, the B6N2 proved to be more effective in this role than its predecessors thanks to its increased top speed. The "Jill" was also occasionally employed as a torpedo-bomber as well.

In February 1945 a B6N2 purportedly from the 702nd Kokutai B6N2 was captured by the US Army at Clark Field. The aircraft was stripped to bare metal and TAIU-SWPA markings, including the striped rudder, were applied. Restored to airworthy condition, the "Jill" underwent technical evaluation and flight testing from Clark Field. The TAIU-SWPA's technical evaluation of the aircraft was recorded in a brief TAIC Summary Manual that appeared in February 1945:

> JILL is a torpedo-bomber designed to replace KATE. Jill 11 is similar to JILL 12 except that JILL 11 uses the MAMORU 11 engine. The performance of the two models is essentially the same except for a higher critical altitude on JILL 12. Maximum speed of JILL is 345mph at 18,600ft.
>
> Ineffective fuel tank protection and light armament together with no evidence of armor indicates that JILL has no decided advantage over KATE except in speed and climb. There is evidence of radar being installed on JILL.[6]

The aircraft was probably scrapped following technical evaluation by the TAIU-SWPA.

OPPOSITE The B6N2 was powered by a Mitsubishi MK4T Kasai 25 radial engine rated at 1,850hp, which TAIU-SWPA test pilots found gave the "Jill" a top speed of 345mph at 18,600ft – admittedly, this aircraft was unarmed and only lightly fueled during these evaluation flights. (*NARA*)

Following the occupation of Japan two more B6N2s were captured by US ground forces at Suzuka airfield. Both "Jills" were amongst the 145 captured Japanese aircraft that were shipped to America on board three US Navy escort carriers for evaluation, the B6N2s departing Yokosuka on the flightdeck of *Barnes* on November 3, 1945. By May 1946 the aircraft were at Middletown, where one of them was later scrapped. Construction number 5350 survived, however, being put on outdoor static display with other Japanese and German aircraft at NAS Willow Grove from 1958. The sole surviving example of its type in the world, the aircraft was acquired by the NASM in 1981 and placed in storage at its Paul E. Garber Facility at "Silver Hill" – it remains here in a dismantled state.

TWIN-ENGINED BOMBERS

Mitsubishi G3M2 "Nell"

In 1933, the IJNAF issued Mitsubishi with the 8-Shi specification calling for the development of a land-based twin-engined long-range reconnaissance aircraft. The company duly built the Ka-9 monoplane, which featured a clean fuselage married to a Junkers-style "double wing" and twin fins and rudders. Powered by two 500hp Hiro Type 91 liquid-cooled engines, the Ka-9 made its first flight in April 1934. Demonstrating exceptional maneuverability and handling characteristics and possessing a range of 3,760 miles, the aircraft so impressed the IJNAF that it issued Mitsubishi with the 9-Shi specification for a fully developed attack bomber capable of carrying 1,764lb of ordnance. The aircraft's defensive armament would consist of three 7.7mm Type 92 machine guns.

The Ka-15 built by Mitsubishi to meet this requirement featured the wing of the Ka-9 combined with a wider fuselage that allowed for the fitting of three retractable turrets, each housing a 7.92mm weapon. The tail surfaces were also enlarged to resolve center-of-gravity issues and improve stability during the bomb-run. The first prototype flew in June 1935, and it was followed by 20 additional Ka-15s completed in six configurations. The principal differences amongst these machines centered on whether their noses were glazed or not and which powerplant was fitted – 750hp Hiro Type 91 or 830/910hp Mitsubishi Kinsei 2/3 14-cylinder air-cooled radial. In June 1936, the aircraft entered production as the G3M1. Featuring a redesigned canopy covering an enlarged cockpit, only 34 G3M1s were built prior to production switching to the improved G3M2 fitted with 1,075hp Kinsei 41 or 42 radial engines.

This variant gave the bomber its combat debut over China on August 14, 1937 when aircraft from the Taipai-based Kanoya Kokutai attacked Hangchow and Kwangteh in the first ever trans-oceanic bombing raid – the aircraft covered 1,250 miles to hit their targets. G3M2s would see considerable combat in China over the next four years, with as many as 130 aircraft assigned to four Kokutais being committed to the Second Sino-Japanese War.

The final bomber variant to enter production in 1941 was the G3M3, built by Nakajima under an IJNAF contract – the company had also previously delivered a large number of G3M2s. Powered by two 1,300hp Kinsei 51 engines and with an increased fuel capacity of 5,182 litres, the G3M3 had a range of 3,871 miles. Like late-build G3M2s, this model

Allied Intelligence personnel investigate and assess the status of captured IJNAF G3M2 "Nell" construction number 197, found at Cape Gloucester airfield on December 30, 1943. The Nakajima-built aircraft, which had been completed in late 1942, had initially been used as a bomber by an unidentified kokutai before it was stripped of most of its armament and employed instead as a transport. A number of "Nells" had flown men and materiel to Cape Gloucester airfield from mid-1943 through to November of that year, and it appears that construction number 197 might have been damaged on the ground here during a strafing attack. (NARA)

Although declared "restorable" by Allied Intelligence, the "Nell" was left where it was found due to the type's obsolescence. (NARA)

also featured improved armament in the form of a large "turtle back" dorsal turret, housing a flexible 20mm Type 99 Model 1 cannon, blister turrets on either side of the fuselage for a flexible 7.7mm machine gun and an additional 7.7mm weapon that could be fired from either side of the cockpit. The front retractable turret fitted in the G3M1 and early G3M2 was retained.

Despite improved armament, the fast, lightweight bomber remained capable of delivering a heavy bombload to its target, while minimizing its time over the target or battlefield. The G3M, however, sacrificed armor protection for its aircrew as well as self-sealing fuel tanks for speed, range, and altitude gains – the aircraft suffered significant losses to Chinese fighters as a result.

At the start of the Pacific War, the IJNAF had more than 250 G3Ms assigned to front-line and secondary units, and the aircraft (codenamed "Nell" by the Allies) was heavily involved in early Japanese successes against US forces on Wake Island, in the Philippines and in the Marianas Islands. Aircraft from the Genzan and Mihoro Kokutais also helped sink the British battleships HMS *Prince of Wales* and HMS *Repulse* off Malaya on December 10, 1941. "Nells" accompanied Japanese forces as they captured territory in the Southwest Pacific islands, although by 1943 most examples had been replaced in the front line by the G4M "Betty."

On December 30, 1943, the US Marine Corps found a G3M2 from an unknown IJNAF unit amongst a number of Japanese aircraft abandoned at an airstrip at Cape Gloucester. The bomber was subsequently evaluated by Allied Intelligence and declared "restorable," although it was decided not to return the "Nell" to airworthiness owing to the type's obsolescence. The Allied Intelligence evaluation produced following the examination of

demolition of the crashed plane. The major differences between the Model 22 and Model 11 were found to be in close accord with the variations that documents and PoWs had already pointed out; removal of side blisters, addition to the nose section for probable accommodation of navigator and/or radar operator, installation of 20mm top power turret (first yet examined), installation of radar, Kasei 21 engines replacing either Kasei 11s or 15s and use of 4-bladed propellers.

Modified Nose

The transparent part of the nose extends from the nose back to more than halfway to the cockpit and completely encircles the plane except for a narrow catwalk at the bottom. The finding of plotting tables in this section leads to the belief that the navigator and/or the radar operator now occupy a position in the nose. Recovered radar equipment is shown in Figs. 9 and 10. The forward radar antenna projects from the center of the nose and the 7.7mm nose gun (electrically powered, according to document) can rotate 360° around the antenna.

New Armament

Nose Armament – Under "armament" on page 8, the original specifications call for two guns in the nose; one 7.7mm electrically operated, revolving turret gun described in the paragraph above and a second 7.7mm gun carried in a rack on the bulkhead of the nose that can be fired through ports on either side of the nose. This second gun was not recovered at either Biak or Tinian and it is not known whether it was specified only for the experimental version or is still considered by the Japs as "standard equipment".

Lateral Guns – In place of side blisters, Betty 22 has on each side a semi-circular sliding rail arrangement behind a transparent door that mounts a 7.7mm gun. In addition to the two side hatch guns, a "third reserve 7.7mm gun" is stated by the document to be carried on the bulkhead in the waist. No trace of this gun has yet been recovered.

Dorsal Turret – The revolving top power turret is aft of the greenhouse and just forward of the trailing edge of the wing; it is reported as probably rotating 360°, with the 20mm gun offset to the left side of the operator allowing space for his head and shoulders. It is believed to be self-contained as there was a complete arrangement of motor, pump and hydraulic reservoir attached to the turret that appeared ready to operate. The operator stands on a platform and must move around as the turret revolves. Elevation is approximately 85°. A piece of 3/8-inch armor plate is used to protect the operator and mechanism.

New Engines

Higher rated Kasei 21 engines developing 1825hp at takeoff (War Emergency Rating) have replaced the Kasei 11s or 15s that were formerly fitted in Betty 11. According to a document, the operation of the water-alcohol injection system is automatic and begins to function at between 36.22 and 36.61 inches of manifold pressure; water-alcohol being injected under pressure through eight metered jets directly in back of the supercharger impeller. At 41.73 inches of manifold pressure, the water-methanol consumption rate is equal to 40 percent of the gasoline consumption rate. Four-blade, constant speed, variable pitch propellers, of the Hamilton type, were recovered at Tinian which confirms the documentary specifications.

Wing Fuselage and Tail Plane

The 82ft span of Betty 22 is identical with that of the Model 11. The length with a rounded tail turret is given as 65ft 7in, but with the "fish mouth" turret found at Tinian it is estimated by TAIC as being 64ft 10in. The Tinian report gave an approximate length of 60ft, but the condition of the crash did not permit an accurate measurement. Photographic assessments indicate that the documentary length of 65ft 7in is probably correct. The shape of the wingtips have been changed and manual specifications state they are removable. Flaps are electrically operated. A previous document had indicated a laminar flow type wing, but this is not borne out by the crash report, or in a newly recovered manual or by photographic coverage. The value of this wing construction to a plane such as Betty would be questionable.

The horizontal tailplane has been redesigned; tips are now rounded comparable to main wingtips and trailing edge is almost straight. Fin and stabilizer are single cantilever type.

Fuel Tankage

Details of fuel tanks and their arrangement could not be determined from the crash. All recovered documents, however, are consistent in showing a maximum tankage of 6,490 liters

(1,715 US gals.). This is a reasonable figure and would represent only a nominal increase over the 1,560-gallon capacity of Betty 11. Performance on Betty 22 shown on page 11 has been computed on the basis of carrying these 1,715 gals in an overload reconnaissance condition.

Documentary Data on Betty 22
Specifications on Betty 22 as taken from a Jap manual (with comments where applicable) are as follows:

Official Japanese Designation
G4M2
Type 1 Land Attack Plane, Model 12 (or 22)
Comment: Now established as Model 22.

Manufactured by
Mitsubishi Jukōgyō K.K., Nagoya Kōkūki Seisakusho.

Type
Twin-engine, all-metal, mid-wing medium bomber.

Function
Torpedo and level bomber. Can also be used for recce.

Crew
Seven – pilot, co-pilot, turret gunner, two waist gunners, tail gunner, bombardier. The bombardier also operates the nose MG.

Wings
Mid-wing cantilever monoplane with stressed skin. Box spar construction of laminated, high-test aluminum alloy. Wing is divided into a center section and inner and outer wing sections. Ten integral gas tanks are fitted, five in each wing. The leading edge of each inner wing contains an oil tank.

Trailing edge flaps on inner wing section. Flaps are electrically operated and are equipped with a crank for manual operation. The flap brackets are mounted perpendicular to the underside of the flap. They hinge on brackets which extend back from the underside of the trailing edge of the wing. Flap does not ride back on a track, but moves in an arc around this hinge point. This type of suspension gives a slot effect when flaps are cracked.

Frise type ailerons with trim tabs on outer wing sections. The ailerons have counterweights on both sides of all hinge joints on the leading edge. Wingtips are removable.

Comment: This document, crash report and photographic assessment show no indication of a laminar flow wing on Betty 22. It is possible that this change may be incorporated in Betty 34.

Fuselage

Elliptical, semi-monocoque fuselage. Transparent Plexiglas nose and tail. All-metal construction, principally of high-test aluminum alloy. The skin is flush riveted. Dorsal turret to rear of greenhouse and just forward of trailing edge of the wing. Rectangular gun openings in each side of the fuselage replace the blisters which were in earlier models.

Comment: Tinian Betty 22 had dual pilot's cockpit.

Tail Unit

Cantilever monoplane type. Aerodynamically balanced elevators and rudder. Elevators and rudder equipped with trim tabs.

Undercarriage

Retractable main landing gear and tail wheel. Main landing gear retracts in a forward direction into the center part of the nacelle. It is retracted by an electric motor in the fuselage and power is transmitted by a series of shafts. System can be manually operated with a crank. The tail wheel is retracted by an electric motor fitted immediately next to the tail wheel housing. It is also equipped with a crank for manual operation.

Comment: Tinian report stated main landing gear retracts "rearward", which is erroneous. Other details coincide.

Fuel Tanks

Ten integral fuel tanks are contained inside the wing; two tanks in the center section, three in each inner wing, and one in each outer wing. Total capacity, 6,490 liters (1,715 US gals.). With the exception of the outboard tank in each wing, the fuel tanks are covered with a self-sealing pad 28mm thick. The wing CO_2 fire-extinguishing line surrounds the outboard tanks on three sides, giving them additional protection.

Comment: Capacity and location of tanks could not be confirmed from Tinian examinations.

Dimensions
Fuselage

Length	20m. (65.616ft.)
Height	6m. (19.68ft.)
Maximum width	2m. (6.56ft.)
Engine CL – CL	6m. (19.68ft.)

Comment: Exact length could not be checked at Tinian. With a "fish mouth" tail turret such as actually found, TAIC estimates length as 64ft 10in.

Wing

Thickness ratio at root	15%
Thickness ratio at tip	10%
Chord at root	5m. (16.40ft.)
Chord at tip	1.250m. (4.10 t.)
Area (Assuming wingtips are squared)	78.125 sq. meters (840.94 sq. feet)
Aspect ratio (Assuming wingtips are squared)	8.0
Span (Given as "approximate")	25m. (82.02ft.)
Mean aerodynamic chord	3.500m. (11.48ft.)

Comment: 82ft span confirmed at Tinian. There was evidence at Tinian of a sealed section in each wing, possibly for flotation.

The G4M2a undertook a handful of evaluation flights from Clark Field, during which it attained a top speed of 345mph when lightly loaded. This "Betty" variant was powered by two 1,850hp Mitsubishi MK4T Kasai 25 radial engines. (*Smithsonian National Air and Space Museum, (NASM 87-15125).*)

Flap

Length (Given as "approximate")	5.250 m. x 2 (17.22 ft. x 2)
Area	4.108 sq. meters x 2 (44.22 sq. ft. x 2)
Angle traversed	45°

Aileron

Length (Assuming wingtips are squared)	6.250m. x 2 (20.51ft. x 2)
Area (Assuming wingtips are squared)	2.05 sq. meters x 2 (22.07 sq. ft. x 2)

Weights and Loadings

Empty	8,000kg. (17,636.8lb.)
Normal	12,500kg. (27,557.5lb.)
Overload	15,395kg. (33,939.8lb.)

Bomb Load

1 x 800kg. (1,763.68lb.) bomb, or
1 x 800kg. (1,763.68lb.) torpedo, or
1 x 500kg. (1,102.30lb.) bomb, or
4 x 250kg. (551.15lb.) bombs, or
12 x 60kg. (132.28lb.) bombs, or
12 x 30kg. (66.14lb.) bombs, or
12 x 10kg. (22.05lb.) bombs, or
12 x 4kg. (8.82lb.) bombs, or
12 x 1kg. (2.20lb.) bombs.

Bombs are released by percussion-cap type bomb release. Bomb-bay doors are installed only when plane is used in recce work. When any bomb load is carried, the bomb-bay doors are removed and a wind deflection plate is placed in the rear of the bomb-bay to cut down wind resistance. When a torpedo is carried, this plate is removed.

Comment: Bomb-bay arrangement similar to Betty 11.

Armament

Nose: 2 x 7.7mm MG, 600 rounds, the transparent nose is actually an electrically-powered revolving turret, giving one gun a considerably greater field of fire. The second gun is carried in a rack on the bulkhead of the nose and can be fired through ports on either side of the nose.

Turret: 1 x 20mm cannon, 270 rounds. Placed in a revolving power turret.

Waist: 2 x 7.7mm MG, 600 rounds per gun. One gun on each side of the ship. Each is mounted on a semi-circular rail behind a sliding transparent door. In addition, there is a reserve 7.7mm MG carried on the bulkhead in the waist.

Tail: 1 x 20mm cannon, 270 rounds. Elevation 35°, depression 55°. Traverse 40° to either side of line extending directly aft.

Comment: No trace of the "second" nose gun or the reserve waist gun was found at Tinian. Other specifications checked.

One of the key recognition features of the G4M2a is clearly visible in this aerial view of the TAIU-SWPA example – the bulged bomb-bay. The first G4M2as had been delivered to the IJNAF in late 1943, and production of the aircraft continued until war's end. (NARA)

Armor

The only armor mentioned is a small plate directly aft of the rear gun magazine storage rack.

Comment: The above was standard with Betty 11. An additional piece of 3/8-inch plate to protect the top turret gunner and the mechanism was recovered at Tinian – size not given.

Automatic Pilot

Plane is equipped with an automatic pilot which controls the plane hydraulically.[7]

It was later discovered that this US Intelligence report erroneously claimed that no laminar flow airfoils were incorporated in the design of the G4M2 Model 22 Betty.

Several "Bettys" were flown by the Allies in 1945, including a 763rd Kokutai G4M2 (tail code 763-12) that was captured by the US Army at

ABOVE Unlike the TAIU-SWPA, the RAF's ATAIU-SEA kept its solitary G4M2a both fully radar-equipped and armed during the series of flights it made with the aircraft from the former IJNAF airfield at Tebrau in 1945-46. The bomber was crewed by RAF and IJNAF personnel during this period. Note the Zero-sen running in toward the "Betty" at the start of a low-level pass over the airfield: this aircraft is one of three A6M3/5s operated by the ATAIU-SEA. (© IWM CF 896)

ABOVE RIGHT One of two "Bettys" that carried Lt Gen Torashiro Kawabe's surrender delegation from Kisarazu to Ie Shima on August 19, 1945 is swarmed over by US airmen, sailors, and Seabees. The IJNAF aircraft remained on Ie Shima overnight while Kawabe and his party were flown on to Manila on board a USAAF C-54, where they received detailed surrender instructions. Both IJNAF aircraft had returned to Japan by August 21; the G6M1-L force-landed near the mouth of the Tenryu River when it ran short of fuel. (NARA)

Clark Field in February 1945. The aircraft was stripped to bare metal and had US TAIU-SWPA markings applied, including the striped rudder. It also had its propeller spinners painted red. The aircraft was then flight tested by the TAIU-SWPA, whose evaluation revealed that although the defensive armament of the G4M2 represented a marked improvement over that fitted to the G4M1, the former still lacked adequate armor protection for its crew or self-sealing fuel tanks. The flight tests of the G4M2 revealed that the aircraft was capable of attaining a top speed of 345mph when lightly loaded. The bomber was almost certainly scrapped following the evaluation.

A G4M3 was shipped back to the US on board the light carrier *Core* in November 1945, although it was never flown. Listed as in storage at Middletown in May 1946, the "Betty" was allocated to the National Air Museum in September of that year. However, it was eventually scrapped – parts of the aircraft survive with the NASM at "Silver Hill."

The RAF's ATAIU-SEA flew a radar-equipped G4M2a fitted with ASV radar from the former IJNAF airfield at Tebrau, near Singapore, immediately post war. Finally, a "Betty" was also reportedly flown to Australia in late 1945 and stored at RAAF Base Fairbairn, in Canberra, for inclusion in the Australian War Memorial (AWM). It too was scrapped in around 1950, however.

Yokosuka P1Y1 "Frances"

The development of what would become the P1Y Ginga ("Milky Way") fast medium bomber commenced in 1940 following the issuing of the 15-Shi specification by the IJNAF for an aircraft capable of carrying out low-altitude, torpedo- and dive-bombing attacks. The Dai-Ichi Kaigun Koku Gijitsusho was tasked with producing a bomber that rivaled the performance of the Junkers Ju 88, North American B-25 Mitchell and Martin B-26 Marauder. The aircraft was expected to have a top speed of more than 345mph, and, unlike previous IJNAF bombers, it would be fitted from the start with protected fuel tanks – eight in total, with a further six unprotected. Armor for the three-man crew consisted of a single 20mm plate behind the pilot's head, and, unlike its German and American contemporaries, the P1Y had only single flexibly mounted guns in the nose and rear cockpit positions. Capable of carrying either a single 1,764lb torpedo semi-internally beneath the fuselage or two 1,102lb bombs in a ventral bomb-bay, the P1Y, like de Havilland Mosquito, had to rely on speed for its survival.

Powered by a pair of 1,820hp Nakajima Homare 11 18-cylinder radial engines, the first of six prototype P1Ys was completed in August 1943 and made its maiden flight shortly thereafter. The aircraft's

These P1Y1 "Frances" medium bombers were found by US troops in a hangar at Kisarazu Naval Air Base in September 1945. The aircraft appeared to be intact, but unserviceable. (NARA)

impressive top speed and maneuverability were popular with test and service pilots alike, and principal constructor Nakajima immediately commenced production of the P1Y1. However, the bomber's hydraulic system and immature engines proved troublesome for groundcrews, resulting in the IJNAF refusing to accept the P1Y1 for service use until October 1944 – by then 453 aircraft had been built.

Amongst the changes made to the P1Y1 in an attempt to improve its reliability was the fitting of two 1,825hp Homare 12 radials, but the engines remained unreliable. The weapons installed in the aircraft also varied, with flexible 20mm Type 99 Model 1 cannon being fitted in the nose and dorsal positions on some Gingas, and others featuring 13mm Type 2 machine guns on single or twin mountings. Five Kokutais would eventually be equipped with the P1Y1, seeing action from land bases in China, Formosa, the Marianas, the Philippines, Ryukyu, Shikoku and Kyushu from late 1944. Codenamed "Frances" by the Allies, the bomber was used both conventionally and as a kamikaze platform, particularly during the Okinawa campaign from April 1945.

A nightfighter variant of the aircraft, the P1Y2-S Kyokko ("Aurora"), was developed by Kawanishi during the spring of 1944. Powered by 1,850hp Mitsubishi Kasei 15a 14-cylinder radials and armed with 20mm Type 99 Model 2 cannon mounted obliquely in the fuselage to fire up and forwards (as well as the 20mm cannon in the rear cockpit – the nose-mounted weapon was removed), the prototype made its first flight in June 1944. Once in service the Kyokko proved to be largely ineffective against B-29s because of the aircraft's poor high-altitude

Flanked by US Navy personnel, IJNAF groundcrew pose for a photograph in front of a hangar at Yokosuka Naval Air Base in the late fall of 1945. Just visible in the hangar behind them is a propellerless P1Y1 "Frances," as well as a Q1W1 "Lorna." These men helped with pre-shipment preparations for the aircraft transported to the US by carrier. (*Aviation History Collection / Alamy Stock Photo*)

performance. Most of the 96 nightfighters that were built ended up being stripped of their angled guns and used as bombers instead, flying alongside the almost 1,000 P1Y1s built by Nakajima.

Early US Intelligence reports created after the examination of an abandoned P1Y1 on Tinian in late 1944 revealed that the Allies were fearful of the "Frances'" capabilities:

***

FRANCES 11 (GINGA) - P1Y1

The service version of the "Ginga" FRANCES is designed for horizontal, torpedo- and dive-bombing, with its principal role expected to be that of a torpedo-bomber, and its secondary role that of a dive-bomber. Document states it is powered by the 18-cylinder Homare 11 engines rated at 1,820 h.p. at takeoff which should make it a fast, maneuverable and dangerous anti-shipping attack plane. This engine installation was confirmed by the crash examinations at Guam and by the photographs taken at Tinian. The Tinian report stated that FRANCES was found with "14 cylinder engines" but apparently a typographical error was made. Performance estimates are being prepared and will be published in the near future.

The bomb-bay is 16ft long with a single release, and the loading schedule from a document indicates that either 1 x 1,870lb. torpedo or 1 x 1,760lb. bomb can be carried. Two external bomb racks are mounted on the wings, one to each side; each believed capable of accommodating a 550lb. bomb (Document lists an alternative loading of 2 x 1,100lb. or 2 x 550lb. bombs).

The only armament positions found were a small caliber flexible gun mount in the nose and a large flexible mount in the rear cockpit, probably for a 20mm cannon (Document called for a 20mm nose gun and a 20mm gun in the rear cockpit). The only armor protection was a piece of 3/8in plate protecting the pilot. With its large fuel capacity, FRANCES should have an overload torpedo range of around 2,000 miles. Dive brakes are fitted and flight limitations shown in the FRANCES handbook limit the speed to 402mph.

While the fire power is insufficient, overall performance should be high. FRANCES, with a steadily increasing production rate, can be expected to participate in future shipping attacks.

FRANCES 11 (HAKKO – ALSO LISTED AS KYOKKO) – NIGHTFIGHTER P1Y1-S

FRANCES 11, the service version of 15 Experimental land bomber, has been modified for use as a "Hei" nightfighter and given the Model/Type symbol P1Y1-S. Its exact Japanese name is not entirely clear as it is translated in Romaji as both Hakko and Kyokko. The dual purpose follows the JUDY-IRVING pattern and is indicative that multi-usage of aircraft will be continued in the future by the Japs. Quite possibly the nightfighter will be designated as Model 12 since it involves an engine change.

The bomber version of FRANCES has been in operation for almost a year and it seems reasonable that some nightfighters might also be in service. A number of crashed FRANCESs were recovered in the Marianas and performance estimates will be issued shortly.

The armament so far revealed by actual investigation has been very limited, one probable 20mm. flexible cannon in the rear cockpit and one electrically controlled revolving gun mount in the nose, caliber undetermined. (Documentary specifications called for 1 x 20 mm. aft cockpit gun and 1 x 20 mm. nose gun, both flexible). The nightfighter version will undoubtedly carry much heavier armament than that found in the torpedo-bomber FRANCES.

Performance of the FRANCES 11 (Hakko or Kyokko) should be extremely good, based on preliminary assessment of its two Kasei 25 engines. With radar installation, increased fire power, and the high speed it is believed capable of, the nightfighter FRANCES should be more effective than IRVING or the Army NICK.[8]

***

This photograph shows one of the three P1Y1s captured at Matsushima airfield aboard *Barnes* transiting through the Panama Canal en route to Norfolk, Virginia, in late November 1945. The "Frances," which had had its outer wing sections removed (they were stored in the ship's hangar bay) so as to reduce its "footprint" on the flightdeck, was liberally sprayed with a special anti-corrosion coating prior to the voyage. The "Frances" also had a tarpaulin drawn over the top of the forward fuselage, indicating that the canopy area was not as watertight as it should have been. (*Aviation History Collection / Alamy Stock Photo*)

Three P1Y1s were captured by US forces at Matsushima airfield in Miyagi Prefecture in September 1945. Given Foreign Equipment (FE) numbers 1700, 1701 and 1702, they were transported to Yokosuka and loaded onto the escort carrier *Barnes*, which sailed for America on November 3, 1945. Although FE 1700 and FE 1701 were scrapped, FE 1702 (construction number 8923) was restored to airworthiness and flown by the

USAAF's Flight Test Section at Middletown from February through to July 1946. The flight revealed that the "Frances" was capable of a top speed of 340mph at an altitude of 19,400ft and was very maneuverable. The aircraft also featured armor protection for its aircrew as well as self-sealing fuel tanks, thus making the P1Y1 eminently more survivable in combat than earlier Japanese twin-engined bomber designs.

Following its evaluation, the aircraft remained at Middletown until the USAAF transferred its ownership to the Smithsonian Institution in September 1948. In January 1949, the bomber was transported to Park Ridge for storage, and it remained there until moved to the NASM's "Silver Hill" in the 1950s. The fuselage now resides at the Paul E. Garber Facility, the wings and engines having been lost some years ago.

Of the three P1Y1s sent to the US, it appears that construction number 8923, seen here at Wright Field, was the only example restored to airworthiness and flown by the USAAF's Flight Test Section from February to July 1946. Wearing the Foreign Equipment code 1702 on its tail, the aircraft remained at Middletown until the USAF transferred ownership of the "Frances" to the NASM in September 1948. (*Wikipedia Commons/public domain*)

Kyushu Q1W "Lorna"

Development of the world's first dedicated anti-submarine patrol aircraft commenced in 1942 following the issuing of the 17-Shi specification for a three-seat machine with long endurance and low speed by the IJNAF, who also emphasized that the type was needed urgently in the front line. In response to the request, K.K. Watanabe Tekkosho created the twin-engined Q1W1 Tokai ("Eastern Sea"), which featured extensive cockpit and nose glazing in order to maximize forward visibility for the three-man crew.

Powered by two 610hp Hitachi GK2C Amakaze-31 nine-cylinder radial engines, the aircraft was to be fitted with an all-new small search radar, but delays in its production meant that the larger Type 3 Model 1

This photograph of one of the Q1W1 "Lornas" captured at Hakata was taken during the flight to Yokosuka for shipment on to America; the ASW patrol bomber had been adorned with US insignia prior to leaving. (*NARA*)

One of the four "Lornas" craned onto the flightdeck of *Barnes* in November 1945, this particular machine was tied down on the port side of the vessel between a Ki-46 and a D4Y2. The aircraft was photographed on board the carrier just prior to it departing Yokosuka naval base for the US. (*NARA*)

MAD (KMX) radar was installed instead. Magnetic anomaly detection (MAD) gear was also fitted to the Q1W1, while its defensive armament consisted of one flexible 7.7mm Type 92 machine gun for a rear gunner and one or two 20mm Type 99 cannon mounted in the nose. The aircraft could also carry two 551lb bombs or depth charges. The prototype Q1W successfully performed its first flight in September 1943, and it was praised for its ease of handling. Capable of launching attacks in a fairly steep dive and blessed with an 835-mile range, the Q1W1 was ordered into production with Kyushu in the spring of 1944.

Just 153 aircraft, given the Allied codename "Lorna," had been built by war's end, with the majority of the Q1W1s being assigned to units based in Japan, Formosa and China that had been charged with protecting convoys bringing urgently needed raw materials and oil from the Dutch East Indies and Malaya. They proved easy prey for Allied fighters, however, owing to their slow top speed (200mph at 4,400ft) and modest defensive armament.

Shortly after VJ Day, four "Lornas" were captured by US occupation forces at Hakata, on the island of Kyushu, and flown northeast to Yokosuka for shipment to the US on board the escort carrier *Barnes* in November 1945. At least one of these aircraft was subsequently flown by the USAAF from Middletown after it had been returned to airworthiness with parts sourced from another "Lorna," the flight testing confirming the Q1W1's top speed of 200mph. The airworthy aircraft and its parts donor ended up at Park Ridge in September 1946 after being allocated to the proposed National Air Museum, while the remaining pair was sent to the AOAMC in Newark. All four "Lornas" were scrapped shortly thereafter.

Mitsubishi Ki-21 "Sally"

In February 1936, the IJAAF issued a specification asking for a twin-engined heavy bomber to replace the Mitsubishi Ki-1 and Ki-20, the new aircraft needing an endurance of more than five hours at 186mph, a top speed of 248mph at 9,845ft and a maximum bomb load of 2,205lb. Defensive armament for the crew of four (with two more seats for additional gunners) consisted of three flexibly mounted 7.7mm Type 89 machine guns in nose, dorsal and ventral positions. Finally, either two 850hp Nakajima Ha-5 or two 825hp Mitsubishi Ha-6 radials were to be used. Two Ha-6-powered Ki-21 prototypes were built by Mitsubishi at the company's Nagoya works, and they commenced manufacturer's flight trials in December 1936.

Four months later, the Ki-21s participated in a competitive trial against two Kawasaki Ki-19s that had also been built in response to the IJAAF specification. Although the Mitsubishi bomber was deemed to have superior performance, the Ki-19 had better flight characteristics and was a more stable bomber. The IJAAF ordered Mitsubishi to fit Ha-5s to a third prototype and improve the aircraft's inflight handling, the company redesigning the rear fuselage and vertical tail surfaces. The revised bomber easily beat the Ki-19 in the second round of trials, with the initial model (Ki-21-Ia) being ordered into production in November 1937.

When the first Ki-21s to reach the front line were delivered to the 60th Sentai in August 1938, the IJAAF now had an aircraft that was as good as the best twin-engined bombers in service anywhere in the world. Early lessons in combat over China resulted in the creation of the Ki-21-Ib and -Ic, which had a single additional 7.7mm gun firing through lateral openings on either side of the rear fuselage and a fifth, remotely controlled, Type 89 mounted as a "stinger" in the tail. The -Ib also had a bigger bomb-bay, larger landing flaps, horizontal tail surfaces of increased size and limited fuel tank protection in the form of laminated rubber sheets. In addition to these changes, the -Ic had an extra lateral machine gun and was fitted with an auxiliary fuel tank. These new variants replaced the Ki-21-I in northern China and Manchuria.

The IJAAF realized that it needed to improve the Ki-21's speed and ceiling in preparation for Japan's wider campaign of conquest in Asia,

Ki-21-II construction number 4492 was built in July 1943 and captured by the USAAF at Kungyang in China's Yunnan Province in the fall of that same year. It was test flown by TAIU personnel, who noted that the bomber was capable of attaining a top speed of 301mph at an altitude of 15,400ft. (PF-(sdasm3) / Alamy Stock Photo)

and it instructed Mitsubishi to produce a more advanced version of the bomber fitted with the company's 1,500hp Ha-101 14-cylinder radial engines. The latter had a larger diameter than the Ha-5, so redesigned nacelles were required – these also allowed the undercarriage to be fully enclosed for the first time. The aircraft's horizontal tail surfaces were enlarged yet again, although armament remained unchanged. Designated the Ki-21-II, the aircraft conducted flight trials in March 1940 and entered service as the -IIa nine months later.

When the Pacific War commenced in December 1940, the Ki-21 units supported the invasion of Thailand, Burma and Malaya, as well as continuing to attack targets in China. Codenamed the "Sally" by the Allies shortly thereafter, the Ki-21-II was at the forefront of operations in Southeast Asia and the Dutch East Indies well into 1942. As opposition from British and American fighters became more organized, so losses amongst "Sally" units began to rise. In an attempt to provide the aircraft with better defenses, Mitsubishi replaced the bomber's distinctive dorsal greenhouse and flexible machine gun with a large conical turret housing a 12.7mm Type 1 machine gun. The revised variant was designated the Ki-21-IIb, and almost 700 were built to bring "Sally" production to more than 2,000 aircraft.

Ki-21-IIb-equipped units were heavily involved in the fighting in New Guinea, the Solomons and India in 1942–43, and the aircraft suffered terrible losses during the defensive campaigns in Southeast Asia from the fall of 1944. By then, the Mitsubishi Ki-67 had entered production, allowing the "Sally" to be relegated to transport and communication roles. It was also employed on special missions, including a suicide attack on Yontan and Kadena airfields on Okinawa in May 24, 1945 by nine Ki-21-IIbs. Each aircraft crash-landed at either site, allowing the 14 heavily armed troops in each "Sally" to attack parked US aircraft and supply dumps.

As previously noted, like most Japanese bombers, the "Sally" suffered from a lack of adequate armor protection for its crew, modest defensive firepower, and poorly protected fuel tanks. The latter were the subject of this mid- to late-war US Intelligence Report:

A test was conducted at Dahlgren, Va. on 3 July 1944 to determine the following by means of .30 to .50 caliber bullet impacts on the fuel tank of a SALLY 2.

a. The ability of the fuel tank to seal bullet holes.
b. The ability of the fuel tank to withstand the effects of hydraulic shock resulting from bullet impacts.

The tank was filled with 100 octane aviation gasoline and firing was conducted with both .30 and .50 caliber aircraft machine gun and A.P. [armor piercing] ammunition. Tests were conducted at a range of 75ft and at ambient temperature. A wooden box placed approximately 3ft in front of the fuel tank was used to tumble bullets.

DESCRIPTION

The SALLY 2 fuel tank consisted of a ductile metallic tank 1/16in in thickness, completely enclosed in a natural rubber outer covering technically defined as a "smoked sheet". The "smoked sheet" was apparently uncured and was approximately 3/8in in thickness. The chemical reaction of gasoline on the "smoked sheet" covering resulted in reasonably effective self-sealing action.

The rubber outer covering was firmly attached to the metallic tank by means of gummed strips of rubber on the inside of the "smoked sheet" which were pressed firmly into rivet heads in the metal tank itself. For the purpose of making the rubber covering completely leak-proof, gasoline-resistant putty was applied around all fittings. The tank when filled held approximately 75 US gallons of gasoline.

The SALLY 2 fuel tank was received at the Naval Proving Ground in very poor condition. It was badly crumpled, all fittings were welded on the tank and all welds were broken or cracked.

After plugging numerous sources of leakage the tank was filled with aviation gasoline and one yawed .30 caliber bullet was fired into the left side. Both entrance and exit leaked heavily. A yawed .50 caliber bullet was fired into the tank above the fuel level and resulted in large holes in the metal with moderately bad tulipping of the metal on the exit. The third impact, a .50 caliber bullet through the fuel tank, resulted in damage extensive enough to render the tank incapable of retaining fuel.

CONCLUSION

Because of its design it is believed that incendiary ammunition fired into the tank would produce an immediate fire.

Based on the results of the subject test, it is the opinion of the Naval Proving Ground that the SALLY 2 type aircraft fuel tank is unable to satisfactorily withstand either .30 caliber AP or .50 caliber AP bullet impacts.

SALLY 3 ARMOR TESTS

A piece of 8mm armor plate taken from a Type 97 twin-engine bomber (SALLY 3) which crashed at Patia, Bengal, on 20 December 1943 has been subjected to firing tests by the Chief Inspector of Small Arms, Ishapore. British .303 AP 2025 f.s. and 22 1/2-degree angle of obliquity, the plate was defeated with lodged core. At 1350 f.s. and 0° angle of obliquity a pinhole penetration resulted. The turret is the only known position of 8mm armor on this aircraft.[9]

During the fall of 1943, Ki-21-II construction number 4492 was captured by the USAAF at Kungyang, in China's Yunnan Province, where it was test-flown and evaluated by TAIU personnel. During the flight testing, it was revealed that the aircraft was capable of a top speed of 301mph at an altitude of 15,400ft. A relatively complete Ki-21 was also delivered to the ATAIU-SEA at Maiden airfield in Calcutta in 1944, and although it was too badly damaged to fly, the aircraft was closely examined by RAF personnel. Three airworthy "Sallys" (a Ki-21-I and two Ki-21-IIs) were also part of the "Gremlin Task Force" flown on reconnaissance and transport duties by Japanese crews (accompanied by RAF aircrew) in French Indochina immediately post war.

The *Armée de l'Air*'s *Groupe de transport* I/34 also flew a solitary Ki-21-I alongside other captured Japanese military types in Indochina in 1945–46.

Finally, a Ki-21-IIa that had carried members of the Japanese surrender delegation from Borneo to Labuan Island, in Malaya, at war's end was flown to RAAF Base Laverton in February 1946. Subsequently stored at RAAF Base Fairbairn for inclusion in the AWM, the "Sally" was eventually scrapped in around 1950.

Kawasaki Ki-48 "Lily"

The Ki-48 was created in direct response to the appearance of the Tupolev SB-2 bomber in Chinese skies in the fall of 1937 during the Second Sino-Japanese War, the IJAAF instructing Kawasaki to design a twin-engined light bomber in December of that same year. The manufacturer was charged with building an aircraft capable of achieving 298mph at 9,850ft with an 882lb bomb load. Powered by two 950hp Nakajima Ha-25 radial engines, the bomber would rely on both speed and three or four flexible 7.7mm machine guns for protection. Heavily influenced by the company's Ki-45 design, the aircraft, designated the Ki-48, featured a mid-wing cantilever configuration to allow for the inclusion of an internal bomb-bay. The bomber had a crew of four, three of whom manned flexibly mounted Type 89 guns in the nose (bombardier), dorsal (radio operator) and ventral (navigator) positions.

Delays with the Ki-45 program meant that the first of four Ki-48 prototypes was not completed until July 1939. Flight trials showed that the aircraft was fast and maneuverable, but that the Ki-48 suffered from severe tail flutter. For two months in the fall of 1939 five pre-production aircraft were used to trial modifications to the tail, and by raising the horizontal flying surfaces and strengthening the rear fuselage the problem was resolved. Production of the Ki-48-Ia commenced shortly thereafter.

The 45th Sentai became the first unit to receive examples of the new bomber in the late summer of 1940, these aircraft replacing the unit's Kawasaki Ki-32s. The 45th gave the Ki-48 its combat debut shortly thereafter on the northern China front, where, faced with little in the way of aerial opposition, the bomber enjoyed notable success. The late production model -Ib began to emerge from the Kawasaki plant in 1941, this

This tailless Ki-48-I "Lily" from the 45th Sentai was found at Munda airfield on New Georgia Island when it was captured in August 1943. The battered remains of the bomber were eventually craned onto a barge moored alongside the runway at Munda and transported to Lunga Point on Guadalcanal. One of several Ki-48-Is found here, this example, being the most complete, was thoroughly examined by TAIU-SWPA personnel. (NARA)

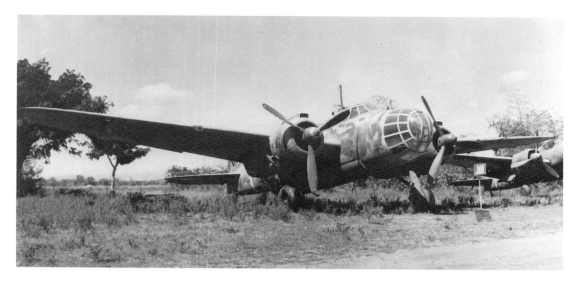

ABOVE This Ki-48-IIa "Lily" medium bomber of the 208th Sentai was found abandoned by US Army troops at Clark Field in February 1945. According to an unnamed IJAAF Ki-48 gunner captured near Hollandia during the summer of 1944, the aircraft's nose mounting was so cramped that its occupant only had a 45-degree field of fire with his 7.7mm machine gun. (NARA)

ABOVE RIGHT A side-on view of the Ki-48-IIa seen in the previous photograph at Clark Field. Stripped of its paint and given TAIU-SWPA markings, this aircraft was flown on several occasions during the spring and early summer of 1945. The bomber attained a top speed of 314mph at 18,375ft during one of these flights. It was eventually scrapped on the airfield. (NARA)

variant having improved gun mountings. Codenamed "Lily" by the Allies, the -Ia and -Ib saw considerable action against Commonwealth forces in Malaya and Burma and American forces in the Philippines during the early stages of the Pacific War, before supporting the invasion of the Dutch East Indies and New Guinea in 1942.

As with other early war Japanese bombers, the "Lily" initially proved effective in combat thanks to Allied fighter units being in a state of total disarray until the dogged defense of Port Moresby commenced in the spring of 1942. From then on Ki-48 units suffered noticeable losses owing to the ineffectiveness of the bomber's defensive armament, lack of crew protection, and vulnerable fuel tanks. Its previously impressive top speed was now being easily overhauled by the increasing number of American fighters in-theater, whilst the aircraft's bombload was also seen as being inadequate. Units were soon forced to operate their Ki-48s at night, which adversely affected the accuracy of their bombing.

By then, an improved version of the aircraft in the form of the Ki-48-II was in the final stages of testing, three prototypes having been completed in February 1942. Powered by two 1,150hp Nakajima Ha-115 radial engines (an advanced version of the Ha-25 with a two-stage blower), the bomber also featured fuel tank protection and armor plating for both the crew and their ammunition magazines. Slightly longer than the Ki-48-I in order to improve the aircraft's stability in flight, the -II could carry double the bombload (1,764lb) thanks to its more powerful engines, but its top speed was increased to only 314mph. Placed in production as the Ki-48-IIa, this variant was also the basis for the -IIb dive-bomber fitted with retractable dive-brakes and the -IIc of 1943 that had its dorsal Type 89 7.7mm weapon replaced with a 12.7mm Type 1 machine gun. Additional flexible Type 89s were also mounted in the nose to be fired from windows on the port and starboard sides of the aircraft.

In spite of these improvements, the Ki-48 remained vulnerable during daylight operations and production ceased in October 1944 following the delivery of the 1,977th "Lily." That same month, Ki-48-IIs were committed to the doomed defense of the Philippines. They also flew night nuisance raids on Okinawa in April 1945. Many more were destroyed in kamikaze attacks against Allied warships off the Okinawan coast, with some being modified (as Ki-48-II KAI) to carry a 1,764lb bombload that was triggered by contact with a target.

A salvaged Ki-48 was delivered to the ATAIU-SEA at Maiden airfield in Calcutta in 1944, and although it was too badly damaged to return to airworthiness, RAF personnel thoroughly examined the aircraft. An airworthy Ki-48-II was also part of the "Gremlin Task Force" that performed reconnaissance and transport duties in French Indochina immediately post war.

In February 1945 a Ki-48-IIa was captured by US Army troops at Clark Field. Stripped of its paint and given TAIU-SWPA markings, the aircraft attained a top speed of 314mph at 18,375ft during flight testing. The lightly loaded bomber also impressed USAAF pilots with its maneuverability. Although this aircraft was later scrapped in the Philippines, two more Ki-48-IIs were captured at Nasuno airfield, just north of Tokyo, and shipped to the US from Yokosuka as flightdeck cargo on board the escort carrier *Barnes* in November 1945. It is unclear whether either of these aircraft was flown after their arrival in America, and both ended up at Middletown Air Depot in September 1946 for inclusion in the proposed National Air Museum. The Ki-48-IIs were scrapped, however.

Nakajima Ki-49 "Helen"

Several months prior to the Ki-21 entering front-line service in August 1938, the IJAAF issued a specification for its replacement. The new bomber would need to be able to operate without a dedicated fighter escort, which meant it had to be considerably faster and better armed than its predecessor. The aircraft had to possess a top speed of 311mph (16 percent higher than the Ki-21's), a range of 1,860 miles, be capable of carrying 2,205lb of bombs and feature one 20mm Ho-1 weapon in a dorsal turret and several 7.7mm Type 89 machine guns in flexible mounts in the nose and ventral, port and starboard positions. A machine gun also had to be installed in a tail turret. Unlike with previous Japanese bombers, this aircraft would have armored protection for its eight-man crew and self-sealing fuel tanks.

These three Ki-49-IIs of the 7th Sentai were captured by the British Army at Kalidjati airfield on Java in the Dutch East Indies following the Japanese surrender. This airfield was used as a forward base for the 18 "Helen" and nine "Lily" bombers, escorted by 22 "Oscars," that attacked Darwin in Australia's Northern Territory on June 20, 1943. (*Military History Collection / Alamy Stock Photo*)

Although Nakajima's Ki-19 had lost to Mitsubishi's Ki-21 in the competitive trial flown the previous year, the former had been given a production contract to build the rival aircraft. This in turn meant that Nakajima was well placed to provide a replacement for the Ki-21, with its Ki-49 Donryu ("Storm Dragon") relying heavily on lessons the company had learned building the Mitsubishi bomber. The design team paid close attention to the aircraft's handling characteristics, with a mid-mounted wing of low aspect-ratio giving the Ki-49 excellent stability and maneuverability at medium to low altitudes. Ordnance would be carried in a fuselage bomb-bay that occupied virtually the entire length of the wing center-section.

After the war, several G5N1/2s were found by US forces in Japan, including two at Atsugi. Following static technical evaluation by TAIU personnel, the "Liz" was deemed to be "underpowered."

Nakajima G8N "Rita"

Despite the failure of the G5N, the IJNAF remained committed to the idea of a four-engined long-range land-based attack bomber flying in support of the fleet and also undertaking deep penetration missions against enemy bases. Consequently, in February 1943, it instructed Nakajima to design such an aircraft to meet the 18-Shi specification. Given the designation G8N1 and named the Renzan ("Mountain Range"), the bomber had to be capable of carrying 8,816lb of ordnance over a distance of 4,600 miles. Its maximum speed was to be

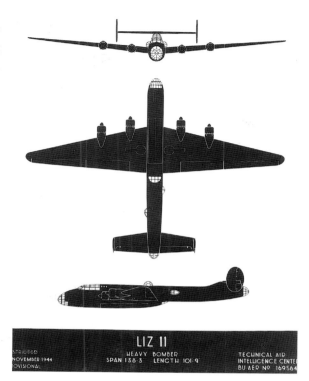

370mph and the bomber needed to be able to climb to a ceiling of 33,450ft. Manned by a crew of 11, the aircraft's defensive armament consisted of two 20mm Type 99 cannon in each power-operated dorsal, ventral and tail turrets, two 13mm Type 2 machine guns in a nose turret and two free-swivelling 13mm Type 2 machine guns in waist gunner positions.

Faced with such a challenging specification, Nakajima chose a mid-mounted wing of relatively small area and high aspect ratio, which also had laminar flow section. The aircraft would be powered by four 2,000hp Nakajima NK9K-L Homare 24 radials equipped with Hitachi 92 turbosuperchargers. These engines drove four-bladed propellers. Equipped with a tricycle undercarriage, the G8N prototype successfully performed its maiden flight on October 23, 1944. Three additional aircraft were subsequently built, and although flight testing showed that the G8N (codenamed "Rita" by the Allies) was a very promising design, enemy air attacks stymied production. Indeed, only three of the four prototypes had been completed by the time the program was canceled owing to a critical shortage of light aluminum alloys. The IJNAF had intended to have an operational fleet of 48 G8N1s by September 1945.

This provisional three-view schematic drawing of the Nakajima G5N1 "Liz 11" was created by the TAIC in November 1944. The artwork was, in the main, quite accurate, although the tail section was too steeply stepped up and the outboard engines not sufficiently canted outwards. (NARA)

After the Japanese surrender, the fourth "Rita" prototype was discovered incomplete at the Nakajima factory at Koizumi, northwest of Tokyo. The aircraft was made airworthy by company workers on US instructions and flown to Yokosuka on December 16, 1945. Shipped to America on board the escort carrier *Bogue*, the bomber was subsequently offloaded in New York the following month and barged to the AOAMC at Newark. From there it was flown to Patterson Field, Ohio, and briefly evaluated during a handful of flights. Originally reserved for the proposed Air Force Museum at this site, the "Rita" was, however, scrapped.

The following USAAF Technical Report was compiled following the G8N1's test flights from Patterson Field:

***

TECHNICAL REPORT ON RITA-11 JAPANESE ATTACK BOMBER
Description

The Rita is a four-engine, cantilever, high mid-wing monoplane of conventional design, with a retractable tricycle landing gear. It was designated a bomber. The airplane is of all-metal stressed-skin construction, with the exception of the control surfaces which are fabric covered. Rudder, elevators, ailerons and trim tabs are provided.

This airplane is equipped with four Homare (HA-45-22) air-cooled, twin-row, 18-cylinder radial engines. The engines are equipped with a low-pressure fuel-injection system, a two-stage internal supercharger, and an exhaust-driven turbosupercharger mounted on the nacelle near the accessory section of the engine. Air scoops are incorporated onto each engine. The dry weight of

The rear fuselage of the second "Rita" prototype had clearly suffered blast damage from exploding ordnance, although it does not appear to have been punctured by shrapnel. The aircraft was scrapped, along with a number of incomplete G8N airframes also discovered at Koizumi. (*NARA*)

each engine without propeller is 1783lb. The German VDM-type propeller is used.

1. Landing Gear

The landing gear is hydraulically operated, incorporating an emergency manually-operated hydraulic pump. An engine-driven hydraulic pump is installed on engines Nos. 2 and 3. These pumps are not self-priming. The hydraulic system is used for actuating the landing gear, brakes, wing flaps and engine cowl flaps.

2. Fuel Capacity

The Rita carries 2,400 US gallons of fuel in the wing cells. In addition, four bomb-bay tanks are installed, but their actual capacity was not checked. All fuel tanks appear to be self-sealing. All fuel may be jettisoned through emergency dump valves.

3. Armament

This aircraft was still in an experimental stage and the major portion of the armament was not installed. The proposed armament consisted of the following:

5 Single-barrel flexible machine guns
45 Machine gun spare ammunition boxes
3,750 Rounds of machine gun ammunition
1 Front machine gun turret
2 Side machine gun turrets
1 Top machine gun turret
1 Tail-gun turret
1 Flexible shell gun
9 Spare ammunition boxes
1 Flexible gun turret

4. Accommodation

A crew of nine is required to operate the aircraft; as a bomber, a crew of eleven is required. The crew accommodations consist of:

1 Pilot's seat
1 Co-pilot's seat
1 Bombardier's seat
1 Radio operator's seat
1 Engineer's seat
1 Shell gun turret seat
5 Machine gunners' seats

The fourth "Rita" prototype was also found at Koizumi in an incomplete state, and was made airworthy by Nakajima workers under the watchful eye of USAAF personnel. The aircraft is seen here at Yokosuka after it was flown in from Koizumi on December 16, 1945 for onward shipment to the US. (NARA)

5. Communication and Radar Equipment

The Rita-11 was equipped with the following types of communication equipment:

a. Radio-telegraph for long range, 1 set

    Frequencies of transmitter, 1,500–8,000 kc

    Transmitting power, 50 w

    Correcting error, 1/5,000

b. Radio for short range, 1 set

    Voltage, 24 v

(No other information available. Regular AAF-type radio has been installed.)

FACTUAL DATA
Dimensions

Span, 103ft 8in.   Length, 74ft 5in.

Height, 25ft 6in.   Wing area, 1202 sq ft

Weight

Gross weight, 60,000lb

Normal takeoff weight, 52,050lb

Power Plants	One Engine	One Engine
Takeoff power	200hp	8,000hp
Rated hp (maximum Continuous power)	1,850hp	7,400hp (at 26,300ft)

Performance

Maximum speed, 371 mph at 26,200ft

Service ceiling, 33,500ft

Landing speed, 115mph

PILOT'S OBSERVATIONS
1. Introduction

This airplane has been restricted to a limited number of test flights. It has been flown under normal conditions and no major flight difficulties were encountered. There has not been sufficient flight time to record accurate data.

The Rita is equipped with hydromatic, full-feathering propellers. The feathering system is unique in that pressure for feathering is supplied from a separate electrically-driven pump and directed to the desired engine through a selector valve located on the engineer's panel. The engineer's panel is located in a compartment aft of the pilot's compartment, and communication must be established by interphone. After the hydraulic selector valve is set, the co-pilot operates a toggle switch to feather the propeller. Care must be exercised that the toggle switch is released as soon as rotation has stopped, since no feathering stop is provided and the propeller will go into reverse pitch. All this procedure necessary to feather a propeller causes considerable delay. This delay would be dangerous in an emergency and the method is not considered satisfactory. It was not possible to unfeather the propellers from the cockpit on this particular airplane, since the solenoids provided for this purpose were not connected.

Transported across the Pacific as flightdeck cargo on board the escort carrier *Bogue*, the "Rita" was offloaded in New York harbor in January 1946 and sent by barge to the AOAMC at nearby Newark Army Airfield. It was photographed there alongside a USAAF C-45F Expeditor. (*USAF*)

The airplane is comparable in size to the American B-24 and the B-17, having one bomb-bay with electrically-operated doors. The bomb capacity is not known.

Hydraulic pressure is provided by two engine-driven pumps located on engine Nos. 2 and 3. The landing gear, wing flaps, and engine cowl flaps are hydraulically operated. There is an emergency hydraulic system for lowering the gear and, in addition, an emergency mechanical system similar in operation to that of the American B-24. The original brakes were so poor that American-type brakes were installed before a flight was attempted.

2. Weight and CG Information

The basic weight of the Rita is 41,819lb. The airplane was ballasted to bring the CG within limits. The first flight was made with full wing tanks and a four-man crew. Takeoff weight was 52,050lb, with the CG located at 23.76% MAC.

3. Flight Characteristics

a. Cockpit Layout. Ingress is through the nose-wheel door. Handles are provided to assist personnel entering and leaving the airplane, but entrance and egress are nevertheless difficult. Entrance is made to the flight engineer's deck from which the pilot proceeds forward to the flight deck. The cockpit is conventionally laid out with a pedestal between the two pilots.

Dual controls are provided. Mixture controls, supercharger controls (inoperative), throttles, and propeller controls are located on the pedestal. Engine energizing and meshing switches are located to the left of the pilot and are push-pull type.

There is only one feathering switch for all four engines; this toggle switch is located to the right of the co-pilot.

The "Rita" was flown from Newark to Patterson Field, Ohio on June 23, 1946, from where it performed a series of test flights following the removal of its dorsal and ventral turrets. The G8N was photographed here towering over a visiting P-51D and an AT-6 on the Patterson Field transient ramp in the summer of 1946. (*NARA*)

Landing-gear and flap controls are located on the lower side of the pilot's pedestal.

b. Taxiing and Ground Handling. The Rita is difficult to taxi because of extremely poor brakes. Nose-wheel action while taxiing is similar to that of the American B-24.

The rudder pedals are attached to a straight cross bar pivoted in the center. This design makes full brake application difficult. The rudder is not effective during taxiing operations.

c. Takeoff and Initial Climb. A takeoff distance of approximately 6000ft with a 10mph wind is required. The fact that the engines would not develop full power, since no turboboost was available, in all probability was responsible for the long ground run. Initial climb was poor and the airplane picked up speed slowly. During taxiing operations and takeoff the airplane felt very heavy.

On one flight, difficulties were encountered when engine trouble developed. Takeoff rpm could not be attained. Inactive turbosupercharger may have been responsible.

d. Climbs. No attempt was made to secure accurate data, but at a power setting of 2400rpm, 35in. Hg and an IAS of 160mph, the airplane showed an indicated rate of climb of 400ft/min; at 150mph the airplane had an indicated rate of climb of 500ft/min.

e. Handling and Control at Various Speeds. Handling and control was investigated only during normal flight, from takeoff to cruising speed (175mph). The control forces were heavy; response to controls was poor. There is noticeable delay between the deflection of a control surface and the desired response of the airplane.

f. Changes in Trim When Operating Landing Gear and Flaps. When lowering the landing gear the airplane becomes slightly nose-heavy, requiring tail-heavy trim. Lowering the wing flaps causes a tail-heavy condition which can be corrected with elevator trim.

g. Control on Reduced Number of Engines. While no engines were feathered, No. 1 engine was throttled back. Under this condition rudder forces became very heavy. However, directional control and altitude were maintained at 150mph and 4,000ft. altitude.

h. Noise and Vibration. The noise level is moderate, but vibration is excessive. The entire airplane vibrates continually at all speeds. The vibration is of low amplitude and high frequency.

i. Comfort. The inadequate adjustment of the seats and the location of the controls contribute to pilot discomfort. The one flight made in this airplane was not of sufficient duration to cause the pilot any appreciable physical discomfort. However, it was the

Although the "Rita" was reserved for the proposed National Air Museum following the completion of its flight testing in the fall of 1946, the bomber was eventually scrapped. (*NARA*)

opinion of the pilot that a normal mission flown in this type of airplane would cause excessive fatigue.

j. Vision. Downward and forward vision from the pilot's compartment is normal for this type of airplane.

k. Approach and Landing. Only one landing was made with this airplane. A power-on approach was used at an IAS of 130–140mph. Rudder forces varied during the approach but it is felt that this was caused by unsynchronized throttles. A full-stalled landing was made. The airplane touched down at an IAS of between 100 and 110mph. Sufficient elevator was available to hold the nose wheel off, and directional control was easily maintained.

4. General Functioning

a. Power Plant and Associated Equipment. The engines functioned satisfactorily, although it was impossible to obtain full power from Nos. 1, 2, and 3 engines. Whether this was because of instrument error or engine malfunction was not ascertained. The engines are rated at 2,800rpm but it was possible to obtain this speed only on No. 4 engine. Engines 1 and 2 turned up 2,500rpm and No. 3 engine, 2,550rpm. All engine controls slip, and must be constantly readjusted. Tachometers oscillated continually; a turn in either direction caused the inside engine to decrease rpm and the outside engine to increase rpm.

From the time the engines were started until the flight was completed, the mixture controls required constant manipulation in order to keep the engines running smoothly. There appeared to be neither auto-rich nor auto-lean settings.

It was necessary to vary the cowl-flap settings in order to keep the cylinder-head temperatures within limits. Number one engine required full-open cowl flaps during all flight operations.

b. Hydraulic, Pneumatic and Electrical Systems. The hydraulic pumps installed on engines Nos. 2 and 3 are not self-priming. A separate hydraulic pump was installed before this flight to prime the engine pumps and to provide some pressure. The brakes were poor and American-type brakes were installed before flight. The hydraulically actuated landing gear, flaps, and cowl flaps operated satisfactorily.

c. Emergency Systems. Landing-gear operating lever in pilot's cockpit must be in down position. The landing-gear lock lever in pilot's cockpit must be in unlocked position. The landing-gear-up lock-release levers at the aft engineer's station must be pulled sufficiently to release "Up" lock. Red light indicates "Up" locks are released.

The emergency landing-gear extension must be turned in a clockwise direction until the green light is on, indicating the gear is down and locked. The lever must be turned in reverse direction about twice after gear is down and locked.

After landing is completed, the lever of each landing gear extension must be turned in the opposite direction (counterclockwise) 45 turns.

WARNING: Each landing gear must be lowered separately.

5. Performance

Stall, performance, and stability investigations were not attempted on this airplane. At 4,000ft pressure altitude, and a power setting of 2,150rpm and 30in. Hg manual-rich, the airplane indicated 175mph.

CONCLUSIONS

The Japanese Rita does not compare favorably with any comparable contemporary American airplane.

The general flight characteristics, excessive maintenance required, risk to personnel, and information gained did not justify further flight tests of this airplane.[10]

***

RECONNAISSANCE AIRCRAFT

Nakajima C6N "Myrt"

In the spring of 1942, following mixed results with attack bombers (usually B5N "Kates") undertaking reconnaissance missions from aircraft carriers during the early stages of the Pacific War, the IJNAF issued the 17-Shi specification to Nakajima. The company was instructed to build a three-seat aircraft with a top speed of 403mph, a maximum range of more than 3,000 miles and a service ceiling of 32,000ft. The resulting design, designated the C6N Saiun ("Painted Cloud"), featured a slim fuselage, forward-canted vertical tail surfaces to allow the aircraft to fit on carrier flightdeck elevators, and a small laminar flow wing that contained four protected and two unprotected fuel tanks. The flying surfaces were also fitted with Fowler and split flaps along their trailing edges, as well as leading-edge slats – these were needed to keep the C6N's landing speed down to the required 81mph. Camera portholes and observation windows were built into the bottom and sides of the fuselage, and a single flexible rear-firing 7.92mm Type 1 machine gun provided the crew with its limited defense, the weapon being manned by the radio operator.

This C6N1 was the first intact example of the Saiun high-speed reconnaissance aircraft to fall into the hands of the Allies following its capture at Clark Field in February 1945. With less than 500 "Myrts" built, the Nakajima machine was a rare find. Like the B6N "Jills" found on Luzon, this aircraft was possibly a survivor from a carrier air group assigned to the First Mobile Force. Despite its rarity, the C6N1 was not restored to airworthiness by the TAIU-SWPA. (NARA)

Fitted with an 1,820hp Nakajima NK9B Homare 11 radial engine driving a four-bladed propeller, the prototype C6N1 made its first flight on May 15, 1943. Some 19 prototypes and pre-production aircraft would eventually be built between March 1943 and April 1944, and these proved that the Saiun was a pleasant aircraft to fly. Its high-altitude performance, however, fell below what had been hoped for by Nakajima, owing to problems with the Homare engine. Nevertheless, the aircraft's

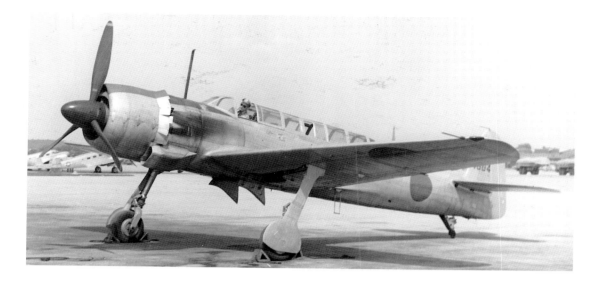

397mph top speed at altitude and 3,000-mile range made the C6N1 far more effective in its designed role than the D4Y2-C that was then being used for carrier-based reconnaissance.

By the time production commenced in the spring of 1944, Nakajima had replaced the Homare 11 with the Homare 21, which drove a three-bladed propeller. The aircraft (codenamed "Myrt" by the Allies) made its combat debut during the First Battle of the Philippine Sea in June 1944, when Saiuns shadowed the US fleet. Thanks to the C6N1s' impressive turn of speed, US Navy pilots flying defensive patrols in F6F Hellcats found them hard to intercept.

Nakajima also developed the C6N1-B carrier-borne attack bomber that was modified to carry a torpedo externally, offset to starboard, beneath the fuselage. However, the destruction of virtually all the IJN's carriers during 1944 halted the aircraft's development prior to production commencing. A small number of Saiuns were modified into C6N1-S nightfighters, with the aircraft's crew being reduced to two and a pair of 20mm Type 99 cannon being mounted obliquely in the fuselage. Although retaining its excellent performance, which made the C6N1-S the fastest of all Japanese nightfighters, the aircraft lacked AI radar, thus greatly reducing its effectiveness.

Less than 500 Saiuns were eventually built, and they saw operational service with five Kokutais. At 0540 hrs on August 15, 1945, a C6N1 was shot down over Tokyo by Lt Cdr T. H. Reidy, CO of F4U-1D-equipped VBF-83 embarked in USS *Essex* (CV-9), to record the last confirmed US air-to-air victory of World War II. Five minutes later, the war officially ended.

Four "Myrts" – including a C6N1-S nightfighter variant – were captured by US troops at Kisarazu post war and flown to Yokosuka for shipment to America. The two C6N1s assigned to the USAAF were returned to airworthiness at Langley Field, Virginia, and flight tested at Middletown. One of those aircraft, FE-4804, was photographed between flights at this location on July 30, 1946 with five-victory P-38 Lightning ace Maj Willard J. Webb in the cockpit. (*NARA*)

ABOVE Its fuselage stained with lead deposits from the exhausts stubs of the 1,870hp Nakajima NK9H Homare 21 radial engine, FE-4804 has clearly been put through its paces during flight testing by the USAAF at Middletown. Three of the four "Myrts," including this machine, were scrapped following their evaluation. (*NARA*)

ABOVE RIGHT C6N1-C construction number 4161 (coded FE-4803 by the USAAF) languishes in the foreign aircraft storage area at Orchard Place Airport in Park Ridge, Illinois during the late 1940s. It had been flown here in August 1946 for inclusion in the proposed National Air Museum, and when this failed to materialize it was acquired by the NASM in 1949 and moved to its "Silver Hill" storage facility, where it remains to this day. (*NARA*)

Following examination of a badly damaged "Myrt" on Tinian in the summer of 1944, US Intelligence reports struck a fearful note with respect to the aircraft's potential as a high-speed torpedo-bomber:

MYRT 11 (Saiun)

MYRT is the service version of 17 Experimental carrier-borne reconnaissance plane with the Model/Type symbol C6N1 and probably manufactured by Nakajima. It is in service, and information received from Tinian examinations and a captured document show that this aircraft is fitted with an 18-cylinder Homare 21 engine rated by the Japs 2,000 h.p. at takeoff and 1,700 h.p. at its critical altitude of 19,680ft. Maximum speed is given as 391mph at critical altitude, cruising speed as 242mph; range with normal loading as 1,840 miles and maximum range with overload fuel as 2,995 miles.

Armament listed in the document and confirmed at Tinian consists of a single 7.9mm. flexible gun mounted in the rear cockpit. A camera port opens through the floor of the center cockpit and flare racks are carried, possibly for night photography. Main wing tanks are protected with a form of self-sealing while others are protected by a carbon dioxide fire-prevention system. No armor is provided nor does there seem to be provision for a bomb load.

Ostensibly MYRT is strictly a fast, maneuverable, long-range and lightly armed reconnaissance plane; however, its close similarity to the torpedo-bombers JILL and KATE cannot preclude the possibility that MYRT may carry an external torpedo. This would greatly curtail its range and lower its performance characteristics but would still make it a potentially dangerous aircraft.

This supposition is by no means conclusive and, in spite of MYRT's apparent suitability, it may be that GRACE is the only new Japanese carrier-borne torpedo aircraft.[11]

The unrestored fuselage of C6N1-C construction number 4161 at the NASM's Paul E. Garber Facility. Its wings are stored nearby on site. (*Photo by Mark Avino, Smithsonian National Air and Space Museum (NASM 2000-9402).*)

Following VJ Day, four "Myrts" were captured by US troops at Kisarazu, in Chiba Prefecture, one of these being a C6N1-S. All these aircraft were flown to Yokosuka by IJNAF personnel under escort by armed US fighters and loaded onto the escort carrier *Barnes* for shipment to America. Offloaded in Norfolk, Virginia, on December 10, 1945, along with 41 other IJNAF and IJAAF types, the aircraft were transported to the nearby Naval Air Station. The two "Myrts" assigned to the USAAF were returned to airworthiness at Langley Field, Virginia, and duly flight tested at Middletown. The evaluation revealed that the aircraft was extremely maneuverable and capable of a top speed of 379mph at an altitude of 20,000ft – a performance comparable with the F6F-5 and F4U-1D. Three of the C6N1s were subsequently placed in storage at Middletown, with the fourth aircraft (presumably having been assigned to the US Navy) being located at the AOAMC in Newark. Three of the "Myrts" were later scrapped, but C6N1-C construction number 4161 survived after it was flown to Park Ridge in August 1946 for inclusion in the National Air Museum. In 1949 the aircraft was acquired by the NASM and moved to its "Silver Hill" storage facility, where it remains to this day.

Mitsubishi Ki-46 "Dinah"

Fast, high flying and ultra-reliable, the Mitsubishi Ki-46 was Japan's most important reconnaissance asset throughout World War II. The aircraft could trace its development history back to December 1937, when the IJAAF issued a preliminary specification for the development of a replacement for the Mitsubishi Ki-15 in the long-range strategic reconnaissance role. Relying principally on speed as its primary means of defense, the aircraft would need a six-hour endurance at a speed of 249mph when flying between 13,125ft and 19,685ft. Its maximum speed was to be 373mph, and the aircraft was to have a single flexible rear-firing 7.7mm machine gun. First flown in prototype form in November 1939, initial production Ki-46-Is were powered by two 900hp Mitsubishi Ha-26-I radials that provided only modest performance. These early machines were relegated to training duties as a result, front-line units being issued with the follow-on Ki-46-II instead. The latter was fitted with two-speed supercharged 1080hp Ha-102 engines, and these allowed the light and nimble Ki-46 airframe to reach speeds of up to 375mph. The -II was the primary production variant of the aircraft, with 1,093 examples being built from March 1941.

Built by Mitsubishi at its Oe-machi plant during late October 1942, Ki-46-II construction number 2251 was assigned to the 76th Dokuritsu Dai Chutai (Independent Squadron) shortly thereafter. Painted overall gray, with *sumire* (violet) characters on the rudder and an air signals emblem on the fin, the "Dinah" was found abandoned at Lae airfield by invading Australian Army troops in late September. It had clearly suffered damage to its starboard wing at some point, leading to the Ki-46-II being withdrawn from service by the IJAAF, although the fuselage of the aircraft was intact. The "Dinah" was eventually towed into a boneyard area on the side of the airfield, where it was left to languish with other captured Japanese aircraft. (*NARA*)

A close up of the tail section of Ki-46-II construction number 2251, which reveals its four-digit construction number in three locations, as well as the *sumire* (violet) characters on the rudder and the crudely applied air signals emblem on the fin. A USAAF P-40 Warhawk can be seen parked behind the "Dinah." (*NARA*)

Ki-46-IIs began to reach front-line units in Manchuria and China from July 1941, where the aircraft's high top speed meant that it could easily avoid interception by enemy fighters. Ki-46-IIs were also sent to French Indochina in October of that year to carry out clandestine reconnaissance flights of the planned amphibious landing sites in Malaya in the final months of peace in the region. Once war had broken out, lone Ki-46s would roam at will across the Pacific, operating in small detachments throughout Southeast Asia. Given the Allied codename "Dinah," a small number of aircraft flown by the IJNAF even traveled as far south as northern Australia.

From late 1942 USAAF P-38Fs started to take a toll on the previously untouchable "Dinahs," and in 1943 newly arrived Spitfire Vs defending Darwin also downed a number of Ki-46-IIs. An improved variant in the form of the Ki-46-III was already undergoing flight trials by then, the aircraft being fitted with 1,500hp Ha-112-II engines that featured direct fuel injection. The -III also had an extra fuel tank to increase duration and offset the higher consumption of the new engines. The most significant change in the aircraft's external appearance centered on its completely redesigned forward fuselage, with a lengthened canopy replacing the cockpit "step" of previous Ki-46 models. First flown in December 1942, the Ki-46-III (611 completed) remained in production until war's end – the last of the -IIs (1,093 delivered) had been completed in late 1944.

From May 1944 a number of Ki-46-IIIs were stripped of their photographic equipment and fitted with two 20mm Ho-5 cannon in the nose and an obliquely-mounted 37mm Ho-203 cannon in place of the top center fuselage fuel tank. Designated the Ki-46-III KAI, the aircraft was issued to air defense units in Japan from November 1944. Operational

ABOVE LEFT ATAIU-SEA personnel operating in the China–Burma–India Theater take notes while investigating the wreckage of an IJAAF Ki-46-III from the Burma-based 81st Kokutai. The aircraft had been shot down by two RAF Spitfire VCs from No 615 Sqn during a reconnaissance mission near Dohazari in eastern India on January 16, 1944. Its pilot, Capt Kuriyama, perished. (NARA)

ABOVE The remarkably intact tail section of the downed Ki-46-III was adorned with the 81st Sentai's distinctive "8" pierced by a stylised "1". This unit had flown "Dinahs" since the fall of 1941, initially in China and then in the Malay Peninsula. It moved to Burma in May 1942, and remained there until war's end. The 81st was equipped with the Ki-46 (and the Mitsubishi Ki-15 "Babs") throughout World War II. (NARA)

Ki-46-II construction number 2485 of the 4th Koukuugun (Air Army) had been built by Mitsubishi at its Oe-machi plant in mid-March 1943. It had force-landed in January 1944 at Sag Sag in western New Britain: the aircraft's right engine was torn off from the firewall and ended up facing backwards, with the propeller blades bent. The Ki-46's nose was also damaged on impact. The fate of its crew is unknown, although they almost certainly survived the crash and fled the scene. According to the TAIC report on this aircraft, "The entire airplane had been painted light gray, and had been polished keenly. The inside of the fuselage was said to be intact, except the radio and a couple instruments had been removed. Internal equipment remaining in the airplane was in excellent condition. Wings and fuselage were in good condition (except for damage visible in photos). Two parachutes were found, as was a log book. The log book was forwarded to ATIS [Allied Translator and Interpreter Services]. Plane is being salvaged." (NARA)

results proved disappointing, however, as the makeshift fighter lacked the rate of climb required to intercept fast, high-flying B-29s.

US Intelligence reports pinpointed the strengths and weaknesses of the "Dinah" as follows:

Dinah 2 Performance and Characteristics
Maximum speed = 365mph at altitude of 21,000ft.

Crew = 2

Construction = All metal

General Data: Maximum armament recovered has been 1 x 7.7mm top rear free gun. One report indicated 2 x 7.7mm free guns. Has used grenade discharge device in tail.

Vulnerability: Unprotected fuel tanks in majority of aircraft. Light armor protection for aircrew (13mm armor plate behind pilot).

Dinah 3 Performance and Characteristics
Maximum speed = 390mph at altitude of 22,000ft.

Crew = 2

Construction = All metal

General Data: Maximum armament recovered has been 1 x 7.7mm top rear free gun. One report indicated 2 x 7.7mm free guns. Has used grenade discharge device in tail.

Vulnerability: Unprotected fuel tanks in majority of aircraft. Light armor protection for aircrew (13mm armor plate behind pilot).[12]

The first fully intact example of the "Dinah" to fall into Allied hands took the form of Ki-46-II construction number 2846 (possibly from the 10th Sentai) captured by US Army troops on April 23, 1944 at

ABOVE On April 23, 1944 Ki-46-II construction number 2846 (possibly from the 10th Sentai) was captured by US Army troops at an airfield near Hollandia. Restored to airworthiness by groundcrew from the A-20 Havoc-equipped 13th BS/3rd BG in September 1944, the aircraft is seen here shortly after making its first flight in USAAF hands. (NARA)

ABOVE LEFT The Hollandia Ki-46-II was flown in its IJAAF blue-gray scheme, but with the addition of US insignia, TAIC titling, and the 13th BS's grim reaper emblem on its nose. (NARA)

LEFT A series of air-to-air photographs of Ki-46-II construction number 2846 were taken prior to the aircraft being shipped to the US. The camera ports left of the fuselage insignia and on the underside of the fuselage near the wing trailing edge can be seen to advantage here, as the Ki-46-II gently banks away from the camera-ship. (NARA)

an airfield near the port town of Hollandia on the northern coast of New Guinea. By September of that year the aircraft was restored to flight-worthy status by groundcrew from the A-20 Havoc-equipped 13th Bomb Squadron/3rd Bomb Group, which was also based in Hollandia. Kept in its IJAAF blue-gray scheme, but with the addition of US insignia, TAIC titling and the grim reaper emblem of the 13th BS on its nose, the Ki-46-II was flown a number of times in-theater before eventually being shipped to the US from Finschhafen, New Guinea, on

The Hollandia Ki-46-II is seen at NAS Anacostia in 1945 following its shipment from Finschhafen, New Guinea, on board the escort carrier *Attu*. The markings applied to the aircraft were briefly retained in the US, including the TAIC 10 code on its fin and 13th BS grim reaper insignia on either side of the "Dinah's" nose. Test flown by TAIC personnel at NAS Anacostia and NAS Patuxent River, and by USAAF Proving Ground Command (which was responsible for testing aircraft weapon systems and munitions) at Eglin Field, the aircraft was last mentioned in official records at the latter location on May 29, 1945 when it was involved in a taxiing accident. (*NARA*)

Both underfuselage camera ports can be seen in this unusual view of the Ki-46-II. Note also that the undercarriage doors appear to be ajar. The central fuselage area of the "Dinah" accommodated a large fuel tank, which separated the two cockpits occupied by the pilot and the radio operator/gunner. (*NARA*)

Amongst the myriad IJAAF and IJNAF aircraft captured at Clark Field in February 1945 was this Ki-46-II of the 55th Dokuritsu Dai Shijugo Chutai. The "Dinah" was one of a number of Ki-46s found here, none of which appear to have been restored to airworthiness by the TAIC-SWPA. (*NARA*)

board the escort carrier USS *Attu* (CVE-102) for further technical evaluation. It was test flown by TAIC personnel at NAS Anacostia, NAS Patuxent River and Eglin Field, where it attained a top speed of 375mph at an altitude of 19,000ft. The aircraft was later scrapped.

An additional five "Dinahs" were shipped to the US on board the escort carrier *Barnes* in November–December 1945, having been found at Kodama airfield, in Saitama Prefecture, and flown to Yokosuka. Four of the aircraft were Ki-46-IIIs and the fifth was one of four Ki-46-IV prototypes fitted with turbosupercharged Mitsubishi Ha-112-II Ru engines rated at 1,100hp at 33,465ft that was test flown in 1944. The aircraft had failed to enter production owing to problems with the turbosupercharging system. As with the Hollandia Ki-46-II, none of the Kodama "Dinahs" escaped the scrapper's torch.

One Ki-46 did survive, however, and it has been a much-prized exhibit in Britain for many decades. Ki-46-III construction number 5439 of the IJAAF's 3rd Chutai was one of a number of Japanese aircraft brought together at Tebrau, in Malaya, in late 1945 for evaluation by the ATAIU-SEA and possible shipment back to Britain – it had been flown in from Kuala Lumpur by an RAF pilot. During the flights that followed (some of which were performed by Japanese pilots), little proper evaluation of the aircraft was carried out. Indeed, it seems that these flights were made primarily for the benefit of the press or visiting VIPs. It was revealed, however, that the "Dinah" was capable of a top speed of 391mph at an altitude of 19,000ft. These flights were almost certainly undertaken to prove the airworthiness of individual aircraft at Tebrau prior to them being shipped to Britain for testing by the Royal Aircraft Establishment at Farnborough.

No fewer than 64 Japanese aircraft were selected by the British Ministry of Aircraft Production and Air Intelligence 2(g) for shipment to Britain, but a lack of available space meant that just four arrived in Portsmouth in

A rear view of the Clark Field Ki-46-II seen in the previous photograph. The "Dinah" is parked with other Japanese types that had been captured intact at the base. The Ki-46-II was the most numerous version of the "Dinah," with 1,093 examples being built between 1940 and 1944. (*NARA*)

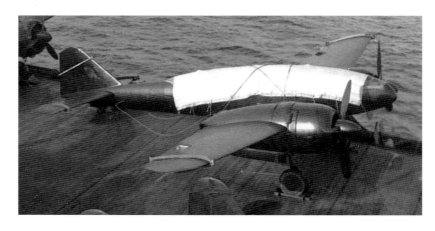

Five "Dinahs" were shipped to the US on board the escort carrier *Barnes* in November–December 1945, after they were found at Kodama airfield in Saitama Prefecture. Four of the aircraft, including this one, were Ki-46-IIIs, while the fifth example was a Ki-46-IV prototype. (*Aviation History Collection / Alamy Stock Photo*)

Shipped to Britain from Malaya in July–August 1946, Ki-46-III 5439 was stored at Stanmore Park from 1948 to 1956, and then displayed at various locations before being returned to storage at St Athan in 1970. The aircraft was moved to Cosford once again in 1989. It was eventually restored in its 81st Sentai colors and placed on display in the RAF museum on site. (*Arjun Sarup*)

August 1946. The "Dinah" was subsequently stored at Stanmore Park from 1948 to 1956, and then displayed at Wroughton, Fulbeck, Biggin Hill, Cosford, and Henlow, prior to being returned to storage at St Athan in 1970. The aircraft was moved to Cosford once again in 1989 following the running down of the St Athan collection, and was restored and placed on display in the RAF museum on site.

Other Ki-46s had fallen into Allied hands both during and after the war, with the ATAIU-SEA having taken delivery of a relatively intact

Ki-46-III construction number 5439 of the 81st Sentai's 3rd Chutai was one of a number of Japanese aircraft brought together at Tebrau in late 1945 for evaluation by the ATAIU-SEA and possible shipment back to Britain. The aircraft is seen here as found at Kuala Lumpur in September 1945, with holes in the rudder fabric and missing cockpit transparencies. IJAAF groundcrew, under the supervision of RAF personnel, returned the "Dinah" to airworthiness, and there is a possibility that the Ki-46-III may subsequently have been part of the RAF's "Gremlin Task Force." Construction number 5439 was eventually flown to Tebrau in 1946. (NARA)

example at Maidan airfield, Calcutta, in 1944. The "Gremlin Task Force" also had several Ki-46s post war, using them to perform reconnaissance and transport flights with Japanese crews (accompanied by RAF aircrew) at the controls in French Indochina – one example was lost in a crash-landing. The *Armée de l'Air*'s *Groupe de transport* I/34 also flew a solitary Ki-46-II alongside other captured Japanese military aircraft in this theater until it too was destroyed in a crash.

CHAPTER 4

EVALUATING SEAPLANES AND FLYING BOATS

These H8K2 "Emily" flying boats of the 801st Kokutai were captured at Takuma seaplane base in Kagawa Prefecture shortly after VJ Day. They were all in airworthy condition, but only a single example was transported to the US. The remaining airframes were unceremoniously scrapped. (*Richard Reinsch*)

Through the flight testing and evaluation of captured IJNAF seaplanes and flying boats, the Allies ascertained that the Japanese design philosophy for these types emphasized versatility, utility and speed. Some seaplane designs were adapted from front-line fighters such as the Zero-sen, while, conversely, the Kyofu was the inspiration behind the outstanding Shiden and Shiden-Kai interceptors – the IJNAF's most potent fighters of World War II. Some flying boat designs such as the H8K2 "Emily" had outstanding range, excellent armor protection for the crew and self-sealing fuel tanks. Indeed, the latter feature was noted and admired by US Air Intelligence experts, as revealed in the following quote from one of their reports: "That the Japs have the knowledge and ability to produce a satisfactory protective lining is attested by the well-constructed form of 'self-sealing' used on the Navy patrol bomber EMILY."[1]

SEAPLANES

Mitsubishi F1M "Pete"

The F1M was designed by Mitsubishi in response to the IJNAF 10-Shi requirement for a catapult-launched short-range observation seaplane needed as a replacement for the Nakajima E8N1. Powered by an 820hp Nakajima Hikari 1 nine-cylinder radial, the prototype F1M1 was a clean biplane design with a central flow and two outboard stabilizing floats. Designed with only a limited number of drag-inducing interplane struts, the aircraft boasted exceptional maneuverability that was markedly superior to a rival aircraft created by Aichi. The F1M1 did, however, porpoise when being taxied on the water, and its directional stability once in the air was rated as poor by service test pilots.

In August 1943 these two F1M2 "Petes" were examined by TAIU personnel at Rekata Bay in the Solomon Islands. A total of four "Petes" were found here, the seaplanes having been operated by the IJNAF from this location until they were damaged in an Allied strafing attack. The aircraft closest to the camera is believed to be construction number 1200, built by Mitsubishi in August 1942 and originally assigned to the 11,200-ton seaplane tender *Chitose*. Behind it is F1M2 construction number 1190, which was also completed in August 1942 and was assigned to the seaplane tender *Kamikawa Maru*. (NARA)

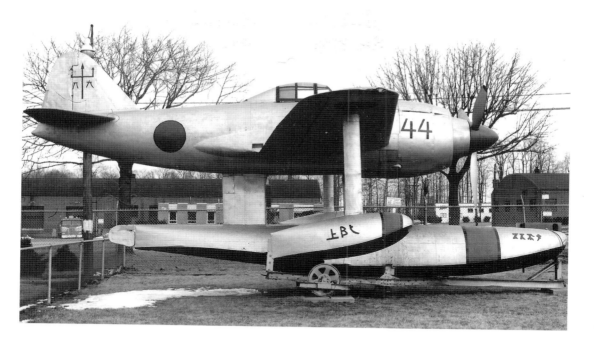

examples were pooled on Lake Biwa in 1945, from where they flew home defense sorties against American bombers. They enjoyed little success.

The following, brief, Allied Intelligence report was compiled on the "Rex" shortly after B-24 crews had been engaged by the floatplane fighter during raids on targets in the Maluku archipelago, west of New Guinea, in early 1944:

> REX 11 is the service model of 15 Experimental fighter seaplane made by Kawanishi and bears the Model/Type symbol N1K1. It is fitted with a Kasei 13 engine made by Mitsubishi and is in production. According to PoWs, early tests were so favorable in regard to speed, climb and maneuverability that it was decided to make a land-based version of the REX seaplane. Necessary modifications were made and the land-based interceptor GEORGE 11 was the result.
>
> REX will probably replace RUFE as the main JNAF float-plane fighter. No performance recognition information is available as yet.[2]

Shortly after VJ Day, US occupation forces found four intact N1K1s possibly from the 951st Kokutai at Kowa, as well as a fifth example at Sasebo, in Nagasaki Prefecture, and had them flown to Yokosuka for shipment to the US on board the escort carrier *Core* on November 14, 1945. Four were assigned to the US Navy and one to the USAAF, and it

Shortly after VJ Day, US occupation forces found four intact N1K1s, possibly from the 951st Kokutai, at Kowa, as well as a fifth example at Sasebo, in Nagasaki Prefecture, and had them flown to Yokosuka for shipment to the US. This particular Kyofu, construction number 565, cheated the scrap man's blowtorch to be put on outdoor display at NAS Willow Grove from 1946 – it is seen here, complete with a fanciful color scheme, in February 1969. (*Author collection*)

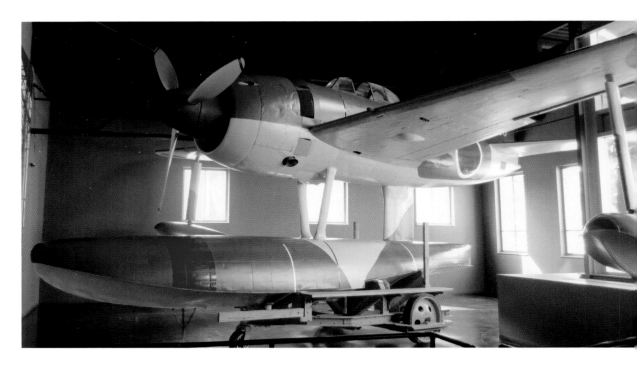

Kyofu construction number 562 also survived destruction to be stored at NAS Norfolk for many years after it had been acquired by the NASM. Now owned by the NNAM, the NIKI fighter was "cosmetically" restored in 2009 and displayed in the newly expanded museum. (*Edward M. Young*)

is unclear whether any of these aircraft were made airworthy following their arrival in America. The USAAF example was recorded as being at Middletown in September 1946, after which it was moved to Park Ridge for inclusion in the National Air Museum. Still at the latter location in 1949, it was scrapped along with many other Japanese aircraft that were here in 1950 following the commencement of the conflict in Korea.

The Sasebo "Rex" was sent to "Pax River" from NAS Norfolk, and then on to the Naval Shipyard in Boston, Massachusetts, for display purposes in October 1946. It too was scrapped. The remaining three N1K1s allocated to the US Navy have survived to this day, however. Construction number 514 also spent time at "Pax River" prior to being put in storage at NAS Norfolk. The Smithsonian Institution obtained the airplane in 1960, although it was not moved to "Silver Hill" for a further 12 years. The floatplane fighter remains here, awaiting restoration.

Construction number 562 was also stored at NAS Norfolk for many years after it too had been acquired by the Smithsonian Institution. It was transferred to the Fleet Admiral Chester W. Nimitz Naval Museum (now the National Museum of the Pacific War) in Fredericksburg, Texas, in February 1976, shortly after which the "Rex's" ownership was switched from the NASM to the NNAM at Pensacola. Once again placed in storage, the floatplane fighter was "cosmetically" restored over a six-month period in 2009 and then put on display in the newly expanded museum.

The last surviving Kyofu is construction number 565, which was on outdoor display at NAS Willow Grove from 1946. Refurbished here in 1982, the aircraft was moved to the NNAM eight years later, where it too is presently held in storage.

Aichi E13A "Jake"

Aichi's E13A1 was the most widely used of all the IJNAF's reconnaissance floatplanes during World War II, and also the most important in terms of numbers built – 1,418 between 1940 and 1945. The aircraft was designed in response to the issuing of the 12-Shi specification in June 1937 that called for a two-seat replacement for the Kawanishi E7K2 three-seat twin-float seaplane. Aichi, Nakajima and Kawanishi responded with the E12A1, E12N1 and E12K1, respectively. While these aircraft were being designed, the IJNAF issued a second 12-Shi specification requesting a three-seat reconnaissance floatplane with a higher speed and longer range. All three companies created additional designs, designated the E13A1, E13N1 and E13K1.

The E13A1 was essentially a scaled-up E12A1, being powered by a 1,060hp Mitsubishi Kinsei 43 14-cylinder air-cooled radial engine. The prototype was completed in late 1938, as were two E12A1 prototypes powered by 870hp Mitsubishi Zuisei 14-cylinder air-cooled radials. Aichi's trials of both types revealed that the E13A1 was the superior aircraft in respect of its performance, stability in flight and maneuverability, despite the aircraft being larger and heavier. The IJNAF also made it known that the three-seater was the preferred choice for front-line service, resulting in the E13A1 being tested in trials against the Kawanishi E13K1. In December 1940 the Aichi design was chosen and production commenced shortly thereafter.

The aircraft changed very little during its production life, relying on the Kinsei 43, which gave it a maximum speed of 234mph. The E13A1 had a range of 1,298 miles and could climb to 28,600ft if required. The floatplane's armament consisted of one flexible 7.7mm Type 92 machine gun for the observer/rear gunner, with a few late production aircraft also being fitted in the field with a flexible 20mm Type 99-2 cannon mounted in a ventral fuselage position that fired downward – these aircraft were modified for operations against US Navy PT boats. The E13A1 was capable of carrying one 551lb bomb or four 132lb bombs or depth charges externally.

The E13A1 made its combat debut in late 1941 when operating from cruisers and seaplane tenders participating in the Sino-Japanese War.

In June 1943, US troops found the substantial remains of two E13A1s in Chichagof Harbor after defeating Japanese forces on Attu Island in the Aleutians. One was dragged ashore by the US Navy and transported to the TAIC at NAS Anacostia. (NARA)

Just a matter of weeks later the aircraft also flew reconnaissance missions during the Hawaiian operation, operating from the cruisers *Tone*, *Chikuma* and *Kinugasa* of the 8th Cruiser Division. Subsequently codenamed "Jake" by the Allies, the E13A1 would prove invaluable to the IJN thanks to its almost 15-hour endurance. Despite lacking fuel or crew protection, and with only a single machine gun for defense, "Jakes" were called on to fly bombing missions when Allied aerial opposition was considered to be light. E13A1 crews also performed air-sea rescue missions, anti-submarine and shipping attack sorties and staff transport flights, and, finally, acted as kamikazes.

From November 1944, a small number of "Jakes" were given upgraded equipment for specific roles, with the E13A1a having improved radios, and the E13A1b being fitted with ASV radar with antennae on the wing leading edges and the rear fuselage sides. Finally, a handful of "Jakes" were modified into ASW platforms through the installation of a magnetic airborne submarine detection device known as Jikitanchiki, details of which were revealed in the following US Intelligence report:

✳✳✳

The Japanese MAD equipment reported herein was recovered from a crashed NELL by Technical Air Intelligence (TAI Field Team) near Putien, Fukien, China (Southeast China Coast Area). NELL is a twin-engine medium bomber used at present by the Japanese for

ABOVE LEFT Much of the "Jake's" fuselage had been destroyed when it was strafed in Chichagof Harbor, the seaplane having clearly caught fire prior to sinking. (NARA)

ABOVE Indeed, only the twin floats and its wing center section were left relatively intact by the time the "Jake" had been beached. (NARA)

LEFT The propeller units from both E13A1s were also salvaged, with one still being very much attached to its 1,060hp Mitsubishi Kinsei 43 14-cylinder air-cooled radial engine. (NARA)

patrol, bombing, transport and troop carrying. Documentary evidence also places MAD equipment in JAKE, GLEN and SLIM. GLEN and SLIM are submarine borne aircraft. JAKE is a twin-float recce plane.

From the above mentioned installations of this equipment, it is apparent that it could be placed in any Japanese aircraft employed on anti-sub patrol. At present there is no direct evidence as to the extent MAD is being used by the Japanese. It is significant, however, that assembly parts for MAD were recovered on Okinawa.

A Japanese prisoner of war interrogation (ATIS, SWPA Serial No. 913, Interrogation Report 750, June 4, 1945, page 9), gives the following on MAD use: "The detector was not used on normal patrols, but only in areas in which submarines had been sighted or suspected. When a submarine was sighted and attacked by a patrol airplane, two marker bombs were dropped, one at the point where the submarine crash dived, and another a short distance away in the direction that it dived. The base was notified of the attack by wireless, and immediately dispatched all available airplanes to the scene and notified other antisubmarine patrol unit bases within an effective distance. These bases would also dispatch all available airplanes.

The airplanes equipped with the magnetic detector, starting at the marker bombs, began a search of the area, flying in formations of three, line abreast. Single airplane and two airplane searches were also made. The distances between each airplane was approximately 300ft."

The formation was in its experimental stage as the effective range of the magnetic detector had not been determined, but the greatest distance that prisoner had seen used between airplanes was 300ft.

An area 20 miles square was searched around the reported location of the submarine. The turning radius of the search airplane was approximately 1,500ft and when the formation made a 180° turn into the new course the area between the old and new courses was left unsearched, and was searched on the return flight.

When the airplane flew directly over a submerged submarine the operator of the magnetic detector received the warning by an electric bell and the flash of a red light. Immediately upon detection a marker bomb was dropped. The airplane flew the same course in the opposite direction and on the second detection another marker bomb was dropped. This procedure was repeated midway between the two marker bombs and at right angles to the line formed by them. The location of the submarine was then known to be within the area indicated by the four marker bombs and a concentrated attack was made.

Installation – The magnetic detector was installed in the wireless operator's cockpit. Prisoner had been near JAKEs equipped with the magnetic detector but did not see any induction coils or antennas attached to the fuselage or wings. The airplanes required only minor alterations for installation of the magnetic detector. They were flown to an unidentified factory at an unidentified location and remained about one week. Prisoner

ABOVE This captured E13A1, having just been craned onto a wheeled trailer at Seletar, was almost certainly flown from here alongside several other IJNAF floatplane and flying boat types in late 1945 or early 1946. Like the land-based aircraft at nearby Tebrau, the "Jake," "Rufe," and other IJNAF types operated from Seletar were flown by Japanese pilots under RAF ATAIU-SEA control. (© IWM CI 1741)

LEFT The wreckage of an E13A1 "Jake" seaplane from an unidentified unit, downed during the US attack on Palawan in the Philippines, is inspected by personnel from USS LST-806 on the shoreline near Puerto Princesa on March 27, 1945. (NARA)

thought it possible that the detector was installed by YOKOSUKA Naval Arsenal at YOKOSUKA Naval Base.

Availability – Magnetic detectors were not available for all airplanes.

Effectiveness – Prisoner did not know to what depth magnetic detector was effective. He stated that until July 1944 his unit had not sunk a submarine. It sank four submarines within a month after the magnetic detector was introduced.

It is desired that any further recovered MAD equipment be forwarded by air to TAIC, with all details of recovery such as plane installed in, etc. Efforts are being made to correlate the extent of use, and subsequent equipment will be tested to determine possible improvement.[3]

***

In June 1943, US troops found the substantial remains of two E13A1s in Chichagof Harbor after defeating Japanese forces on Attu Island, in the Aleutians. One of the aircraft, which had belonged to the 452nd Kokutai, was salvaged by the US Navy and transported to the TAIC at NAS Anacostia. The aircraft was eventually scrapped post war. No fewer than six "Jakes" were used by *Escadrille* 85 of the *Aéronavale* in Indochina following the Japanese surrender, these aircraft having their IJNAF insignia replaced by French Red Cross markings.

Aichi E16A "Paul"

Chosen as the replacement for the E13A1 in response to the IJNAF's 14-Shi specification of 1939, the E16A1 Zuiun ("Auspicious Cloud") was in fact an independent design by Aichi following disagreements within the naval staff with respect to the roles to be performed by the new reconnaissance floatplane. With ongoing delays in finalizing the specification requirement preventing manufacturers from submitting designs, Aichi chose to press on with its AM-22 design regardless, and the IJNAF in turn drafted a new 16-Shi specification based on the company's proposal.

In addition to operating as a reconnaissance aircraft, the two-seat E16A1, as it was designated by the IJNAF, was intended to serve as a dive-bomber. Indeed, to perform this challenging role, the floatplane was equipped with hydraulically-operated dive brakes located in the front leg of the float N-struts. Like the E13A1 it was due to replace, the E16A1 featured upward-folding wings to allow the aircraft to be more easily stored aboard cruisers and seaplane tenders – the principal vessels from which the Zuiuns would operate. Powered by a 1,300hp Mitsubishi MK8A Kinsei 51 14-cylinder air-cooled radial engine and with armament consisting of two 20mm Type 99-2 cannon in the wings and a flexible 13mm Type 2 machine gun for the rear gunner, production aircraft would also be capable of carrying 551lb of bombs. Finally, the floatplane had a remarkable 1,500-mile range.

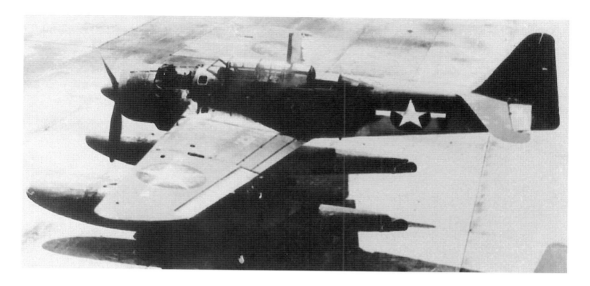

The prototype successfully performed its maiden flight on May 22, 1942 and the seaplane went into production in January 1944. Codenamed "Paul" by the Allies, early examples used the Kinsei 51 as was fitted to the prototype but later production aircraft featured the Kinsei 54, which also produced 1,300hp. Only 256 "Pauls" had been completed by VJ Day, and they suffered heavy losses during the Philippines campaign to marauding US fighters. A number were also expended in kamikaze attacks in the bitter defense of Okinawa.

The first "Paul" to fall into Allied hands was an aircraft from the 634th Kokutai that was captured by US Army troops on December 7, 1944 at Ormoc Bay during the Battle of Leyte. The aircraft, still in flight-worthy status, was evaluated by the US Navy. During flight tests it was revealed that the "Paul" was capable of a top speed of 274mph. The aircraft was later scrapped. A second E16A1 from the 634th Kokutai was found in Japan shortly after VJ Day and it was shipped to the US on board the escort carrier *Core* in November 1945. Subsequently sent to "Pax River" for evaluation, the seaplane was later transferred to NAS Norfolk in January 1947 for onward shipment to Floyd Bennett Field in Brooklyn, New York, where it was briefly put on display. The "Paul's" final fate remains unrecorded.

Aichi M6A1 Seiran

In 1942 Aichi was instructed by the IJNAF to design an aircraft to meet its newly issued 17-Shi specification that called for a Special Attack Bomber that could be carried aboard the IJN's I-400 Class submarines,

This E16A1 from the 634th Kokutai was found in Japan shortly after VJ Day and shipped to the US on board the escort carrier *Core* in November 1945. Following evaluation at "Pax River," it was put on public display at Floyd Bennett Field in Brooklyn, New York, for a short period of time. (*US Navy*)

The last of just 26 M6A1s built, construction number 1600228 was transported across the Pacific on board the escort carrier *Core* and subsequently tested at "Pax River," where its top speed was recorded as 295mph. The Seiran was eventually acquired by the NASM, and it is presently on display in the museum's Steven F. Udvar-Hazy Center in Chantilly, Virginia. (*Smithsonian Institution, National Air and Space Museum, (NASM 2004-49847)*.)

which displaced 4,500 tons and had a cruising radius of almost 48,000 miles. Each vessel could carry three aircraft in a watertight hangar, with a catapult for launching them on the forward deck. Eighteen I-400s were planned, but only five of the class were ordered with the hangar owing to the IJN's urgent need for more conventional submarines.

The original 17-Shi requirement stated that the aircraft was to have no undercarriage, although this was changed so that it could be fitted with twin detachable fins. The resulting design, given the model number AM-24 by Aichi and designated the M6A1 Seiran ("Clear Sky Storm") by the IJNAF, was powered by a 1,400hp Aichi AE1P Atsuta 30 12-cylinder inverted-vee liquid-cooled engine – essentially a license-built Daimler-Benz DB 601. The Seiran could carry a 1,874lb bombload or a 1,764lb torpedo, and its defensive armament consisted of a flexible 13mm Type 2 machine gun for the rear gunner. To make the aircraft submarine-compatible, its wings swivelled on their rear spar so that they could lie flat against the fuselage, the vertical tail tip folded to starboard and the horizontal tail surface folded downward. The M6A1 could be made ready for flight in seven minutes by four trained personnel. Aside from the floatplane-equipped Seiran, Aichi also created the M6A1-K Nanzan ("Southern Mountain") trainer fitted with a retractable undercarriage.

The first of six prototypes was completed in November 1943, followed by two M6A1-Ks. With production examples (fitted with Atsuta 32 engines) of the Seiran beginning to reach the IJNAF in October 1944, plans were drawn up for the deployment of four submarines (I-400 and I-401, carrying three M6A1s each, and I-13 and

I-14, with two C6N1s apiece) to the Panama Canal so the aircraft could bomb its lock gates. However, the target was eventually changed to the US Navy's key western Pacific anchorage at Ulithi Atoll, in the Caroline Islands, with the submarines – all part of the 1st Submarine Flotilla – putting to sea in late July 1945. The war ended before the aircraft could carry out this daring attack. Only 26 M6A1s and two -1Ks had been built by then.

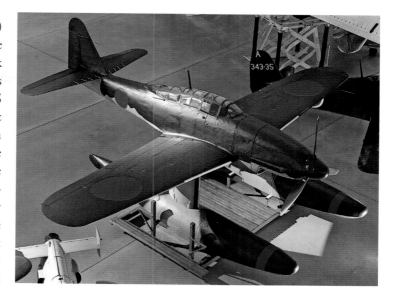

An overhead view of the restored Seiran on display in the NASM's Steven F. Udvar-Hazy Center on November 6, 2007. (*Photo by Dane A. Penland, Smithsonian National Air and Space Museum, (NASM 2013-02980).*)

Single examples of the M6A1 and M6A1-K were shipped back to the US for evaluation. M6A1 construction number 1600228 – the last Seiran built – was flown to Yokosuka from Fukuyama by IJNAF pilot Lt Kazuo Akatsuka, who surrendered the seaplane to US forces upon landing. Transported across the Pacific on board the escort carrier *Core*, it was initially tested at "Pax River," where its top speed was recorded as 295mph. The Seiran was transferred to NAS Alameda in October 1946 for display purposes until it was eventually sent to the NASM facility at "Silver Hill" in 1962. Restoration work on the aircraft was undertaken between June 1989 and February 2000, and it is presently on display in the Steven F. Udvar-Hazy Center in Chantilly, Virginia.

The M6A1-K was shipped from Yokosuka on board the escort carrier *Barnes* on November 3, 1945, bound for Virginia. It too was sent to "Pax River," after which the aircraft was transported to NAS Seattle, Washington, in October 1946 and scrapped shortly thereafter.

FLYING BOATS

Aichi H9A

In January 1940, the IJNAF instructed Aichi to design a twin-engined flying boat specifically for the advanced training of future crews destined to fly the Kawanishi H8K1 maritime reconnaissance flying boat.

A solitary H9A1 twin-engined flying boat, specifically built for the advanced training of future crews destined to fly the H8K1 maritime reconnaissance flying boat, was captured by US troops at Yokosuka and technically evaluated here by the TAIU-SWPA. Subsequent flights revealed that it had a top speed of 197mph at 9,845ft. The H9A1 was not considered important enough to ship back to the US, however, and it was scrapped at Yokosuka. (*Richard Reinsch*)

Featuring a parasol monoplane wing, the aircraft – designated the H9A by the IJNAF – was powered by two 710hp Nakajima Kotobuki 41 Kai 2 nine-cylinder air-cooled radial engines and had semi-retractable tricycle beaching gear. The flying boat typically had a five-man crew consisting of the pilot, co-pilot, observer, flight engineer and radio-operator, with additional seating for three pupils. The H9A could also be fitted with single flexible 7.7mm machine guns in the bow and dorsal open positions, and it could carry two 551lb depth-charges.

Three prototypes were built, with the first performing its maiden flight in September 1940. Poor flying and alighting characteristics resulted in Aichi having to mount the engines lower on the wings. It also modified the flaps and increased both the span and area of the wings. With the H9A now cleared for front-line service, Aichi was contracted to build 24 examples at its Eitoku plant. These were delivered as H9A1s in 1942–43, with four more being completed by Nippon Hokoki K.K. in 1944. The H9A became operational in 1942, and, aside from performing the task for which it was designed, the flying boat also served in the ASW patrol role, as a troop transport, paratroop training aircraft and on liaison tasks.

An airworthy solitary H9A1 was captured by US troops at Yokosuka during the occupation of Japan, the aircraft being technically evaluated by the TAIU-SWPA. Flight evaluation of the H9A1 revealed that it had a top speed of 197mph at 9,845ft. The aircraft was not considered important enough to ship back to the US, however, and it was eventually scrapped at Yokosuka.

Kawanishi H8K "Emily"

Both fast and well armed, the H8K was arguably the best large flying boat of World War II. Designed in 1938 by Kawanishi in response to the IJNAF's 13-Shi specification for a replacement for the company's previous H6K, which was just entering service, the H8K prototype flew for the first time on December 31, 1940. The IJNAF had requested a flying boat that was 30 percent quicker and had a range 50 percent greater than the H6K, and although Kawanishi delivered on the former, it could not attain the latter. Early testing revealed that serious hull modifications were needed to eradicate chronic porpoising in the water, but once these were achieved through the addition of a second step to the planing hull, the definitive H8K was the most advanced aircraft of its type.

Powered by four 1,530hp Mitsubishi MK4A Kasei 11 radial engines and with a crew of ten, the initial production variant, the H8K1, had a

maximum range of 4,475 miles and a top speed of 269mph at 16,400ft. The type marked its service entry with a night bombing raid on Oahu, Hawaii, on March 4–5, 1942, after which the flying boat was christened "Emily" by the Allies. Just 17 H8K1s had been built when production switched to the H8K2 in 1943, which was powered by four 1,850hp Mitsubishi MK4Q Kasei 22 radial engines fitted with water injection – this variant also had a modified vertical tail. The H8K2 possessed excellent defensive armament consisting of five 20mm Type 99 cannon, located in the bow, the dorsal turret, tail turret and left and right fuselage waist blisters. The aircraft also had five 7.7mm Type 92 machine guns located in fuselage hatches. The H8K2 was capable of carrying two 1,764lb torpedoes, eight 551lb bombs or 16 132lb depth-charges. The H8K2 variant quickly became the IJN's standard long-range maritime patrol flying boat. Capable of performing missions which could last for up to 24 hours, the "Emily" was always treated with cautious respect by Allied pilots who happened to intercept one when on patrol over the Pacific. Most late-production H8K2s were also fitted with ASV radar.

In service from 1943, 112 H8K2s had been built by war's end. Assigned to nine front-line units, the "Emily" was seen by Allied fighter pilots as the most difficult Japanese aircraft to shoot down, owing to its impressive top speed and powerful defensive armament.

H8K2 construction number 426 of the 801st Kokutai was the "Emily" chosen for shipment to America on board the seaplane tender USS Cumberland Sound (AV-17). It was offloaded at NAS Whidbey Island, Washington – where this photograph was taken – in December 1945. Three Martin PBM5 Mariners are sat on their beaching gear behind the "Emily" at the NAS's Oak Harbor facility. (NARA)

TOP The "Emily's" interior was extensively photographed once the aircraft was at "Pax River." This view looks forward toward the cockpit of the flying boat. (*NARA*)

CENTER A close-up of the co-pilot's seat and controls in H8K2 construction number 426. (*NARA*)

BOTTOM The flight engineer's position in the H8K2. The majority of these gauges and levers were directly associated with the "Emily's" four 1,850hp Mitsubishi MK4Q Kasei 22 radial engines. (*NARA*)

FAR RIGHT The H8K2's capacious fuselage looking aft toward the tail turret. The underside of the dorsal turret can be seen protruding into the fuselage just forward of the centrally placed doorway. (*NARA*)

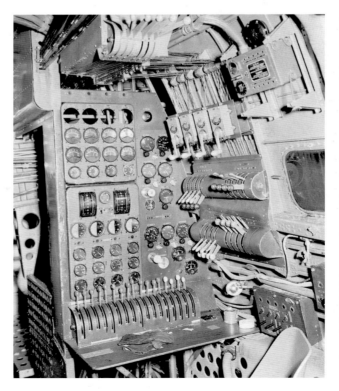

CHAPTER 5

EVALUATING TRANSPORT AIRCRAFT

In early May 1945, US Army troops captured this L2D3 at Zamboanga airfield on Mindanao in the Philippines. It was subsequently flown to Clark Field and put through its paces by TAIU-SWPA personnel. The additional flightdeck windows added to the "Tabby" were one of the design's key recognition features. (*US Navy*)

When a small number of IJNAF and IJAAF transport aircraft were evaluated post war, it soon became evident that Japanese designs had been influenced by successful types used by the USAAF and, to a lesser extent, the Luftwaffe. The most extreme example of this was the Showa/Nakajima L2D "Tabby," which was essentially a license-built Douglas DC-3, while the Kokusai Ki-76 "Stella" was Japan's version of the highly successful Fieseler Fi 156 Storch light-observation/liaison aircraft. The latter was not, however, a copy of the German machine, for its design had commenced a full ten months before an example of the Fi 156 arrived in Japan. Finally, the IJAAF's only glider to see combat appeared to be influenced by the Waco CG-4A that was widely used by the USAAF in World War II.

Showa/Nakajima L2D "Tabby"

In February 1938, Mitsui and Company Ltd acquired the license rights from the Douglas Aircraft Company to build and sell DC-3s in Japan. Separately, it also purchased parts for two unassembled DC-3s. The latter aircraft, and the license, had in fact been purchased by Mitsui on behalf of the IJNAF – Douglas was totally unaware of this fact. When the unassembled aircraft arrived in Japan they were delivered to Showa Hikoki Kogyo K.K., which was instructed to build them and tool up for further production. Nakajima was also asked to participate in their construction.

The first aircraft, designated L2D1, was ready by October 1939, with the second following in April 1940. While these were being built, Showa and Nakajima modified the DC-3 for Japanese production techniques and for the fitting of 1,000hp Mitsubishi Kinsei 43 radials in place of the imported 1,000hp Pratt & Whitney SB3G engines used by the L2D1. Given the designation L2D2, 71 examples would be built by Nakajima between 1940 and 1942 – the first Showa aircraft to this specification was completed in March 1941. Production switched exclusively to Showa after Nakajima built its final example, by which time the L2D2 (codenamed "Tabby" by the Allies) had become the standard IJNAF transport aircraft. Showa also introduced a cargo transport variant with a reinforced floor and large cargo-loading doors on the port side of the rear fuselage. The follow-on L2D3 and 3a were powered by 1,300hp Mitsubishi Kinsei 51 and 53 radials, respectively, and featured additional glazed windows behind the cockpit. Finally, the L2D4 and 4-1 were personnel and cargo transport aircraft that featured a dorsal turret housing a flexible 13mm Type 2 machine gun.

ABOVE This Ki-76 "Stella" artillery spotting and liaison aircraft was found hidden away in the undergrowth on the edge of Clark Field in February 1945. It was closely examined by the TAIU-SWPA, although almost certainly not flown. (NARA)

LEFT Although much of the "Stella's" fabric was missing from its fuselage, the aircraft was intact enough to be worthy of evaluation by TAIU-SWPA personnel. (NARA)

CHAPTER 6

EVALUATING TURBOJET AND ROCKET-POWERED AIRCRAFT

A small assembly line of Kikka twin-engined jet fighters was discovered at Nakajima's Koizumi plant northwest of Tokyo when it was occupied by US forces on October 6, 1945. Note the G8N "Rita" heavy bomber fuselages in the background. Several Kikkas were trucked from here to Yokosuka for onward shipment to the US. (*NARA*)

When Japan's Axis ally Germany began to develop its "wonder weapon" (turbojet and rocket-powered) aircraft during the early 1940s, Japanese Naval Air Attachés in the Third Reich took great interest in these programs. They were soon instructed by the military staff in Japan to pursue ways that would allow the IJNAF to gain access to such revolutionary technologies that would help with the defense of the home islands. The two German aircraft that the Japanese were most interested in were the turbojet-powered Messerschmitt Me 262 Schwalbe ("Swallow") and the rocket-powered Messerschmitt Me 163 Komet ("Comet"). The Naval Air Attachés sought to obtain examples of or plans for these aircraft, as well as to purchase the license from Messerschmitt to build both potentially game-changing aircraft.

TURBOJET-POWERED AIRCRAFT

Nakajima Kikka

Following the demonstration of the Me 262 to members of the Japanese military in 1944, the IJNAF requested that Nakajima undertake the development of a similar turbojet-powered type to serve as a high-speed attack fighter. The IJNAF stipulated that the new machine had to be easy to produce, with wings that could be folded to ensure that aircraft could be hidden from Allied aerial attacks in caves and tunnels. Prominent Nakajima aircraft designers Kazuo Ohno and Kenichi Matsumura duly conceived a fighter that looked very much like a scaled-down Me 262, but with straight instead of moderately swept wings.

Propped up on wooden trestles, the incomplete second Kikka prototype – fitted with two operable Ne-20 turbojet engines – was the subject of limited ground technical evaluation testing at "Pax River" in 1946. (US Navy)

ABOVE A close up of an Ishikawajima Ne-20 axial flow turbojet fitted to an incomplete Kikka found at Nakajima's Koizumi plant. A copy of the BMW 003 engine fitted to the Me 262, the Ne-20 was rated at 1,047lb thrust. (*NARA*)

LEFT A handful of uninstalled Ne-20 turbojet engines were found sat on wooden trestles alongside bare Kikka airframes in the Koizumi plant. These were also sent to the US for testing. (*NARA*)

Initially, the aircraft was to be powered by two 441lb thrust Tsu-11 Campini-type engines, but these were quickly replaced by more powerful 750lb thrust Ishikawajima Ne-12s. When these engines also proved incapable of producing sufficient thrust, Ishikawajima set about building copies of the BMW 003 fitted to the Me 262 based on detailed photographs obtained by IJNAF engineer Cdr Eichi Iwaya. Designated the Ne-20, the axial flow turbojet was rated at 1,047lb thrust. By then christened Kikka ("Orange Blossom"), the fighter was capable of a top speed of 432mph at 32,800ft. Armed with two 30mm Type 5 cannon, it could also carry either a 1,102lb or 1,764lb bomb.

The Kikka successfully performed its first and only test flight, which lasted just 20 minutes, on August 7, 1945 from Kisarazu Naval Air Base, the aircraft using rocket-assisted takeoff gear to help it get airborne. Japan surrendered shortly thereafter, thus preventing additional flight testing. A second prototype was nearing completion at war's end, and American forces discovered around 23 Kikkas under construction at Nakajima's main factory building in Koizumi, in Gunma Prefecture, and at a site on Kyushu Island.

Kikka airframes 3, 4 and 5, as well as several Ne-20 engines, were shipped to America in late 1945, where they underwent technical evaluation. The second Kikka prototype, complete with two Ne-20 turbojet engines, was also transported to the US, and it underwent limited ground testing at "Pax River" in 1946. An additional pair of Ne-20s were sent to the Chrysler Corporation that same year, and the company managed to assemble one working powerplant by combining parts from both turbojets. This was run for 11 hours and 46 minutes, and the official Chrysler Ne-20 Turbojet Report, entitled "Japanese NE-20 turbo jet engine. Construction and performance." is presently on display at the Tokyo National Science Museum.

Although two of the four Kikkas sent to America were scrapped, the remaining pair were placed in long-term storage at NAS Norfolk from the late 1940s. Both aircraft were moved to "Silver Hill" in September 1960, and the fuselage and center wing section of one of the airframes was put on static display – minus its engines – in the Steven F. Udvar-Hazy Center in March 2016. The second Kikka remains in storage. Ne-20 turbojet engines are also currently on display at the Tokyo Science Museum and the NNAM in Pensacola.

ROCKET-POWERED AIRCRAFT

Mitsubishi J8M1 Shusui

In late 1943, Japan and Germany reached an agreement whereby the latter would supply its Axis ally with an example, blueprints, and motors for the revolutionary rocket-powered Me 163 Komet interceptor. In addition, supplemental technical information regarding the aircraft's manufacturing process was also to be supplied to Japan. Both the IJNAF and IJAAF expressed strong interest in building licensed copies of the Me 163 to help thwart anticipated USAAF B-29 Superfortress bombing raids of the Japanese home islands.

After learning about the Komet and its capabilities, Japanese military attachés obtained a Walter HWK 109-509 rocket engine license from the Germans for 20 million Reichsmarks. Despite these arrangements, Japan experienced setbacks when it came to acquiring a complete Me 163. A disassembled example, and its rocket engine, were loaded on board the Japanese submarine *RO-501*, which departed Kiel, Germany, on March 30, 1944, destined for Kobe, Japan. *RO-501* was sunk in the middle of the Atlantic Ocean on May 13, 1944 by US Navy ASW aircraft operating from the escort carrier *Bogue*. Additionally, Me 163 technical data, blueprints and engines loaded onto the Japanese submarine *I-29* were also lost when the I-Boat was sunk by the submarine USS *Sawfish* (SS-276) on July 26, 1944 off the Philippines.

As a direct result of these setbacks, the Japanese were forced to build their own version of the Komet by utilizing a general Me 163 instructional manual obtained by IJNAF engineer Cdr Eichi Iwaya. The resulting aircraft, designated the J8M1 Shusui ("Sharp Sword") by the IJNAF and the Ki-200 by the IJAAF, were to be built by Mitsubishi. The Japanese also built their own version of the Walter HWK 109-509 engine at the

Mitsubishi had completed a total of seven J8M1s by war's end, and several other partially built airframes were discovered by US occupation forces in the company's No. I Plant at Nagoya shortly after VJ Day. Key parts and sub-assemblies from these rocket-powered interceptors were crated up and shipped to the US for detailed evaluation. (NARA)

OPPOSITE TOP Three complete J8M1s were transported to the US on board the escort carrier *Barnes* in November 1945, and two of them were subsequently sent to "Pax River" for detailed evaluation. Each Shusui was marked with a crudely applied A-prefixed two-digit number for recognition purposes: this particular airframe is A23. The third J8M1 shipped from Japan, it was assigned to the USAAF and sent to Wright Field. Photographed here in 1946, the Shusui is sat in a specially built wheeled cradle (the J8M1 lacked a conventional undercarriage). (*NARA*)

OPPOSITE BOTTOM A23 was the only J8M1 to survive the wholesale scrapping of Axis aircraft that took place in the US between 1946 and 1950, and it is seen here on display in the Planes of Fame Museum at Chino. (*Edward M. Young*)

1st Naval Air Technical Arsenal in Yokosuka. The Arsenal also constructed three J8M gliders, designated the MXY8 Akigusa ("Autumn Grass"), to obtain basic aerodynamic and handling information for the rocket-powered fighter. The MXY8 successfully completed its maiden flight on December 8, 1944 in the skies above Hyakurigahara airfield, with Lt Cdr Toyohiko Inuzuka serving as the test pilot on this initial flight. By then Japanese engineers had succeeded in producing their own version of the Walter HWK 509A rocket engine, the 3,307lb thrust Toko Ro.2. Finally, the J8M1 was to be armed with two 30mm Ho-105 cannon capable of firing 400 rounds per minute.

The prototype J8M1 performed its first, and only, powered flight on July 7, 1945 at a tremendous cost. Lt Cdr Inuzuka completed a successful rocket-powered takeoff, upon which the undercarriage dolly was jettisoned and the aircraft rocketed upward at a 45° angle. However, when the aircraft reached an altitude of 1,300ft, the engine shut down, causing the J8M1 to stall. Inuzuka was just moments away from successfully gliding the aircraft back to the airfield when he struck a small building near the runway and the J8M1 crashed and was consumed by flames. Inuzuka succumbed to his injuries the following day. All future J8M1 flights were postponed until the Ro.2 engine could be modified and the problem corrected. Flight testing was slated for resumption, as well as commencement of the development of the J8M2, when the war ended on August 15, 1945. A total of seven J8M1/Ki-200s had been produced by then.

Three J8M1s were recovered by US occupation forces from Mitsubishi's No. 1 Plant at Nagoya shortly after VJ Day, these aircraft being shipped to America in November 1945. Two of them were sent to "Pax River" for detailed evaluation, after which one was scrapped there. The other was transported to NAS Glenview, Illinois, in October 1946 and put on display – it too was later scrapped. The third Shusui was allocated to the USAAF and evaluated at Wright Field, after which it was transferred to Hollywood, California, also for public viewing. This aircraft was acquired by Ed Maloney from a Los Angeles fairground in 1948 and eventually included in his pioneering Air Museum in Claremont, California. It has remained a part of this collection ever since, being restored and presently displayed in the Planes of Fame Museum at Chino.

An unfinished J8M1 was recovered from a cave at Sugita, near Yokosuka, in 1961 and presented to the Japanese Air Self-Defense Force two years later. Left unrestored for many years, the aircraft was refurbished by Mitsubishi in 1997–2001 and is now on display within the company's museum in Komaki Minami.

CHAPTER 7

EVALUATING SPECIAL AERIAL WEAPONS

One of the Yontan Ohkas is carefully removed from its jungle hideaway with the help of a wheeled dolly and a GMC CCKW "Deuce-and-a-half" 6x6 truck in April 1945. (*Richard Reinsch*)

Like its Axis ally Germany, Japan also designed and developed innovative special aerial and "smart" weapons during the final stages of World War II. These included incendiary bomb balloons, specially designed kamikaze piston-engine aircraft, the dreaded Ohka manned aerial bomb, air-to-air rockets, "I-go" guided air-to-surface missiles and specially designed aerial torpedoes that glided to their targets.

SPECIAL AERIAL WEAPONS

Fire Balloons

A captured Japanese fire balloon that was launched during the Fu-Go ("balloon bomb") campaign against the American and Canadian mainland in 1944–45 is seen in flight during US Army testing. A complete example can be seen at the Canadian War Museum in Ottawa, Ontario. (US Army)

During the last two years of World War II, the Japanese unleashed a largely ineffective fire balloon or Fu-Go ("balloon bomb") campaign against the American and Canadian mainland. The Fu-Go was essentially a hydrogen balloon that carried either one 33lb anti-personnel bomb, one 26lb incendiary bomb, or four 11lb incendiary devices. The Fu-Go offensive against North America represented an inexpensive means of attacking the civilian population of Japan's enemies by utilizing the jet stream high above the Pacific Ocean. War planners hoped that their fire balloons would heavily damage both American and Canadian metropolitan areas, forests and farmland, causing panic and terror among inhabitants.

Between late 1944 and April 1945, in excess of 9,300 fire balloons were launched by the Japanese, destined for North America. Only 300 of them reached their target, however, most falling prey to adverse weather conditions. Seven American citizens fell victims to the fire balloons, all of them losing their lives in one lone incident in the state of Oregon on May 5, 1945. Aside from this tragic loss of life, little damage was done by the Japanese fire balloons in the US.

Two fire balloon variants were developed by the Japanese. One was known as the "Type B Balloon," the brainchild of the IJNAF. It was made of rubberized silk, spanned 30ft in diameter and was the first fire balloon variant to be launched at North America. Some of these were also used to study weather patterns affecting the continent, and to gauge the chances of the "bombed-up" balloons reaching their intended targets. The other variant was the actual bomb-laden balloon, which spanned 33ft in diameter and contained 19,000 cu ft of hydrogen at the time of complete inflation. Fire balloons were launched from various sites along the east coast of Honshu, the main Japanese island.

Under the direction of Maj Gen Sueyoshi Kusaba, the Imperial Japanese Army's Ninth Army Number Nine Research Laboratory perfected the fire balloon concept. They were launched by Japan for the first time on November 3, 1944 and discovered in Alaska, Arizona, California, Colorado, Idaho, Iowa, Kansas, Michigan, Montana, Nebraska, Nevada, North Dakota, Oregon, South Dakota, Texas, Utah, Washington, Wyoming, Mexico and Canada. The last Japanese fire balloon was released at North America in April 1945. The seven victims of a single fire balloon were killed after encountering a landed balloon in the Gearhart Mountain forest in southern Oregon.[1]

Although they were largely ineffective, the Japanese fire balloons achieved a milestone in the history of modern warfare by participating in the longest-ranged raids ever mounted in the history of aerial warfare. This record remained intact until surpassed by the RAF's Operation *Black Buck* (Avro Vulcan bomber raids) attacks on the Falkland Islands during the conflict with Argentina in 1982. A complete Japanese fire balloon is presently on display at the Canadian War Museum in Ottawa, Ontario.

Nakajima Ki-115 Tsurugi

Anticipating the inevitable Allied invasion of Japan, the IJAAF instructed Nakajima on January 20, 1945 to develop a simple, inexpensive single-seat piston-engined aircraft to be used exclusively as a suicide or kamikaze weapon. The company responded with the creation of the Ki-115 Tsurugi ("Sabre"), which had all-metal wings, a fuselage made of steel and wooden, fabric-covered, tail surfaces. The non-retractable undercarriage, made of

Four Ki-115s were found by US occupation forces in Nakajima's No. 1 Plant at Ota, in Gunma Prefecture. All of them were shipped to the US, where they were technically evaluated by the USAAF at Wright Field in 1946. (*NARA*)

The crudeness of the Tsurugi's construction is plainly obvious from this photograph, the suicide aircraft featuring all-metal wings, a fuselage made of steel, and wooden, fabric-covered, tail surfaces. (NARA)

tubular steel, was to be jettisoned in flight as a weight saving measure. The Ki-115 was fitted with a 1,151hp Nakajima Ha-35 Type 23 radial engine, and provision was made for the fitting of two solid-fuel rocket units under each wing to boost the aircraft's performance in its final dive on Allied ships. The Tsurugi was capable of carrying a bomb of up to 1,764lb in size attached to a recessed crutch beneath the fuselage center-section.

Although the Ki-115 successfully performed its maiden flight in March 1945, and more than 100 had been built between March and August 1945, no Ki-115s ever participated in actual combat prior to the war ending.

Following the cessation of hostilities, four Ki-115s were captured by US occupation forces at Nakajima's No. 1 Plant at Ota, in Gunma Prefecture. All of these machines were shipped to the US and evaluated by USAAF personnel. They found the Ki-115 to possess "crude" instruments and controls, and to be generally a poor performer. Visibility was atrocious over the nose from its open cockpit and takeoffs and landings risky, unless undertaken by an experienced pilot. Nevertheless, USAAF evaluators agreed that had these aircraft been deployed in massed fleets, they might

This Ki-115 was displayed outside the USAF HQ building at Yokota Air Force Base until 1953, when it was transferred to the Japanese Aeronautical Association. Its present whereabouts remains unknown. (USAF)

have wreaked havoc on an Allied invasion fleet. Only one of these Ki-115s survived scrapping to be passed on to the Smithsonian Institution in 1949. Construction number 1002 was stored at Park Ridge until moved to "Silver Hill" in 1970, where it remained until loaned out to the Pima Air and Space Museum in Tucson, Arizona, in 2011.

A second Ki-115 was displayed outside the USAF HQ building at Yokota Air Force Base, Japan, until 1953, when it was transferred to the Japanese Aeronautical Association. Its present whereabouts remain unknown, however.

Only one of the four Ki-115s shipped to the US in 1945–46 survived being scrapped, and it was passed on to the Smithsonian Institution in 1949. Construction number 1002 was stored at Park Ridge until moved to "Silver Hill" in 1970, where it remained until loaned out to the Pima Air and Space Museum in Tucson, Arizona in 2011. (*Steve Ozel*)

Yokosuka MXY7 "Baka"

By the late summer of 1944, the Japanese cause in World War II had become so desperate that it resorted to the development of specialized suicide or kamikaze aircraft to repel Allied invasion fleets. The IJNAF requested the development of a rocket-powered, manned flying bomb that was to be air-launched from a G4M2e Model 24J "Betty" or other heavy bomber. This revolutionary weapon became known as the Yokosuka MXY7 Ohka ("Cherry Blossom"), which was given the Allied codename "Baka" ("Fool" or "Idiot") bomb. The Ohka, which was the brainchild of the 405th Kokutai's Ens Mitsuo Ohta and the University of Tokyo's Aeronautical Research Institute, successfully performed an unpowered (glide) flight in October 1944 and a successful powered flight the following month.

A detailed TAIC Intelligence Report captured the intriguing details of this revolutionary aerial weapon, and the grave threat it represented to the Allies:

***

SUMMARY

BAKA is a Japanese rocket propelled suicide aircraft bomb launched by a parent plane. Carrying a 2645lb. S.A.P. warhead, BAKA can attain a maximum level speed of 540mph for a minor portion of its flight and is capable of a horizontal range of 55 miles if released from 27,000ft. – the maximum service ceiling of a launching aircraft such as BETTY.

Allied Code Name – BAKA (Fool)

PERFORMANCE

In assessing the performance of BAKA, it must be borne in mind that this suicide weapon is first of all a glider and, secondarily, a powered plane.

Although the rockets greatly increase its speed for a short time, they cause only a slight range increase over its maximum glide range. The solid curve shows that the maximum horizontal range when released at 27,000ft. is 55 miles. Fifty-two of these miles would be traveled at a glide speed of 230mph and at a minimum glide angle of 5° 35'; during the remaining three miles, the use of rockets would accelerate the speed to 535mph in level flight. At a 50° or greater diving angle, terminal velocity will be 620mph with rockets. Without rocket power, the same speed would be reached at a diving angle of 88°–90°. Whether the rockets were used at the end of the run, or whether they were used to climb, would not

This MXY7 Ohka flying bomb was captured by the US Marine Corps at Yontan airfield on Okinawa following the invasion of the island on April 1, 1945. It was one of more than ten examples that were hastily shipped back to the US to undergo technical evaluation as the Allies strived to find the best way to defeat the potentially deadly aerial weapon. This particular Ohka survived to be put on display at the US Marine Corps Air-Ground Museum in Quantico, Virginia. (NARA)

appreciably affect the maximum range. However, under certain circumstances, it is possible to have an increase in BAKA's horizontal range while using rocket propulsion. The conditions necessary for this increase are as follows:

1. **Lower airspeeds** at which minimum drag would be commensurate with maximum rocket duration. This could occur at
2. **Very low ambient temperatures**, which would necessitate
3. **Firing of rockets** at high altitudes immediately after release from the parent aircraft. This could increase the maximum range to 60 miles.

Against ships, the rockets will presumably be used at the end of the run in a torpedo approach in an attempt to score a hit close to the water line. If launched from a distance, however, BAKA would be vulnerable to attack by fighters before reaching a position to complete effectively its own attack. Lacking maneuverability, BAKA could take but little evasive action in its unpowered glide, and its only method of escape would be to fire one or more of its rockets. In this event, the increased velocity secured from the rocket would partially dissipate before BAKA could reach its target and its final terminal velocity would be substantially decreased.

The destruction of the parent aircraft is extremely important inasmuch as special fuselage modifications are undoubtedly necessary, and the available supply of adaptable parent aircraft controls the number of BAKAs that can be launched.

From range graph the estimated range of BAKA when launched from any determined altitude can be found. The speed curve shows estimated impact speed at varying diving angles both with rocket

As part of the TAIU-SWPA's analysis of the Yontan Ohkas, this example was adorned with tape that allowed the flying bomb to be measured when photographed. Sub-assemblies from two other MXY7s can be seen in front of and behind the subject aircraft. (*NARA*)

BETTY-22

This three-view schematic of a G4M2 "Betty 22" carrying a "Baka" flying bomb was also included in the TAIC report on the MXY7. (*NARA*)

power and without. Although all BAKAs have fuselage rockets, one variation has been found with provision for two additional rocket units under the wing. The performance curves have been computed on the basis of power being applied only by fuselage rockets. The additional drag caused by the mounting of wing units would almost offset their extra propulsive thrust and only increase the horizontal range approximately two miles from 27,000ft. without materially affecting the speed.

In the "Speeds at Impact" chart, it has been assumed that a typical attack would consist of, first, a glide to sea level and then a level run under rocket power.

POSSIBLE LAUNCHERS OF BAKA

In addition to BETTY, the following aircraft are believed to be suitable for launching BAKA or could be made satisfactory without major modifications:

PEGGY 1	Satisfactory. May need extended tail wheel.
HELEN 2	Possible. Would need longer tail wheel assembly or cut in bomb-bay for horizontal stabilizer. (A recent report indicates that BAKA may also have been launched from HELEN).
SALLY 2	Possible. Would need extended (back) bomb-bay and longer tail wheel assembly.
TAIZAN	16 Exp. Land Attack Plane. Expected successor to BETTY and could undoubtedly be used. May be in limited production.
RITA 11	Possibly more than one BAKA.
FRANCES 11	May carry modified version of BAKA.

CONSTRUCTION DETAILS

BAKA is constructed in the following five major assemblies:

1. Warhead and warhead fairing
2. Central fuselage
3. Wings
4. Tail Unit
5. Rocket Installation

BAKA

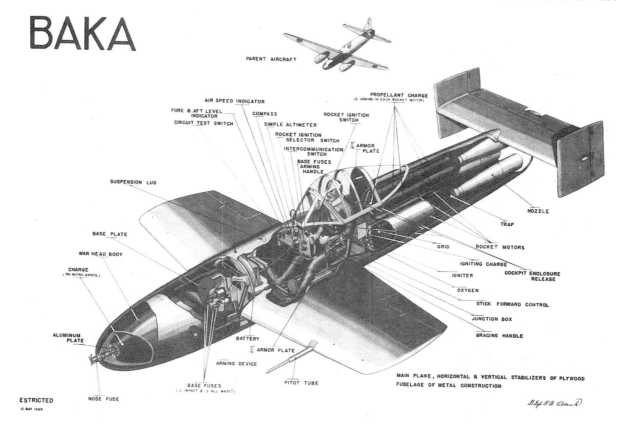

PARENT AIRCRAFT

PROPELLANT CHARGE
(6 GRAINS IN EACH ROCKET MOTOR)

AIR SPEED INDICATOR

FORE & AFT LEVEL
INDICATOR
CIRCUIT TEST SWITCH

COMPASS

SIMPLE ALTIMETER

ROCKET IGNITION
SELECTOR SWITCH

ROCKET IGNITION
SWITCH

INTERCOMMUNICATION
SWITCH

ARMOR
PLATE

BASE FUSES
ARMING
HANDLE

NOZZLE

SUSPENSION LUG

TRAP

GRID

ROCKET MOTORS

BASE PLATE

WAR HEAD BODY

IGNITING CHARGE

IGNITER

COCKPIT ENCLOSURE
RELEASE

CHARGE
(TRI NITRO ANISOL)

OXYGEN

STICK FORWARD CONTROL

JUNCTION BOX

ALUMINUM
PLATE

BRACING HANDLE

BATTERY

ARMOR PLATE

ARMING DEVICE

PITOT TUBE

MAIN PLANE, HORIZONTAL & VERTICAL STABILIZERS OF PLYWOOD
FUSELAGE OF METAL CONSTRUCTION

ESTRICTED
10 MAY 1945

NOSE FUSE

BASE FUSES
(2 IMPACT & 3 "ALL WAYS")

Warhead and Fairing

Characteristics of Warhead

Total weight – 2645lb.

Length – 68 3/8 in.

Diameter – 23 5/8 in.

The warhead of BAKA shown in cross section in Fig. 6 resembles that of a torpedo but is made specifically for this installation. It consists of the body, base plate, explosive filling, a cushion plate, and five fuzes. Although tests have not yet been completed, the US Naval Proving Grounds (Dahlgren, VA) states that the warhead will probably not be detonated by gunfire.

Body

The body is made in one piece machined from a forging. Wall thickness varies from 13/16 inches to 2 1/2 inches. The first 5 7/16 inches of the nose is solid. A hole in the nose is made with standard nose fuze threads and a set screw is provided to lock the fuze in place after assembly. The internal surfaces of the body and

Working from detailed photographs and a written description of the Yontan Ohkas, TAIC artist SSgt R. B. Aldrich created this cutaway drawing of a "Baka" – and its "Betty" bomber mother aircraft – in May 1945. The artwork was a key component of the intelligence report on the flying bomb that was supplied to front-line units in the Pacific Theater during the final months of the war. (*NARA*)

base plate are heavily lacquered to prevent contact between the explosive filling and the bare metal; standard practice on Japanese bombs. External coloring is the same as that used on Navy general purpose bombs: Green nose, brown band, and blue-gray body color.

Section Thru Warhead

Base Plate

The warhead is attached to a tubular framework on the forward bulkhead of the central fuselage. The lugs on the base plate are machined from the parent forging and are fitted with four 3/4 inch bolts. The base plate is screwed into the body and locked by a set screw. A raised boss on the plate contains four equally spaced fuze cavities for the base fuzes and a threaded hole for the arming device.

Cushion Plate

An aluminum plate 1 3/8 inches thick is placed in the front end of the body. This is believed to act as a cushion and prevent the detonation of the explosive by the shock of impact. A similar aluminum plug is found in the 800kg Japanese Navy armor piercing bomb.

Explosive

The explosive filling is trinitroanisol (Japanese Type 91 explosive), which has about the same power and sensitivity as TNT. It is one of the common Japanese Navy bomb fillings. The explosive is poured into the body in a liquid form and solidifies as it cools. A document indicates that it is poured in three successive increments in the nose section and a single pouring fills the cylindrical section of the body. The recess of the base plate is filled separately and sealed with wax before it is assembled to the body. Picric "surrounds" are placed around the gaines recesses in the base plate filling to serve as boosters.

Nose Fuze

The nose fuze is a slight variation of the standard A-3(d) which is one of the common nose fuzes used in large Japanese Navy bombs. This fuze does not have the nose cap or starting wire usually found on the A-3(d) and the body is made of plated steel instead of brass. The brass shear wire is replaced by a heavy steel shear pin. It is possible that this simplified design will become the standard form of the A-3(d).

Arming is accomplished by the rotation of the vanes. This screws the spindle sleeve forward to the limit of its travel and upon impact the sleeve and spindle are driven in, breaking the shear pin and allowing the striker to stab the primer. Before BAKA is released, the arming vanes are prevented from rotating by an arming wire. The wire is attached permanently to the parent plane and hooked through the hole in one of the arming vanes. Upon release the wire is automatically pulled out of the vane which is then free to rotate. Gaines are used in both nose and tail fuzes and are made with delays ranging from instantaneous to 1.5 seconds. The gaine with the desired delay is screwed into the pistol before it is assembled to the warhead.

Fairing

The nose section of the warhead fairing, which is about two feet in length, is of monocoque welded construction, while the remainder – to which the nose section is flush rivetted – is of semi-monocoque construction and also flush rivetted. Aluminum alloy is used throughout. Fairing is attached to the main fuselage section at eight points of support on the first frame.

Central Fuselage

The main, and central, section of the fuselage incorporates the cockpit and pilot controls, instrument panel, rocket tubes, armor plating, battery and mountings for the wing and warhead.

Of aluminum alloy, semi-monocoque construction, this section is of four-longeron design, with bent up angle section stiffeners. There are seven bent angle strengtheners spaced 5 3/4" and bent up hat-sections and zees spaced about 11" apart are used for the frames.

A fifth hat-section at 12 o'clock which is interrupted by the cockpit and between the bead sight and suspension lug is in effect a false longeron. This is used as a stiffener and a support for the No. 3 (upper) rocket tube aft, and as a stiffener forward of the cockpit.

The fuselage skin is of .025" – .040" thickness. Flush rivets are used throughout except for a section in the region of the empennage.

Double concave sheets are employed extensively and are often of large size. Clad duralumin sheets are used similar to 24 SRT clad.

A mounting for the warhead is provided at the front end of the center fuselage section. This is built

The TAIC also created this two-view schematic of the G8N "Rita" carrying a "Baka" flying bomb, even though Nakajima never test flew the bomber with the MXY7. The IJNAF had indeed ordered the company to make the Tenzan Ohka-compatible. (NARA)

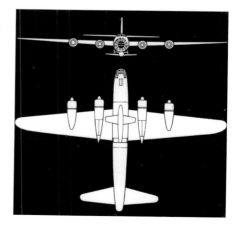

As part of the "Baka" report created by TAIC, evaluators looked into the flying bomb's areas of vulnerability. The key zones were then identified in these artworks, which were studied by ships' gunnery officers and Allied fighter pilots alike. (*NARA*)

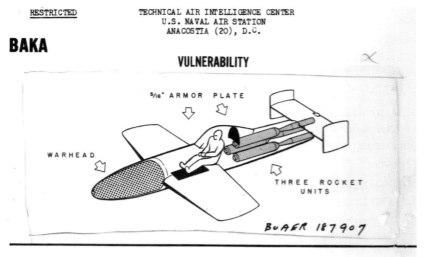

PROTECTION AFFORDED PILOT BY WARHEAD AND ARMOR PLATE ON FLOOR
¾-front view from below

PROTECTION AFFORDED PILOT BY BACK ARMOR PLATE AND THE ROCKET UNITS
¾-rear view from above

of welded steel tubes of 1.75" and 2.00" O.D. and machined steel fittings, and ties into the four longerons. Four warhead support points are provided.

A conventional type Plexiglas canopy encloses the cockpit and the center sliding hood is fitted with four quick-release latches for jettisoning, although the jettison arrangement has been neither complete nor serviceable as such on any models examined to date. The windscreen is of straightforward angular design with plain glass panels.

Aft of the cockpit, on the bottom of the center fuselage section, twin-rail type supports are fitted for the support of two of the rocket units. The third rocket unit is suspended from the top by two lugs on the fifth (false) longeron. Further steadying brackets are provided.

Immediately aft of the pilot's seat, a thin aluminum alloy staggered bulkhead, with three asbestos-fringed holes is installed, and the entire fuselage aft of this is occupied by the rocket units and rocket venturis.

The pilot's seat is of the bucket type with a plywood back. Armor protection is provided underneath and to the rear (see Armor). The suspension lug that attaches BAKA to its launching parent plane is 7' 8 1/2" of the nose, midway between the ring and bead sights.

The control surfaces of BAKA are operated by a standard joystick (mounting a switch for firing the rockets) and a foot rudder bar. Provision is made to lock all controls while being carried, and a spring tension regulator is installed for assistance in holding the joystick forward when free. Cables are used for rudder control and a combination of cables and push-pull tubes for the ailerons and elevators.

Wings

Of wood, incorporating high density wood beams at approximately the 20% and 50% chord points. The leading edge is of five-ply wood held in shape by ribs with approximately 12" spacing, and the trailing edge is of similar construction. The ailerons are also of wood, mass balanced, push-pull controlled, with leading edges normal to the longitudinal axis. This results in a narrow chord at the tip and a wide chord inboard (with recesses to take the balance weights into the undersurface). All plywood surfaces are fabric covered.

The complete wing assembly is recessed at the center section and bolted to brackets on the front fuselage frames. The wing supports are not integral with the warhead mounting. An electrically heated pitot tube is fitted to the port wing.

Rocket Motor

Results to date are summarized as follows:

At temperatures between -40°F and 5°F "chuffing" resulted, that is, propellant burned in cyclic bursts.

In a full scale motor at 63°F burning was continuous.

In a 1/6 scale motor at 104°F a slight chuff resulted toward the end of the burning period; it is expected, however, that in the full scale motor, burning would be continuous, or nearly so, between 63°F and 104°F.

Tests are continuing in the range between 5°F and 63°F.

Time of burning varied considerably with temperature, being 30 secs. at -40°F and about 9 sec. at 104°F.

Throughout the range of temperatures mentioned, integrated impulse (Thrust in lbs. x time in sec.) is fairly constant, the range being about 13,000 to 15,000lb. sec. (full scale motor).

The full scale motor tested at 63°F gave an average thrust of 1,500lbs., maximum thrust of 4,500lbs., duration 9.7 sec. and an integrated impulse of 14,600lbs. sec. These figures correspond closely to those given in PACMIRS DOC. No. 1641 which relates to BAKA.

Pressures, in general, are quite low compared to other powders, the average pressure at 104°F being only 154 lbs/sq."

Propellant

Each fuselage and wing rocket is charged with six grains of "500 special FDT-6" powder having the following physical characteristics:

Length of grain	500mm (19.6")
Outside diam.	110mm (4.3")
Diam. of single axial perforation	10mm (.39)
Weight	7.4kg. (16.2lbs.)
Chemical analysis is as follows:	
Nitro Glycerine	26.9%
Nitro Cellulose	59.9%
(11.54% Nitrogen)	
Graphite	Nil
Ash	2.8%
Potassium Sulphate	2.9%
Ethyl Centralite	2.9%
Alpha Nitro Naphthalene	6.1%
Di Nitro Naphthalene	Trace
Total Volatiles	1.3%
Heat of Explosion	820 cal/g

The following information is extracted verbatim from a technical analysis of the fuselage rockets:

"Observation of the small scale firing showed that the gases were not cooled sufficiently by expansion to prevent secondary combustion. The flame, however, was not very strongly luminous. A moderate amount of gray smoke is produced. The use of the smoke and flash patterns observed from the ground as identifying characteristics would not be reasonable since the high velocity of BAKA would modify them greatly. Flash might be useful at night, but the smoke would be dispersed over a long distance and would probably be of very low visibility in the daytime. This unit is evidence for the existence of a well-trained, able rocket engineering group in Japan. While it evidently does not have the advantage of some of our designs for similar purposes, it is a well-engineered rocket device."

EQUIPMENT
Armament

None

Armor

The pilot's seat is of the bucket type with a plywood back. Above it and to the rear, a single flat piece of armor plate 1' 2 1/2" high, by 1' 6 3/4" wide at the base, by 5/16" thick, is fitted to protect the head and shoulders. Two additional pieces of armor plate are installed in the bottom of the cockpit extending from a position even with the front end of the pilot's seat to the bulkhead just forward of the rudder bar. The forward piece measures 15 7/8" long and the aft piece 9 5/16" long, both are 12 3/16" wide by 5/16" thick.

There is an opening in the after plate (approx. 5" x 3.5") for movement of the control stick.

Weights of armor pieces are as follows:

Head and Shoulder	21lbs.
Bottom Fuselage – Forward	18.5lbs.
Bottom Fuselage – Aft	11lbs.

This Ohka 22 was found in the Dai-Ichi Kaigun Koku-Gijitsusho factory in Yokosuka after VJ Day. This improved version of the flying bomb had been built specifically for carriage by the P1Y1 Ginga fast bomber. Its wingspan was reduced because of the limited clearance provided by the P1Y1 in comparison with the G4M2, the Ohka 22 also having a smaller 1,323lb warhead. Finally, the new variant was fitted with a Tsu-11 jet engine so that the flying bomb could be launched further from its target, thus reducing the P1Y1's vulnerability to enemy fighters. Just 50 Ohka 22s had been built by war's end. (NARA)

VULNERABILITY OF BAKA AGAINST VECTORED FIGHTER (VF) ATTACK

Although the armor effectiveness is good at the ranges and speeds shown below, all bullets should defeat the armor installation, providing the bullet initially passes through only the glass cockpit covering, or dural, but not heavier surfaces.

All estimates are based on firing .50 cal. A.P. projectiles with a muzzle velocity of 2,750 f.p.s. from a Browning type gun with the VF chasing BAKA.

VF Speed	Alt. (feet)	Range (yards)	BAKA Speed
400mph	S.L.	550	200mph
	5,000	650	(powerless glide)
	10,000	750	
	20,000	1000	
400mph	S.L.	450	300mph
	5,000	500	
	10,000	600	
	20,000	800	

INSTRUMENTS

A small shock-mounted instrument panel forward of the pilot's seat includes, reading from the left and from top to bottom:

Intercommunication Switch and Lights
Rocket Ignition Selector Switch
Altimeter (Model 3 Simple Aneroid; Limits 0–8,000 meters)
Compass and Deviation Card (Navy Model 12 Type 92 used in ZEKE 52)
Air Speed Indicator (Model 6. 0–600 knots)
Turn and Bank Indicator (Not installed)
Fore and Aft Indicator (Model 2 inclinometer +5° to -25°
Card Holder – empty
Circuit Test Switch

Above the instrument panel and offset slightly to the left is a pull handle for arming the warhead base fuzes.

Below panel and to the right a small electric horn is installed as part of an intercommunication system. Communication between the BAKA pilot and the parent aircraft is possible only before launching, since there is no radio gear. This communication system comprises a horn by which the BAKA pilot may audibly receive code messages, with a push button for sending dot-dash in a similar

Another view of an Ohka 22, this time taken in a hangar at Yokosuka with an Ohka 11 and two J8M1s Shusui rocket-powered interceptors in the background. All of these machines were later shipped to the US for evaluation. (*NARA*)

manner to the parent aircraft, and a light is provided so that the BAKA pilot may visually observe his message being sent. A Gosport speaking tube has also been fitted. After launching, the electrical circuits and speaking tube connections are broken and no further communication is possible.

At pilot's left hand is the control stick spring tension regulator. To the left of this, and below, are two switches; the left one is the main circuit cut-out, while the right-hand one, when closed, completes a 12-volt circuit to a two-prong detachable socket mounted in a rib near the left rudder bar. The intended purpose of this plug is unknown. A light is included in the circuit to indicate when it is closed. The only other electrical circuit is the ignition circuit, discussed under the heading "Method of Ignition."

LANDING GEAR
No landing gear or skids are fitted.

PORTABLE OXYGEN BOTTLE
Although TAIC examination has not revealed a connection between BAKA and the oxygen system of the parent plane, a portable walkaround oxygen bottle which can be strapped to the suicide pilot has been located. The bottle bears the following information:

Weight	1.83kg. (4lbs.)
Volume	1.02 liters (72.2 cu.in.)
Pressure	150 atmospheres (2,130lbs/sq.in.)
Estimated Endurance	
Altitude	Duration
19,680ft.	28.2min.
26,240ft.	25.4min.

SIGHTS

Ring and bead sights are mounted forward of the cockpit; the ring sight immediately forward of windshield and the bead sight 2' 5 1/4" forward of the ring sight; instructions for their adjustment are stenciled on the outside of the fuselage. The sighting is parallel with the axis of BAKA.

TRANSPORTING DOLLY

The tricycle hydraulic dolly used both for transporting BAKA and for raising it into position in the parent aircraft.

SPECIFICATIONS

Weight Analysis

Fuselage with Fairing	71.5lbs.
Wing	367
Tail	120.5
Nose Fairing	40
Sub-total	5,999 lbs.
Warhead	2,645lbs.
Rocket Unit	768lbs.
Pilot	120lbs.
Oxygen bottle	4lbs.
TOTAL	4,136lbs.

Dimensions

Wing Span	16' 5"
Length	19' 10" (less nose fuze)
Span, Tail Plane	7' 1"
Wing Area	64.7 sq. ft.
Aileron Area (both ailerons)	3.2 sq. ft.
Wing loading	Approx. 70.2 lbs/sq. ft.
Max. height fuselage, nose sect.	2' 6 1/2"
Max. height fuselage including canopy	3' 10 1/4"
Max. height fuselage, tail section	2' 3 3/4"

MODEL/TYPE SYMBOL

The "Model/Type Symbol" for BAKA appears to be MXY7. It is known that "M" is the Japanese Navy's designation for "Special Aircraft" and the letter "X" stands for research or experimental.

"Y" is the manufacturer's symbol, namely Air Technical Depot at Yokosuka and the number "7" stands for the seventh modification to the aircraft. A previous reference has been made to an "MXY3 Glider." It now seems that BAKA has gone through considerable experimentation and MXY3 was probably an earlier prototype.

TENTATIVE ASSESSMENT

BAKA is so constructed that it seems possible for various designs of wings to be fitted to the one basic design fuselage. This presents several development possibilities.

A. Attaching alternative warheads, or even an engine to the basic combined wing and warhead strongpoints.

B. Versions such as deck launching gliders, land based gliders or training gliders may be in existence or projected for the future. The flexibility of the structural and control design would lend itself to such variations.

C. A jet unit similar to the "V-1 robomb" launched from land or ship deck ramps by rockets or by a parent aircraft. BAKA in its present form does not seem adaptable for this usage but a modification impulse jet version is a strong possibility.

D. Remote control rocket equipment comparable to the Hs 117 or Hs 293 and later developed German guided missiles. The same manufacturing facilities that produce BAKA could be utilized for these missiles.

E. A liquid rocket unit such as the Me 163.[2]

An Okha 43 K-1 flying bomb trainer glider, with anti-corrosion coating applied, has been lashed down to the flightdeck of the escort carrier *Core* ready for shipment to the US. Christened the Wakazakura ("Young Cherry") by the IJNAF, the Okha 43 K-1 had the warhead replaced by a second cockpit and the addition of flaps and a retractable skid for landing. Only 45 Okha 43 K-1s (both single- and two-seat versions) were built. Note the Ki-67 "Peggy" bomber parked in the background. (*US Navy, Naval History and Heritage Command*)

There are four Ohkas displayed in museums in Britain, at least one of which was shipped back from Seletar in April 1946 for evaluation by the Royal Aircraft Establishment at Farnborough. This particular MXY7 has been a part of the RAF Museum Cosford collection for many years. (*Arjun Sarup*)

This single-seat Okha 43 K-1 was brought back to the US for evaluation post war. Its landing skid can clearly been seen here in the extended position. The K-1 carried water ballast in place of the warhead and rocket motors of the operational Ohka 11, and this had to be expelled before landing. Nevertheless, the K-1's high landing speed of 130mph challenged the novice pilots charged with flying it. This particular K-1 is displayed at the National Museum of the US Air Force in Dayton, Ohio. (*Arjun Sarup*)

✳ ✳ ✳

The MXY7 Ohka made its combat debut during the US invasion of Okinawa, examples being air-launched via "Betty" bombers at US Navy vessels with the intention of sinking or badly damaging as many capital warships as possible. While the Ohkas were successful in sinking several destroyers and badly damaging a minesweeper, they failed to score any hits on capital warships due to the US Navy's timely application of defensive measures, including the proper deployment of vectored carrier fighter aircraft to intercept and shoot down the "Betty" parent aircraft carrying the Ohkas, and the proper deployment of picket destroyers that put up a barrage of anti-aircraft fire, preventing the rocket-propelled suicide aircraft from scoring direct hits on US aircraft carriers, battleships, or cruisers.

On April 12, 1945, nine "Betty" bombers launched a successful Ohka attack on the US fleet off Okinawa, sinking the destroyer USS *Mannert L. Abele* (DD-733) and causing so much damage to the destroyer USS *Jeffers* (DD-621) that it was put out of commission. On

d. Only one control could be applied at one time.

e. A control box with a stick was used.

2. Receiver:

a. The receiver used amplitude modulation and had the following control frequencies:

(1) Up	3,000
(2) Down	2,600
(3) Right	2,200
(4) Left	1,800

b. There were 220 receivers built of which 100 were dropped, and the rest destroyed.

c. Control was achieved by electrically shifting the gyro centering point which caused the servos to move the missile until the gyro centered again.

d. The batteries which operated the receiver consisted of 24 cells linked in series, 12 to a bank, and the two banks connected in parallel.

(1) From 30 minutes to 3 hours after filling the battery, the no load voltage was 27 to 29 volts. With a load of four to six amps, the voltage was 24 to 26 volts. The useful life of the battery was five minutes.

D. Motor and Fuel System:

1. The jet motor was designed by the Mitsubishi engine laboratory at KYOTO and delivered ten ton-second thrust using hydrogen peroxide and a catalyst.

2. The fuel system was as follows:

a. Compressed air at 150 kg/cm^2 (206 lbs/in^2) stored in a 26.8 (.95 cu ft) liter tank for forcing H_2O_2 and catalyst into the motor.

b. Two needle valves, electrically operated, admitted air from the tank to a reducing valve. Two valves were used to ensure operation in case of the failure of one.

c. From the reducing valve, a line ran to the H_2O_2 tank and the catalyst tank.

d. The H_2O_2 tank was made of steel and plated on the inside with tin. The tank was cylindrical in shape with hemispherical ends. The capacity was 83.7 liters (22 gal).

e. The catalyst tank was spherical and of the same construction as the H_2O_2 tank. The capacity of this tank was 5.4 liters (1.4 gal).

f. All lines were of dural.

3. Operation:

a. The air was turned on, pressurizing the system and forcing the H_2O_2 and the catalyst to the motor.

b. A flow of H_2O_2 was started before the flow of catalyst to prevent possible flow of the catalyst back up in the H_2O_2 lines.

c. The H_2O_2 sprayed out through holes around the periphery of the back end of the motor and impinged on a baffle plate mounted in the combustion chamber of the motor. Guide vanes had been used previously but were abandoned in favor of the baffle plate arrangement.

d. The catalyst was sprayed from holes in the center of the ring of H_2O_2 holes. Striking the baffle plate, the two combined.

e. A Level type nozzle completed the motor.

f. The amount of fuel listed was sufficient to give a thrust of 150kg (330lbs) for 80 seconds.

II. General Remarks:

A. Although the system of control is inferior, in general, to American designs, the fact that this missile was designed, built, and tested within four months is remarkable and indicates a close organization between the Army and the contractors.

B. The elimination of rate gyros and the use of electrical damping is of interest.

C. The people concerned were emphatic in their assertions that no information on German guided missiles was ever made available to them.

D. Future work in this field was to have included the installation of radar seekers, etc. One project to have been studied was that of launching missiles from the ground to attack enemy installations. It is interesting to note that both the Germans and the Japanese turned to this type of warfare after the destruction of their air forces. Apparently the Japanese learned nothing from the Germans in this respect since at the close of the war, no work had been started on a V-1 type missile.

E. Originally the "I-go" incorporated a radio altimeter to skim at a fixed height above the ground. This did not work, however, and was removed.

F. Complete wind tunnel tests on full, and one half scale models of "I-go" were run. These tunnel tests including tunnel tests of the missile attached to the mother plane (Ki-48) are being translated and will be included in this report as an appendix when available.[6]

Airborne Anti-Submarine Circling Torpedo

Another highly innovative aerial weapon developed by the Japanese during World War II was the Airborne Anti-Submarine Circling Torpedo. Interesting facts concerning this aerial weapon were revealed in a post-war ATIG report that documented an interview, conducted on November 16, 1945, between former IJN officer Lt Cdr Takeda Niiro and the ATIG's Lt E. G. Oxton:

Summary: From April to December 1944, the Japanese Navy was developing and testing a winged, anti-submarine torpedo containing a 220-lb. charge and designed to be dropped from 327ft. (100m), assume a linear trajectory with a glide ratio of approximately three-to-one, enter the water, and spiral downward describing circles 260ft. (80m) in diameter spaced at depths of 260ft.

Test drops showed such instability in flight that it was concluded that a gyroscope stabilization system was necessary but no research was done on the weapon after the end of 1944.

Designation: Air Torpedo No. 6.

Weight: 597lbs. (270kg)

Description: Except for a metal nose section, to take the force of impact, and two small wing braces, the entire torpedo was made of wood.

Wings and rudder were glued to the wooden torpedo case. Wings remained attached until detonation.

The case was constructed of interlocking spirals of wooden strips 3.3 inches (13mm) thick.

Guiding System: Rudder was fixed at eight degrees, causing torpedo to circle counterclockwise in 260ft. circles. It sank because of its specific gravity of 1.4. To prevent the eight-degree rudder displacement from affecting flight, the rudder was covered by a hollow fairing between the torpedo body and tailplane. This hollowed section of fairing was attached by means of an aluminum pin which was sheared at impact, unsheathing the rudder.

Propulsion: None. The weapon was unpowered both in flight and in the water.

Warhead: 220lbs. (100kg) explosive charge 98.

Fuzing: It was planned to use a magnetic proximity fuze, but its development was a separate project on which research was incomplete.

Arming: Fuze was to be air armed by a vane which would be allowed to spin when arming wire was pulled.

Aiming: Visual. No sighting device used.

Parent Plane: Torpedo bomber TENZAN (JILL 11 or 12) with a capacity of one torpedo.

Launching: Standard torpedo racks were used; no modifications necessary.

Tests and Operational Use: Forty drops were made to test the torpedo's stability in flight. Fifteen of the forty tumbled or spun in. Wing width was reduced to four feet, and the dihedral was increased from 15 to 20 degrees. These modifications helped somewhat, but stability was still unsatisfactory.

"Many" rudderless torpedoes were dropped over the side of a boat to test the rate of descent in water. The specimens traveled at five to six knots in a dive of 17 degrees. A recorder was attached to indicate rate and angle of descent. The recorder was especially built but operated on the same principles as recorders used on regular torpedo tests. There was no good method of recording the circle traveled by torpedoes dropped with rudders.

Limitations: Maximum pressure the torpedo can withstand is that at a depth of 327ft. (100m).

Manufacture and Production Data: 100 of the missiles were made. The First Technical Arsenal at YOKOSUKA made all iron parts and the wooden rudder. The wooden torpedo case and wings were made by the Marunimoko Co. in FUTSUKAISHI, Hirsohima Prefecture.

Development Agency and Key Personnel: Research on the project was under the supervision of Commander FUKUBA of the First Technical Arsenal Branch at KANAZAWA.

Lt. Comdr. NIIRO, 28 Gazembo, TOKYO, the officer interviewed, had the liaison mission between the Naval Air Arm and Commander FUKUBA. NIIRO was a torpedo engineer at the Kure Naval Base from February 1941 to January 1944. He is a Navy regular with ten (10) years service.

CONCLUSION OF INTERVIEWING OFFICER: Knowledge of the attempt at such a weapon by the Japanese is of value at least for

USAAF and Navy Intelligence records. Its value to our research on similar missiles requires further investigation.

RECOMMENDATIONS: Samples forwarded to the US require further study for a true evaluation of the weapon.

EQUIPMENT, LOCATION AND DISPOSITION: Technical Air Intelligence Unit acquired, crated, and listed two mock-ups of the airborne anti-sub circling torpedo. These were contained in boxes M3 and M3A shipped from YOKOSUKA aboard the USS Barnes, marked for the Technical Air Intelligence Center, NAS, Anacostia, D.C.[7]

Aerial Heat Homing Bomb

Yet another highly innovative aerial weapon developed by the Japanese was the Aerial Heat Homing, or Infra-Red Bomb. Interesting facts concerning this aerial weapon were revealed in a post-war ATIG report that documented an interview, conducted on December 12, 1945, between former IJA Maj Tetsuo Shirakura, Army Ordnance HQ, Capt Takeo Akiba, 1st Army Technical Laboratory, and the ATIG's Lt Ernest G. Oxton and Mr. H. H. Moore, US Naval Technical Mission to Japan:

***

BRIEF OF MATERIAL DISCUSSED:

The fuzing system of the heat homing bomb, KEGO, consisted of four air-armed initiating trains, two instantaneous for deck impact and two with 0.3- to 0.5-second delay for underwater explosion.

The two instantaneous initiating trains fired one booster located in the rear of the main explosive charge, and each of the two delay trains fired its own booster, similarly located.

Material discussed included the operation of the fuzing system, composition of explosive trains, and research leading to the modifications of the standard fuzes used.

CONCLUSION OF INTERVIEWING OFFICER: Fuzing system looks good on paper but is difficult to evaluate because no heat-homing missile with live charge was tested against a solid target.

RECOMMENDATIONS: Similar dual detonating systems, including water discriminating, simple, shear pin type fuze should be studied for use in VB and VB-6.

EQUIPMENT, LOCATION, AND DISPOSITION: All of the fuzes were claimed by officers interviewed to have been destroyed. No samples have yet been found.

APPENDIX "A"
Detailed Description

Arming: Firing pins of the two initiating trains to the instantaneous booster protruded beyond the heat seeking nose and were armed by means of vanes which were spun off three to five seconds after the arming wire was pulled, assuming a wind velocity of 40 meters per second (131ft/sec).

The two delay fuzes were armed by means of Robinson cup anemometers which extended into the wind stream on the dorsal and ventral surfaces.

(NOTE: Because of language difficulties these Robinson cup anemometers were referred to as "Robinson Couples" in the overall report on KEGO, the Japanese Heat Homing Bomb, ATIG report no. 146.)

Operation: The delay fuzes for underwater explosion were standard Model 4 (1944) which had been modified by the addition of a 0.3- to 0.5-second, pressed black powder delay. Primer, detonator, and booster were all self-contained in the two fuzes which were located in the tail of the main charge.

Water discriminating initiators for instantaneous explosion at deck impact were made from standard Model 12 (1933) fuzes modified with an iron shear pin to hold the firing pin away from the primer. This shear pin had an experimentally determined diameter, 1.2mm (.472in.), such that water impact would not fire the fuze but the greater force of impact with a deck would cause instantaneous detonation in the following manner:

Firing pin would shear the shear pin and strike the mercury fulminate primer (Raikoo) which exploded, setting off a detonating mixture (Boofun) of antimony sulphide. This mixture in turn fired a booster (Melayaku) of tetra nitro methyl aniline which set off a detonating cord (Syoei) with a burning rate of 4,000 to 5,000 meters per second (4,400 to 5,500ft/sec). Each of the two initiators was connected by a detonating cord to the middle booster in the tail of the main charge. The detonating cord entering the main charge first set off another tetra nitro aniline booster which fired a charge of molded picric acid (1st Tanooyaku), and that finally exploded the main charge of picric acid.

Tests: Tail fuze was tested and found satisfactory on 10kg (22lb) bombs and on live heat seeking missiles (uncontrolled) dropped into the water 20 or 30 miles off the coast of HAMAMATSU.

Shear pins of various diameters were tested for the instantaneous fuze. 19kg (42lb) test shells were fitted with test fuzes and fired from a 120mm (4.7in) mortar. Specifications for the pin required that it shear at terminal velocities of not more than 100 meters per second (327ft/sec) upon ground impact and not less than 200 meters per second (654ft/sec) upon water impact.

Key Personnel: Capt. Takeo AKIBA, 899 3 Cho-me, Setagaya-Ku, TOKYO, an engineering graduate of Tokyo Imperial University in 1942; assigned to fuze Section, First Army Technical Laboratory.

Maj. Tetsuo SHIRAKURA, 3629 Nerima-Minimachi-2 Itabashi-Ku, TOKYO, graduated from the Tokyo Military Academy in 1937; assigned to Army Ordnance Headquarters.[8]

CHAPTER 8

WHAT WAS GAINED FROM THE EVALUATIONS

A rare color view of the assorted IJNAF fighter aircraft (most of which are wearing 302nd Kokutai tail codes) abandoned at Atsugi in September 1945. Amongst the A6M5/7s and J2M3s are P1Y2-S Kyokko and J1N1 Gekko twin-engined nightfighters. (*Donald Nijboer collection*)

It is quite clear that the Allies gained much from the evaluation of captured Japanese aircraft and aerial weapon systems, gauging the strengths and weaknesses of IJAAF and IJNAF types, as well as aerial weapons. The technical evaluations enabled the Allies to develop tactics for combating and defeating Japanese aerial threats. They also provided a valuable insight into Japanese aircraft and aerial weapon design philosophy and manufacturing practices. Finally, the study of captured aircraft and aerial weapon systems provided the Allies with a metric against which to gauge the state of Japanese aeronautics, and technological development and advancement during World War II.

The results of this exhaustive evaluation was summed up in a USAAF Air Technical Intelligence Review Report entitled "Description of Experimental Aircraft and Experimental Engines under Development by the Japanese Army and the Imperial Japanese Navy," published in July 1946:

✳✳✳

In the case of the Army experimental aircraft it will be noted in Appendix I that the greater portion of development work was being concentrated on fighter types. The range of maximum speeds and critical altitudes for the experimental fighters is considerably lower than those under development by the AAF, even when the Japanese versions of the Me-163 and Me-262 are considered. Wing loadings for army fighters are also below the range now considered practical by AAF. The experimental bombers under development by the Army are of interest in that only one four-engine aircraft was being developed.

The most modern heavy bombers were under development by the Navy. Improving the reliability and performance of the Ki-84, Ki-100 Type II, Ki-102A and C fighters was a major objective of the Army. Range extension of the Ki-67 by providing additional tanks and further tests of the Ki-74 were the most important bomber problems being considered at the end of the war. The Ki-115 attack airplane was delayed by landing gear trouble and over-weight. The most important observation or recce problem was to increase the critical altitude of the Type 100 as indicated by the construction of the Ki-46 Type IV. The shortage of aluminum and the substitution of wood is reflected in the transport type Ki-110 which was a wood edition of the Ki-54. The first Ki-110 was destroyed by an air raid.

It will be noted that very few new engines were being considered, the majority being improved types based on older models. One of the first liquid-cooled engines to be used in Japanese Army Aircraft was the Ha-40 which resulted from a study started in 1939 on a German Daimler-Benz by Kawasaki. This engine was in production in 1942 for fighters as the Type-3, and employed fuel injection. The Ha-140 was started in 1941 and put into production in 1944. By connecting two Ha-40s in tandem and using contrarotating propellers, the Ha-201 was evolved. The first fighter flight test of this engine in 1943 resulted in a crash, and no further work was done on this project.

At the request of the Army, the Nakajima Co. began trial production of the Ha-45 air-cooled engine in 1940. This engine was later installed in the Ki-84 fighter with methanol injection, but was not completely developed for combat by the end of the war. With the object of turning out a small air-cooled engine of high rating the Hitachi Co. completed the first Ha-51 in 1944, but test results

OPPOSITE More than 60 N1K2 Shiden-Kais of the 343rd Kokutai go up in flames at Omura on December 30, 1945. Except for a few types that were preserved for technical air intelligence purposes, all captured Japanese aircraft had been destroyed by early 1946. Initial destruction methods of enemy aircraft employed by the occupation forces are detailed in the following account from an unidentified officer serving with the US Army's XI Corps Artillery at "Mito-Two." "More than 1,500 Japanese aircraft have been destroyed during the past 12 days by men of the 637th Tank Destroyer Battalion, which is located just northeast of Tokyo. Moving in on 12 airfields, and covering a ground area of 800 square miles, these men have organized into what they call 'Destruction Incorporated' crews. A crew consists of five men, a Japanese full track prime mover and a gas pump spray mounted on a Japanese truck. The system for destruction is simple, but believed to be foolproof. Two men on the prime mover pull the planes to the selected burning area. One man searches the entire plane for bombs and ammunition. Another member punctures all gas tanks to prevent explosion. The remaining man stands by the gas pump spray and at the signal 'all clear' sprays Japanese synthetic gas over the plane to be destroyed. It is then ignited and the crew moves on to the next aircraft." (Author collection)

were so unsatisfactory the project was canceled. In the 1,000-hp air-cooled class, the Ha-102 was successfully applied to the Ki-46 fighter in 1940. The Ha-115 engine in this same class was installed in the Ki-43 fighter in 1942. In the 1,500-hp class the Ha-101 completed in 1943 was used in the Ki-21 Mark II aircraft. The Ha-505 and Ha-50 were engines intended for heavy bombers and power ratings above 2,000 hp. The Ha-505 was canceled in 1944 after preliminary tests and the Ha-50, a double row radial of 22 cylinders and a rating of 3,000 hp, was started by Mitsubishi in 1943. Air raids destroyed the experimental model in 1944.

The Navy was apparently in a superior position to the Army with regard to research and development facilities and available funds.[1]

***

However, this report fails to make reference to the fact that the IJNAF was pursuing further development of the excellent Nakajima Homare radial piston engine for advanced fighters and heavy bombers. In addition, the IJNAF was urging the development of more powerful versions of the Ne series of turbojet engine and Ro rocket engines that would have brought the Nakajima Kikka and Mitsubishi Shusui closer to the Me 262 and Me 163 in terms of their performance capabilities.

The Allies also benefited from captured Japanese aircraft evaluations in that they obtained valuable aircraft aerodynamic and design data. For example, through technical evaluation of the H8K2 "Emily" flying boat, the US Navy was able to glean important hull step design information that it then applied to the design of some of its future large flying boats, such as the Convair R3Y Tradewind, during the mid-1950s. In addition, Allied countries were also able to gain important aerodynamic and design data regarding jet fighter and rocket-powered tailless, swept-wing aircraft designs from the Kikka and Shusui evaluations.

APPENDICES

APPENDIX A
Roster of surviving Japanese aircraft and their disposition

Mitsubishi A6M Zero-sen

Restored Zero-sens on display in Australia:
Construction number 840 – Remains, including forward fuselage, inboard wings, engine, and propeller, displayed at the Australian Aviation Heritage Centre, Winnellie, Northern Territory.
Construction number 5784 – Displayed at the Australian War Memorial, Canberra, Australian Capital Territory.

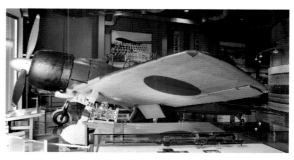

A6M3 construction number 3621 on display at the Tachiarai Peace Memorial Museum in Chikuzen, Fukuoka. (*Arjun Sarup*)

Restored Zero-sens on display in Japan:
Construction number 1493 – Displayed at the Kawaguchiko Motor Museum in Fujikawaguchiko, Yamanashi.
Construction number 3621 – Displayed at the Tachiarai Peace Memorial Museum in Chikuzen, Fukuoka.
Construction numbers 4168/4240/4241 – Displayed at the Yushukan in Chiyoda, Tokyo.
Construction number 4685 – Displayed at Hamamatsu Air Base, Hamamatsu, Shizuoka.
Construction number 4708 – Displayed at the Mitsubishi Heavy Industries Museum, Komaki, Aichi.
Construction number 31870 – Two-seat trainer on static display at the National Museum of Nature and Science, Taito, Tokyo.
Construction number 62343 – Displayed at the Chiran Peace Museum for Kamikaze Pilots in Chiran, Kagoshima.
Construction number 82729 – Displayed at the Yamato Museum, Kure, Hiroshima.

A6M5 construction number 4240 on display at the Yushukan in Chiyoda, Tokyo. (*Arjun Sarup*)

Construction number 91518 – Displayed at the Kawaguchiko Motor Museum, Fujikawaguchiko, Yamanashi.

Construction number 92717 – Displayed at the Kawaguchiko Motor Museum, Fujikawaguchiko, Yamanashi.

Restored Zero-sen on display in New Zealand:
Construction numbers 3835/3844 – Displayed at the Auckland War Memorial Museum, Auckland.

Zero-sens on display in the United Kingdom:
Construction number 196 – Fuselage center section on static displayed at the Imperial War Museum, London.
Construction number 3685 – Unrestored fuselage on static display at the Imperial War Museum Duxford, Cambridgeshire.

Zero-sens on display in the United States:
Construction number 1303 – Stored at the Flying Heritage Collection, Everett, Washington.
Construction number 2266 – Nihau Incident Zero-sen remains displayed at the Pacific Aviation Museum, Honolulu, Hawaii.
Construction number 3618 – Stored at Fantasy of Flight, Polk City, Florida.
Construction number 3852 – Babo Airfield, Indonesia-based Zero-sen that underwent restoration by the Flying Heritage Collection, Everett, Washington. This aircraft possesses a Pratt & Whitney engine.
Construction number 4043 – Stored at Fantasy of Flight, Polk City, Florida.
Construction number 4340 – Restored Zero-sen flight tested at Wright Field, Dayton, Ohio, and displayed at the NASM, Washington, D.C.
Construction number 4400 – Stored at Flying Heritage Collection, Everett, Washington.
Construction numbers 5356/5451 – Displayed at the Pacific Aviation Museum in Honolulu, Hawaii.
Construction number 5357 – Flightworthy restored Zero-sen once flight tested at NAS Patuxent River, Maryland, and now based at the Planes of Fame Air Museum, Chino, California. This aircraft still possesses its original Sakae radial engine.

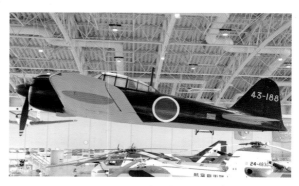

A6M5 construction number 4685 on display at Hamamatsu Air Base in Hamamatsu, Shizuoka. (*Richard Vandervord*)

A6M5 construction number 62343 on display at the Chiran Peace Museum for Kamikaze Pilots in Chiran, Kagoshima. (*Arjun Sarup*)

A6M7 construction number 82729 on display at the Yamato Museum in Kure, Hiroshima. (*Arjun Sarup*)

Construction number 5450 – Displayed at the National Naval Aviation Museum, Pensacola, Florida. Construction number 23186 – NASM-restored Zero-sen loaned to the San Diego Air and Space Museum, San Diego, California, for display. Construction number 51553 – Century Aviation restoration project Zero-sen displayed at the National Museum of the US Air Force at Wright-Patterson Air Force Base in Dayton, Ohio.

A6M2 construction number 51553 on display at the National Museum of the US Air Force at Wright-Patterson Air Force Base in Dayton, Ohio. (*Arjun Sarup*)

Nakajima Ki-43 "Oscar"

Ki-43-I construction number 750 – Alpine Fighter Collection restored aircraft on display with the Flying Heritage Collection, Everett, Washington.

Ki-43-II construction number 5465 – Nose and tail (unrestored) displayed at the Australian War Museum, Canberra, Australian Capital Territory.

Ki-43-IIb construction number 6430 – NASM-restored aircraft loaned to and displayed at the Pima Air and Space Museum, Tucson, Arizona.

Ki-43-IIIa – New build displayed at Museum of Flight, Seattle, Washington.

Ki-43 – Based at GossHawk Unlimited, Casa Grande, Arizona.

Ki-43 – Restoration project at The Fighter Collection, Duxford, United Kingdom.

Ki-43-II – Displayed at Central Indonesian Air Force Museum, Yogyakarta, Java.

Ki-43-II – Displayed at the Chiran Peace Museum for Kamikaze Pilots in Chiran, Kagoshima.

Ki-43 – Restoration project at Kawaguchiko Motor Museum, Kawaguchiko, Yamanashi.

Ki-43-I construction number 750 on display with the Flying Heritage Collection in Everett, Washington. (*Edward M. Young*)

Kawasaki Ki-61 "Tony"

Ki-61-II construction number 379 – Stored at Fantasy of Flight, Polk City, Florida.

Ki-61-II construction number 640 – Flightworthy AvSpecs of Ardmore, Auckland, New Zealand restored aircraft destined for the Military Aviation Museum, Virginia Beach, Virginia.

Ki-61-II-Kai construction number 5017 – Kawasaki Heavy Industries restored aircraft displayed at Kagamigahara Aerospace Science Museum, Kagamigahara, Gifu.

Ki-43-IIb construction number 6430 on display at the Pima Air and Space Museum in Tucson, Arizona. (*JHM collection*)

Nakajima Ki-84 "Frank"

Ki-84 construction number 1446 – Flightworthy Air Museum (Planes of Fame Museum) restored aircraft displayed at Tokko Heiwa Kinen-kan Museum, Kagoshima Prefecture.

Kawasaki Ki-100 Goshikisen

Ki-100-Ib – Restored aircraft displayed at RAF Museum Cosford, Shropshire.

Ki-61-II-Kai construction number 5017 on display at the Chiran Peace Museum for Kamikaze Pilots in Chiran, Kagoshima. (*Arjun Sarup*)

Mitsubishi J2M "Jack"

J2M3 construction number 3014 – Restored aircraft displayed at Planes of Fame Museum, Chino, California.

Kawanishi N1K1 "Rex"

N1K1 construction number 514 – Stored at NASM Paul E. Garber Facility, Suitland, Maryland.
N1K1 construction number 562 – Restored aircraft displayed at National Museum of the Pacific War, Fredericksburg, Texas.
N1K1 construction number 565 – Stored at the NNAM, Pensacola, Florida.

Kawanishi N1K2-J "George"

Restored "Georges" on display in the United States:
N1K2-Ja construction number 5128 – Displayed at the NNAM, Pensacola, Florida.
N1K2-Ja construction number 5312 – Displayed at the National Museum of the US Air Force, Wright-Patterson Air Force Base, Dayton, Ohio.
N1K2-Ja construction number 5341 – Displayed at the NASM Steven F. Udvar-Hazy Center, Chantilly, Virginia.

Ki-84 construction number 1446 on display at the Tokko Heiwa Kinen-kan Museum in Kagoshima Prefecture. (*Arjun Sarup*)

Restored "George" on display in Japan:
N1K2-Ja – Displayed at Nanreku Misho Koen, Ehime Prefecture, Japan.

Kyushu J7W Shinden

J7W1 – Forward fuselage displayed at NASM Steven F. Udvar-Hazy Center, Chantilly, Virginia. Remaining parts of aircraft in storage at Paul E. Garber Facility, Suitland, Maryland.

N1K2-J construction number 5128 on display at the NNAM in Pensacola, Florida. (*Greg Goebel*)

Kawasaki Ki-45 "Nick"

Ki-45 KAIc – Restored fuselage of aircraft once flight tested at Wright Field, Dayton, Ohio, and NAS Anacostia displayed at NASM Steven F. Udvar-Hazy Center, Chantilly, Virginia.

Nakajima J1N1 "Irving"

J1N1-S construction number 7334 – Restored aircraft displayed at NASM Steven F. Udvar-Hazy Center, Chantilly, Virginia.

Mitsubishi Ki-46 "Dinah"

Ki-46-III construction number 5439 – Restored aircraft displayed at RAF Museum Cosford, Shropshire.

Yokosuka D4Y "Judy"

D4Y1 construction number 4316 – Restored aircraft displayed in the Yasukuni Jinja Yushukan Shrine, Tokyo, Japan.
D4Y3 construction number 7483 – Restored aircraft, possessing a Pratt & Whitney R-1830 engine, displayed at Planes of Fame Air Museum, Chino, California.

Aichi B7A "Grace"

B7A construction number 816 – Fuselage of aircraft once flight tested by US Navy following World War II, stored at NASM Paul E. Garber Facility, Suitland, Maryland.

Nakajima B6N "Jill"

B6N construction number 5350 – Remains of aircraft once flight tested at NAS Anacostia, Washington, D.C., stored at NASM Paul E. Garber Facility, Suitland, Maryland.

Nakajima Ki-115 Tsurugi

Ki-115 construction number 1002 – NASM aircraft displayed at Pima Air and Space Museum in Tucson, Arizona.
Ki-115 – Displayed outside USAF HQ building at Yokota AFB until 1953 when transferred to Japanese Aeronautical Association. In storage, whereabouts unknown.

N1K2-J (construction number unknown) on display at Nanreku Misho Koen in Ehime Prefecture. (*Edward M. Young*)

J1N1-S construction number 7334 on display at the NASM Steven F. Udvar-Hazy Center in Chantilly, Virginia. (*Arjun Sarup*)

Ki-46-III construction number 5439 on display at RAF Museum Cosford in Shropshire. (*Arjun Sarup*)

Yokosuka P1Y "Frances"

P1Y1 construction number 8923 – Intact, disassembled aircraft stored at NASM Paul E. Garber Facility, Suitland, Maryland.

Mitsubishi G4M "Betty"

G4M1 – Remains displayed at Planes of Fame Air Museum, Chino, California.

G4M2 – Restored fuselage displayed at Kawaguchiko Motor Museum, Yamanashi Prefecture, Japan.

G4M2 – Forward fuselage stored at NASM Paul E. Garber Facility, Suitland, Maryland.

Ki-115 construction number 1002 on display at Pima Air and Space Museum in Tucson, Arizona. (*Steve Ozel*)

Aichi M6A Seiran

M6A1 construction number 1600228 – Restored aircraft displayed at NASM Steven F. Udvar-Hazy Center, Chantilly, Virginia.

Kawanishi H8K "Emily"

H8K2 construction number 426 – Restored aircraft static displayed at the Japanese Maritime Self-Defense Force Naval Aviation Museum at Kanoya naval air base, Kagoshima Prefecture, Japan.

Nakajima Kikka

Kikka – Displayed at NASM Steven F. Udvar-Hazy Center, Chantilly, Virginia.

M6A1 construction number 1600228 on display at the NASM Steven F. Udvar-Hazy Center in Chantilly, Virginia. (*Arjun Sarup*)

Mitsubishi J8M Shusui

J8M – Displayed at Planes of Fame Museum, Chino, California.

J8M – Displayed at Mitsubishi museum in Komaki Minami, Japan.

Yokosuka MXY7 Ohka

Restored examples on display in India:

Model 11 – Displayed at Indian Air Force Museum, Palam, New Delhi.

Restored examples on display in Japan:

Model 11 – Displayed at Yushukan War Museum, Yasukuni Shrine, Tokyo.

H8K2 construction number 426 on display at the Japanese Maritime Self-Defense Force Naval Aviation Museum at Kanoya naval air base in Kagoshima Prefecture. (*Richard Vandervord*)

Handbook Interim Report No. 2 (Project No. NAD-25), Prepared by R. J. Groseclose, Captain, Air Corps, Headquarters Air Materiel Command, Wright Field, Dayton, Ohio, January 1947, US National Archives at College Park, MD, Textual Reference Branch.

8. RG 38 Records of the Office of the Chief of Naval Operations, Office of Naval Intelligence, Air Intelligence Group (Op 16-v) Serials and Publications, TAIC Summaries, 1943–45, Box 10, *Technical Air Intelligence Summary No. 33 (OPNAV-16-V-T133): GEORGE 11*, Technical Air Intelligence Center, Naval Air Station Anacostia, D.C., July 1945, US National Archives at College Park, MD, Textual Reference Branch.

9. RG 255 NACA Classified File 1915–58, 1001 Mitsubishi Box No. 243, projno. NND, 836516, Folder 1001 Mitsubishi Nick 2_1, *Nick II (Ki-45) Japanese Night Fighter (Project No. NTE-23)*, R. J. Groseclose, Captain, Air Corps, Headquarters Air Materiel Command, Wright Field, Dayton, Ohio, January 1947, US National Archives at College Park, MD, Textual Reference Branch.

10. RG 255 NACA Classified File 1915–58, 1001 Mitsubishi Box No. 243, projno. NND, 836516, Folder 1001 Mitsubishi Rita 11_1, *Technical Report on Japanese "Rita" Airplane (Project No. DA-8)*, Robert W. Shivadecker, Headquarters Air Materiel Command, Wright Field, Dayton, Ohio, March 1947, US National Archives at College Park, MD, Textual Reference Branch.

BIBLIOGRAPHY

Angelucci, Enzo and Paolo Matricardi. *World Aircraft: World War II, Volume II*. Sampson Low Guides, Maidenhead, 1978

Butler, Phil. *War Prizes – An illustrated survey of German, Italian and Japanese aircraft brought to Allied countries during and after the Second World War.* Midland Counties Publications, Leicester, 1994

Chambers, Mark with Tony Holmes. Osprey Combat Aircraft 119 – *Nakajima B5N 'Kate' and B6N 'Jill' Units.* Osprey, Oxford, 2017

Francillon, Ph.D., René J. *Japanese Aircraft of the Pacific War*, Putnam & Company Ltd., London, 1970, second edition 1979

Goodall, Geoff. *Warbirds Directory* – http://www.goodall.com.au/warbirds.htm

Green, William. *Warplanes of the Second World War, Volume Three: Fighters.* Macdonald & Co. Ltd., London, 1961 (seventh impression 1973)

Green, William and Gordon Swanborough. *WW2 Aircraft Fact Files: Japanese Army Fighters, Part 1*. Macdonald & Jane's Publishers Ltd., London, 1976

Izawa, Yasuho with Tony Holmes. Osprey Aircraft of the Aces 129 – *J2M Raiden and N1K1/2 Shiden/Shiden-Kai Aces.* Osprey, Oxford, 2016

Nohara, Shigeru. *Aero Detail 7: Mitsubishi A6M Zero Fighter.* Dai-Nippon Kaiga Co. Ltd., Tokyo. 1993

Rearden, Jim. *Cracking the Zero Mystery: How the U.S. Learned to Beat Japan's Vaunted WWII Fighter Plane.* Stackpole Books, Mechanicsburg, Pennsylvania, 1990

Rearden, Jim. *Koga's Zero: The Fighter That Changed World War II.* Pictorial Histories Publishing Company, Missoula, Montana, 1995

ENDNOTES

CHAPTER 1

1 RG 38 Records of the Office of the Chief of Naval Operations, Office of Naval Intelligence, Air Intelligence Group (Op 16-V) Serials and Publications, Air Battle Notes, Subject Index to Air Intelligence Material, and other Technical Papers, Box No. 8, *Technical Air Intelligence Center Summary No. 1: Technical Air Intelligence Organization and Functions*, OPNAV-16-V T 101, August 1, 1944, Technical Air Intelligence Center, Naval Air Station Anacostia, D.C., US National Archives at College Park, MD, Textual Reference Branch, p. 1.
2 Ibid.
3 Ibid.
4 Ibid., pp. 1–2.
5 Ibid., p. 2.
6 Ibid., p. 7.
7 Ibid.
8 Ibid.
9 Ibid.
10 "Air Technical Intelligence." Air Force Historical Studies Office. 2008.
11 Trojan, David. "Technical Air Intelligence. Wreck Chasing in the Pacific during the War." http://www.j-aircraft.com/research/David_Trojan/Technical%20Air%20Intelligence%20Wreck%20chasing%20in%20the%20Pacific%20during%20the%20war.pdf (accessed February 16, 2011).
12 Ibid.
13 Starkings, Peter (2011). "The End of the JAAF and JNAF." http://www.j-aircraft.com/research/jas_jottings/end_of_the_jaaf_and_jnaf.htm (accessed February 16, 2011).

CHAPTER 2

1 *New Japanese Aircraft Developments* (Extracts from *Technical Air Intelligence Summary No. 26*, Navy Department, Washington, D.C., July 1944). Microfilm IRISRef. A2203, Frame 1751, US Department of the Air Force, Air Force Historical Research Agency, Maxwell Air Force Base, Alabama.
2 Ibid.
3 Ibid.
4 Ibid.
5 http://www.wwiiaircraftperformance.org/japan/p5016.pdf. General Technical Data and Flight Characteristics of the Japanese Zero Fighter Airplane, Correspondence from Headquarters 23rd Fighter Group, Office of the Commanding Officer, A.P.O. 627, New York, NY, Air Corps Lt Col B. K. Holloway to Commanding General, China Air Task Force, February 6, 1943, WWII aircraft performance.org, Archives of M. Williams, p. 7 (accessed June 19, 2017).
6 Ibid.
7 Ibid.
8 Rearden, Jim. *Koga's Zero: The Fighter That Changed World War II,* second edition. Pictorial Histories Publishing Company, Missoula, Montana, 1995. Originally published as *Cracking the Zero Mystery: How the U.S. Learned to Beat Japan's Vaunted WWII Fighter Plane.* Stackpole Books, Mechanicsburg, Pennsylvania, 1990, p. 72 (also see Appendix II).
9 Ibid., p. 73.
10 http://www.wwiiaircraftperformance.org/japan/hamp-eb201.html. USAAF Flight Test Engineering Branch Memo Report No. Eng-47-1726-A, Performance Flight Test of a Japanese Hamp, AAF No. EB-201, March 28, 1944.

Compiled by Mike Williams and Neil Stirling. (Accessed June 19, 2017.)

11 Ibid.

12 Nohara, Shigeru. *Aero Detail 7: Mitsubishi A6M Zero Fighter*. Dai-Nippon Kaiga Co. Ltd, Tokyo, 1993, p. 78.

13 RG 38 Records of the Office of the Chief of Naval Operations, Office of Naval Intelligence, Air Intelligence Group (Op 16-v) Serials and Publications, TAIC Reports, 1944–45, & TAIC Manual, Box 11, *Technical Air Intelligence Center Report No. 17: Combat Evaluation of Zeke 52 with F4U-1D, F6F-5, and FM-2*, By US Naval Air Station Patuxent River, MD, OPNAV-16-V.T217, November 1944, Technical Air Intelligence Center, Naval Air Station Anacostia, D.C., US National Archives at College Park, MD, Textual Reference Branch, pp. 1–2.

14 Ibid., p. 2.

15 Ibid., p. 3.

16 Ibid.

17 http://www.wwiiaircraftperformance.org/japan/ptr-1111.pdf. *Technical Air Intelligence Center Report No. 17: Combat Evaluation of Zeke 52 with F4U-1D, F6F-5, and FM-2*, By US Naval Air Station Patuxent River, MD, OPNAV-16-V.T217, November 1944, Technical Air Intelligence Center, Naval Air Station Anacostia, D.C., pp. 4–5. Archives of M. Williams. Compiled by Mike Williams and Neil Stirling. (Accessed June 19, 2017.)

18 Ibid., p. 5.

19 RG 38 Records of the Office of the Chief of Naval Operations, Office of Naval Intelligence, Air Intelligence Group (Op 16-v) Serials and Publications, TAIC Reports, 1944–45, & TAIC Manual, Box 11, *Technical Air Intelligence Center Report No. 38: Comparative Performance Between Zeke 52 and the P-38, P-51, P-47*, By Army Air Forces Proving Ground Command, Eglin Field, Florida, OPNAV-16-V.T238, April 1945, Technical Air Intelligence Center, Naval Air Station Anacostia, D.C., US National Archives at College Park, MD, Textual Reference Branch, p. 1.

20 Ibid.

21 Ibid., p. 3.

22 RG 38 Records of the Office of the Chief of Naval Operations, Office of Naval Intelligence, Air Intelligence Group (Op 16-v) Serials and Publications, TAIC Summaries, 1943–45, Box 10,

Technical Air Intelligence Summary No. 7 (OPNAV-35 No. T11): Recent Developments in Japanese Fighters, Air Technical Analysis Division, Office of the Chief of Naval Operations, Navy Department, Washington D.C., January 1944, US National Archives at College Park, MD, Textual Reference Branch, p. 5.

23 Ibid., pp. 5–6.

24 RG 255 NACA Classified File 1915–58 1001 Jaruzzi thru 1001 Junker Box 233, Folder 1001 Japan/6, *Technical Air Intelligence Center Summary No. 25 (OPNAV-16V-T125): New Japanese Aircraft Development*, Technical Air Intelligence Center, Naval Air Station Anacostia, D.C., March 1945, US National Archives at College Park, MD, Textual Reference Branch, p. 15.

25 New Japanese Aircraft Developments (Extracts from Technical Air Intelligence Summary No. 26, Navy Department, Washington, D.C., July 1944). Microfilm IRISRef. A2203, Frame 1751, US Department of the Air Force, Air Force Historical Research Agency, Maxwell Air Force Base, Alabama.

26 http://www.wwiiaircraftperformance.org/japan/Ki-84-TSFTE-2001.pdf. *Army Air Forces, Air Materiel Command Memorandum Report on Frank I, T-2, Serial No. 302*, "Pilot's Comments and Handling Characteristics of Frank I," Prepared by Arthur Murray, 1st Lt, Air Corps, Pilot, Fighter Operation Section, July 16, 1946, pp. 1–9. Archives of M. Williams. Compiled by Mike Williams and Neil Stirling. (Accessed June 19, 2017.)

27 RG 255 NACA Classified File 1915–58 1001 Morane-Saulnier thru Nicholas Beagley, Box No. 245, Folder 1001 Nakajima 04_1, *Frank-1 (KI-84) Pilot's Handbook Interim Report No. 2 (Project No. NAD-25)*, Prepared by R. J. Groseclose, Captain, Air Corps, Headquarters Air Materiel Command, Wright Field, Dayton, Ohio, January 1947, US National Archives at College Park, MD, Textual Reference Branch, pp. 18–20.

28 Ibid, p. 26.

29 Taken from a 1946 TAIC report attributed to an "Allied field grade evaluation pilot," quoted in "The Asiatic Thunderbolt," *Air Enthusiast*, Vol 1, No 2, December 1971, pp. 67–73.

30 "TAIC Manual." *US Technical Air Intelligence Command*, May 1945.

31 RG 38 Records of the Office of the Chief of Naval Operations, Office of Naval Intelligence, Air

Intelligence Group (Op 16-v) Serials and
Publications, TAIC Summaries, 1943–45, Box 10,
*Technical Air Intelligence Summary No. 33
(OPNAV-16-V-T133): GEORGE 11*, Technical
Air Intelligence Center, Naval Air Station
Anacostia, D.C., July 1945, US National Archives
at College Park, MD, Textual Reference Branch,
pp. 1–2, 10.

32 RG 255 NACA Classified File 1915–58, 1001
Mitsubishi Box No. 243, projno. NND, 836516,
Folder 1001 Mitsubishi Nick 2_1, *Nick II (Ki-45)
Japanese Night Fighter (Project No. NTE-23)*, R. J.
Groseclose, Captain, Air Corps, Headquarters Air
Materiel Command, Wright Field, Dayton, Ohio,
January 1947, US National Archives at College
Park, MD, Textual Reference Branch, pp. 1–5,
7–8.

33 RG 38 Records of the Office of the Chief of Naval
Operations, Office of Naval Intelligence, Air
Intelligence Group (Op 16-v) Serials and
Publications, TAIC Summaries, 1943–45, Box 10,

*Technical Air Intelligence Summary No. 5 (OPNAV-
16-V-T105): New Japanese Fighters and Torpedo
Bombers*, Technical Air Intelligence Center, Naval
Air Station Anacostia, D.C., September 1944, US
National Archives at College Park, MD, Textual
Reference Branch, pp. 6, 8.

34 Francillon, Ph.D., René J. *Japanese Aircraft of the
Pacific War*. Putnam & Company Ltd., London,
1970 (second edition 1979), p. 192.

35 Green, William. *Warplanes of the Second World
War, Volume Three: Fighters*. Macdonald & Co.
Ltd., London, 1961 (seventh impression 1973),
p. 58.

36 Green, William and Gordon Swanborough. *WW2
Aircraft Fact Files: Japanese Army Fighters, Part 1*.
Macdonald & Jane's Publishers Ltd., London,
1976, pp. 53, 56.

37 Unknown. *Famous Aircraft of the World, first series,
No. 76: Japanese Army Experimental Fighters* (1).
Bunrin-Do Co. Ltd., Tokyo, August 1976, p. 50.

CHAPTER 3

1 *New Japanese Aircraft Developments* (Extracts from
Technical Air Intelligence Summary No. 26, Navy
Department, Washington, D.C., July 1944).
Microfilm IRISRef. A2203, Frame 1751, US
Department of the Air Force, Air Force Historical
Research Agency, Maxwell Air Force Base, Alabama.

2 Use of Water Injection on Jap Aircraft Engines
(Extract from Air Operations Memorandum
No. 29, April 20, 1944, Navy Dept., Washington,
D.C.). Weekly Informational Intelligence
Summary No. 67-6, June 24, 1944, Office of the
Intelligence Officer, Headquarters, Air Service
Command, p. 5. Microfilm IRISRef. A2203,
Frame 1575, US Department of the Air Force, Air
Force Historical Research Agency, Maxwell Air
Force Base, Alabama.

3 Huggins, Mark. "Falling Comet: Yokosuka's Suisei
Dive-Bomber." *Air Enthusiast, No. 97*, January/
February 2002, p. 66.

4 RG 255 NACA Classified File 1915–58 1001
Jaruzzi thru 1001 Junker Box 233, Folder 1001
Japan/6, *Technical Air Intelligence Center Summary
No. 25 (OPNAV-16V-T125): New Japanese
Aircraft Development*, Technical Air Intelligence
Center, Naval Air Station Anacostia, D.C., March
1945, US National Archives at College Park, MD,
Textual Reference Branch, pp. 8–11.

5 RG 38 Records of the Office of the Chief of Naval
Operations, Office of Naval Intelligence, Air
Intelligence Group (Op 16-v) Serials and
Publications, TAIC Summaries, 1943–45, Box 10,
*Technical Air Intelligence Summary No. 5 (OPNAV-
16-V-T105): New Japanese Fighters and Torpedo
Bombers*, Technical Air Intelligence Center, Naval
Air Station Anacostia, D.C., September 1944, US
National Archives at College Park, MD, Textual
Reference Branch, pp. 11–12.

6 RG 255 NACA Classified File 1915–58 1001
Jaruzzi thru 1001 Junker Box 233, Folder 1001
Japan/5, *Japanese Aircraft Performance &
Characteristics, TAIC Manual No. 1*, Technical
Air Intelligence Center, Naval Air Station
Anacostia, D.C., February 10, 1945, US
National Archives at College Park, MD, Textual
Reference Branch.

7 RG 38 Records of the Office of the Chief of Naval
Operations, Office of Naval Intelligence, Air
Intelligence Group (Op 16-v) Serials and Publications,
TAIC Summaries, 1943–45, Box 10, *Technical Air
Intelligence Summary No. 7 (OPNAV-16V-T107): Betty
22–G4M2*, Technical Air Intelligence Center, Naval
Air Station Anacostia, D.C., September 1944, US
National Archives at College Park, MD, Textual
Reference Branch, pp. 1–8.

8   RG 38 Records of the Office of the Chief of Naval Operations, Office of Naval Intelligence, Air Intelligence Group (Op 16-v) Serials and Publications, TAIC Summaries, 1943–45, Box 10, *Technical Air Intelligence Summary No. 5 (OPNAV-16-V-T105): New Japanese Fighters and Torpedo Bombers*, Technical Air Intelligence Center, Naval Air Station Anacostia, D.C., September 1944, US National Archives at College Park, MD, Textual Reference Branch, pp. 8 and 12.

9   RG 38 Records of the Office of the Chief of Naval Operations, Office of Naval Intelligence, Air Intelligence Group (Op 16-v) Serials and Publications, TAIC Summaries, 1943–45, Box 10, *Technical Air Intelligence Center Summary No. 3 (OPNAV-16-V-T103): Miscellaneous Japanese Aircraft Development*, Technical Air Intelligence Center, Naval Air Station Anacostia, D.C., August 1944, US National Archives at College Park, MD, Textual Reference Branch, pp. 1–25.

10   RG 255 NACA Classified File 1915–58, 1001 Mitsubishi Box No. 243, projno. NND, 836516, Folder 1001 Mitsubishi Rita 11_1, *Technical Report on Japanese "Rita" Airplane (Project No. DA-8),*

Robert W. Shivadecker, Headquarters Air Materiel Command, Wright Field, Dayton, Ohio, March 1947, US National Archives at College Park, MD, Textual Reference Branch, pp. 1–6.

11   RG 38 Records of the Office of the Chief of Naval Operations, Office of Naval Intelligence, Air Intelligence Group (Op 16-v) Serials and Publications, TAIC Summaries, 1943–45, Box 10, *Technical Air Intelligence Summary No. 5 (OPNAV-16-V-T105): New Japanese Fighters and Torpedo Bombers*, Technical Air Intelligence Center, Naval Air Station Anacostia, D.C., September 1944, US National Archives at College Park, MD, Textual Reference Branch, p. 12.

12   RG 38 Records of the Office of the Chief of Naval Operations, Office of Naval Intelligence, Air Intelligence Group (Op 16-v) Serials and Publications, TAIC Summaries, 1943–45, Box 10, *Technical Air Intelligence Center Summary No. 3 (OPNAV-16-V-T103): Miscellaneous Japanese Aircraft Development*, Technical Air Intelligence Center, Naval Air Station Anacostia, D.C., August 1944, US National Archives at College Park, MD, Textual Reference Branch, pp. 1–25.

CHAPTER 4

1   *New Japanese Aircraft Developments* (Extracts from *Technical Air Intelligence Summary No. 26*, Navy Department, Washington, D.C., July 1944). Microfilm IRISRef. A2203, Frame 1751, US Department of the Air Force, Air Force Historical Research Agency, Maxwell Air Force Base, Alabama.

2   RG 38 Records of the Office of the Chief of Naval Operations, Office of Naval Intelligence, Air Intelligence Group (Op 16-v) Serials and Publications, TAIC Summaries, 1943–45, Box 10, *Technical Air Intelligence Summary No. 5 (OPNAV-16-V-T105): New Japanese Fighters and Torpedo Bombers*, Technical Air Intelligence Center, Naval

Air Station Anacostia, D.C., September 1944, US National Archives at College Park, MD, Textual Reference Branch, p. 8.

3   RG 38 Records of the Office of the Chief of Naval Operations, Office of Naval Intelligence, Air Intelligence Group (Op 16-v) Serials and Publications, TAIC Reports, 1944–45, & TAIC Manual, Box 11, *Technical Air Intelligence Center Report No. 45: Japanese MAD Equipment (OPNAV-16-V-T245),* Technical Air Intelligence Center, Naval Air Station Anacostia, D.C., July 1945, US National Archives at College Park, MD, Textual Reference Branch, p. 1.

CHAPTER 7

1   "Balloon Bombs." *The Oregon Encyclopedia.* https://oregonencyclopedia.org/articles/balloon_ bombs/#.WcMJVYvF-rg (accessed December 26, 2013).

2   RG 38 Records of the Office of the Chief of Naval Operations, Office of Naval Intelligence, Air

Intelligence Group (Op 16-v) Serials and Publications, TAIC Summaries, 1943–45, Box 10, *Technical Air Intelligence Center Summary No. 31 (OPNAV-16-V-T131): BAKA,* Technical Air Intelligence Center, Naval Air Station Anacostia, D.C., June 1945, US National Archives at College

Park, MD, Textual Reference Branch, pp. 1–24.
(Accessed June 19, 2017.)

3 Japanese Parachute Cable Bomb, Weekly
Information Intelligence Summary No. 72, July
29, 1944. Microfilm IRISRef. A2203, Frame
1675, US Department of the Air Force, Air Force
Historical Research Agency, Maxwell Air Force
Base, Alabama.

4 RG 38 Records of the Office of the Chief of Naval
Operations, Office of Naval Intelligence, Air
Intelligence Group (Op 16-v) Serials and
Publications, TAIC Summaries, 1943–45, Box 10,
*Technical Air Intelligence Center Summary No. 32
(OPNAV-16-V-T132): Evolution of Zeke*, Technical
Air Intelligence Center, Naval Air Station
Anacostia, D.C., June 1945, US National
Archives at College Park, MD, Textual Reference
Branch, p. 15.

5 Ibid, p. 17.

6 http://www.fischer-tropsch.org/primary_
documents/gvt_reports/USNAVY/USNTMJ%20

CHAPTER 8

1 RG 255 NACA Classified File 1915–58 1001
Jaruzzi thru 1001 Junker Box 233, Folder 1001
Japan/9, Air *Technical Intelligence Review No.
F-IR-101-RE: Description of Experimental Aircraft
and Experimental Engines under Development by
the Japanese Army and the Imperial Japanese Navy*,
Air Technical Intelligence Group Advanced
Echelon FEAF, Headquarters Air Materiel
Command, Wright Field, Dayton, Ohio, August
5, 1946, US National Archives at College Park,
MD, Textual Reference Branch, pp. 1–2.

Reports/USNTMJ-200D-0550-0575%20
Report%200-02.pdf (accessed June 19, 2017) via
http://www.aviationofjapan.com/2013/04/
hasegawa-kawasaki-ki-48-ii-otsu-lily.html
(accessed June 19, 2017). *Japanese Guided Missiles:
"Intelligence Targets Japan" (DNI) of 4 Sept. 1945,
Fascicle O-1, Target O-02, Japanese Radio
Controlled Flying Bomb "I-go,"* US Naval Technical
Mission to Japan, Air Technical Intelligence
Group, November 20, 1945, pp. 20–25.

7 Ibid., *Japanese Guided Missiles: "Intelligence Targets
Japan" (DNI) of 4 Sept. 1945, Fascicle O-1, Target
O-02, Japanese Airborne Anti-Submarine Circling
Torpedo*, US Naval Technical Mission to Japan, Air
Technical Intelligence Group, November 16,
1945, pp. 16–17.

8 Ibid., *Japanese Guided Missiles: "Intelligence Targets
Japan" (DNI) of 4 Sept. 1945, Fascicle O-1, Target
O-02, Heat Homing Bomb, Fuze System*, US Naval
Technical Mission to Japan, Air Technical
Intelligence Group, December 12, 1945, pp. 7–8.

INDEX

Page numbers in **bold** refer to illustrations and captions.